Vault Reports Guide to Mastering Chemistry

™

TEAM

DIRECTORS

H.S. Hamadeh   Samer Hamadeh   Mark Oldman

EXECUTIVE EDITOR

Marcy Lerner

MANAGING EDITOR

Edward Shen

SENIOR WRITERS

Doug Cantor
Hans Chen
Michael Hasday
Elizabeth Morgan
Mat Johnson
Nikki Scott

LAYOUT PRODUCTION

Hans Chen
Robert Schipano
Jake Wallace

RESEARCH ASSISTANTS

Faisal Anwar
Alex Apelbaum
Stacy Cowley
Kaila Hale-Stern
Abigail Jackson
Sylvia Kovac
Shirley Lin
Austin Shau
Angela Tong

CUSTOMER RELATIONS

Archana Chand

WEB SITE DESIGN

James Ford

ADVERTISING

Kirsten Fragodt

VAULT REPORTS, INC.

80 Fifth Avenue
11th Floor
New York, NY 10011
212 366-4212
www.vaultreports.com

Vault Reports Guide to Mastering Chemistry

JASON CHIN

Houghton Mifflin Company

Boston • New York 1998

For information about permission to reproduce selections from this book, write to Permissions, Houghton Mifflin Company, 215 Pa rk Avenue South, New York, New York 10003 or contact Vault Reports Inc., P.O. Box 1772, New York, New York 10011-1772, (212) 366-4212.

Library of Congress CIP Data is available.

ISBN 0-395-86174-8

Printed in the United States of America

KPT 10 9 8 7 6 5 4 3 2 1

ACKNOWLEDGEMENTS

My gratitude goes to Samer Hamadeh and Mark Oldman for their encouragement while writing this book.

I would like to thank Mohammed Shamji for contributing many questions. Stacey Rutledge for her extensive editorial support and answers to questions. Margaret Chin for proof reading and editing every chapter with an imaginative and witty eye, and for making my explanations clearer. I also thank Douglas Fordham and Andrew Pomerantz for their comments on earlier chapters. My continuing regards go to my parents, and my good friends on both sides of the pond. Keep passing the open windows.

Vault Reports greatly appreciates the efforts of the following: Marnie Cochran, Jake Wallace, Rob Schipano, Ed Shen, Marcy Lerner, David Chalfant, Megan Sercomb, Mark Hernandez, Glenn Fischer, Ravi Mahtre, Jay Oyakawa, Lee Black, and Flannery's Bar (205 West 14th Street, New York City).

CONTENTS

INTRODUCTION

The Vault Reports Guide to Mastering Chemistry is designed to clarify and reinforce a standard college chemistry textbook. This guide will serve as a valuable weapon in your arsenal as your course progresses and as youstudy for exams. This book has been composed to show you how chemistry can explain the world that surrounds us in a powerful and revealing way. Remember, every chemistry course is taught in a slightly different way. This study guide cannot replace your textbook and course lectures; it can, however give you an edge because it makes the most important and complicated concepts much easier to grasp.

The guide is aimed at making chemistry intuitive, and shows you how to use deductive reasoning in combination with simple facts to solve problems.

ORGANIZATION

Each chapter of this Vault Reports Study Guide begins with a brief overview of the concepts to be covered. The chapter then outlines and explains the concepts that will be critical to your success. Note the Vault Reports icons designed to help you navigate your way through the text. At the conclusion of each chapter, you will have the chance to test your knowledge with asection of Thrills, Chills, & Drills.

Key Concept: These are the main ideas of the chapter, explained and supported with examples. These concepts should not be skipped, since they usually form the building blocks for future chapters. If you still have trouble with a key concept after reading a chapter, you should refer back to your text or seek help from your professor.

Commonly Tested Subject: This icon flags important ideas that often appear on exams. Be prepared!

Brownie Points: Once you have a firm understanding of the basics, you can add the bells and whistles. This icon flags some slightly advanced concepts that will earn you a little extra notice on an exam.

Difficult Terrain! While most chemistry is surprisingly straightforward, some topics can get a bit slippery. This icon will alert you to concepts that are easily misunderstood or confused. As with any difficult terrain, take your time and you'll be fine.

Key Terms: The most important terms in every chapter are defined in the Key Terms section. They can also be found in the glossary at the back of the book.

Thrills, Chills, and Drills: So how are you doing so far? Test yourself with Thrills, Chills, and Drills at the end of each chapter. This section is designed to test the Key Concepts of each chapter with atleast 20 True/False questions, at least 20 multiple choice questions, and several longer questions. Answers and explanations are provided in the back of each chapter. Good luck!

CHAPTER

THE PROPERTIES OF MATTER: WHAT MATTERS?

1

OVERVIEW

Chemistry can be broadly defined as the study of the matter that makes up the universe, and the transformations this matter can undergo. Central to an understanding of chemistry is an appreciation of the properties of matter.

You probably already have an intuitive grasp of some of the properties of matter. For example, you can distinguish between a solid, liquid and a gas. Some of the distinctions chemists make between different types of matter are more subtle than our knowledge of solids, liquids, and gases, but they are equally important when it comes to understanding the properties of matter. This chapter introduces the language that chemists use, and the concepts they invoke, when discussing the properties of matter.

In this chapter we will sharpen our understanding of everyday terms such as solid, liquid and gas. We will learn to differentiate between physical properties and chemical properties of matter, and between pure substances and mixtures. We also will look deeper and distinguish between two different types of pure substances, known as elements and compounds. Finally, we will distinguish between different types of mixtures known as heterogeneous and homogeneous mixtures and show how each type of mixture may be seperated into pure substances.

CONCEPTS

The States of Matter

Matter can exist in three states: solid, liquid, and gaseous.

SOLID MATTER HAS A SHAPE INDEPENDENT OF ITS CONTAINER AND IS NOT EASILY COMPRESSIBLE.

Ice is a solid. We cannot easily squeeze an ice cube into a smaller volume, so we say that it is incompressible. Ice also maintains its shape (as long as it remains cold enough): When we put an ice cube in a glass, it does not take the shape of the glass but remains a cube.

LIQUIDS ARE FLUIDS THAT TAKE THE SHAPE OF PART OF THEIR CONTAINER AND ARE NOT EASILY COMPRESSED.

The most important liquid on earth is water; without it we could not live. When we pour a glass of water the bottom of the glass fills first, taking the shape of its container. Also, we cannot easily make the liquid take up less space in the glass. Like ice, water cannot be compressed.

GASES ARE FLUIDS THAT FILL THEIR CONTAINERS AND ARE EASILY COMPRESSED INTO A SMALLER VOLUME.

The air around us is a gas. The oxygen we inhale, and the carbon dioxide we exhale are both gases. The compressed air in a car tire fills the tire (its container). That air is compressed — it occupies a fraction of the volume that it would in the atmosphere.

ICE, WATER, AND STEAM ARE ALL COMPOSED OF THE SAME MOLECULES.

At first it may seem that solids, liquids, and gases are worlds apart, but a moment's thought tells us this is not the case. When we say "water is a liquid," we mean that this is its state at room temperature (and at a certain atmospheric pressure). At the **freezing point** of water, 0°C, it becomes ice. At 100°C, the **boiling point** of water, it becomes steam. Importantly, these changes are reversible. When we cool steam to below 100°C, it condenses again into to water. Similarly, when we warm ice to above 0°C it becomes water again.

A simple explanation of these phenomena is that solid, liquid and gaseous water are made of fundamentally the same thing — water molecules. We observe the organization of water molecules in different ways — or rather, in different states of matter — at different temperatures.

How do we explain the different properties of ice, water, and steam in terms of water molecules? In ice, water molecules are directly linked together in a 3-dimensional array with the position of each water molecule fixed. This explains both the rigidity of ice and its incompressibility. When ice melts, the water molecules break free of the ice lattice and form liquid water. Liquid water is incompressible, because its molecules are already **close** together; it is a fluid because its molecules can move around each other freely. At water's boiling point, the molecules move **apart** from each other. In the gas phase, water molecules fly around independently and therefore fill any container. In fact, steam is compressible because of the large amount of space between the gaseous molecules.

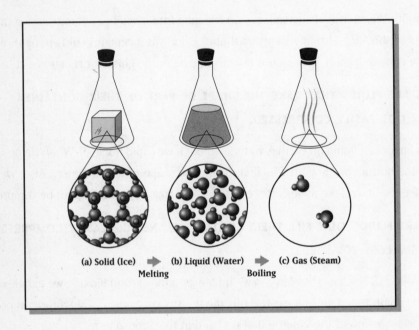

(a) Solid (Ice) ➡ (b) Liquid (Water) ➡ (c) Gas (Steam)
Melting   Boiling

This discussion is the basis of the **kinetic theory** of atoms and molecules, which explains the properties of matter in terms of the atoms and molecules from which it is made.

Chemical and Physical Properties of Matter

Scientists distinguish between the chemical and physical properties of matter.

PHYSICAL PROPERTIES OF MATTER CAN BE OBSERVED WITHOUT CHANGING THE CHEMICAL PROPERTIES OF THE MATTER.

The state of matter is one very important physical property. Other physical properties include color, ductility (the ability of metals to be pulled out into wires), hardness, and luster (metallic shine).

A yellow color is a physical property of the element sulfur. The fact that iodine turns directly from a solid to a gas, without becoming a liquid en route (we say it **sublimes**), is a physical property of iodine. The magnetism of iron is a physical property, because iron is not chemically changed into another substance by magnetization. A physical property of gallium metal is that it melts at 30°C, so you can melt it with the heat of your hand. A physical property of sugar is that it dissolves in a cup of coffee. However, the tendency of iron to rust is not a physical property since rusting involves the **chemical** change of iron into iron oxide.

PHYSICAL PROPERTIES MAY BE EXTENSIVE OR INTENSIVE. EXTENSIVE PROPERTIES ARE DEPENDENT UPON THE AMOUNT OF MATTER INVOLVED. INTENSIVE PROPERTIES ARE INDEPENDENT OF THE AMOUNT OF MATTER.

The mass (M) of a sample of matter is an extensive property, because mass varies with the amount of the sample. Volume (V) is an extensive property for the same reason. However, density (ρ) = M/V is an **intensive** property. As the sample size increases the mass increases, but so does the volume. The density of a sample (ρ), which is defined as the mass per unit volume, does not increase with sample size.

Color is an intensive property, but this point is more complex than you might think. An observer can see color independent of the amount of matter associated with that color. A red ladybug is no redder than a red bus. In fact, a single atom or molecule of a colored substance has color! However, the **intensity of color** we see is an **extensive** property. Our eyes, for example, are not nearly sensitive enough to detect color from a single atom. (The color from a single atom can be detected using an instrument known as a spectrometer.)

CHEMICAL PROPERTIES DESCRIBE THE WAY MATTER BEHAVES THROUGH CHEMICAL CHANGE.

One chemical property of iron is that it combines with oxygen to form rust (iron oxide); a chemical property of wood is that it burns in air. We can represent a particular chemical change, or **chemical reaction**, in terms of **a chemical equation**. On the left-hand side of the equation are the reactants. Reactants (as their name suggests) react to form **products**, which are represented on the right-hand side of the equation:

$$\text{iron} + \text{oxygen} \rightarrow \text{iron oxide}$$

It is due to a chemical property of the Statue of Liberty that it has turned a greenish color since it was first erected. The statue is covered with copper — a reddish metal — which over years of weathering took on a greenish coating of copper carbonate. This process is described by the chemical equation:

copper + water + oxygen + carbon dioxide → copper carbonate

When we pass an electric current through water, hydrogen peroxide and hydrogen are given off. We can write:

$$\text{water} \xrightarrow{\text{electric current}} \text{hydrogen peroxide + hydrogen}$$

In this process, water is converted into two new chemical species, hydrogen peroxide and hydrogen. A chemical reaction has occurred. The equation represents a reaction that defines one chemical property of water.

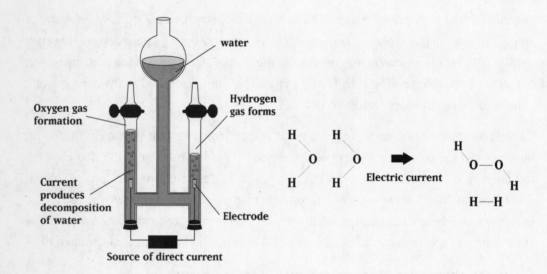

water

Oxygen gas formation

Hydrogen gas forms

Current produces decomposition of water

Electrode

Source of direct current

Electric current

The chemical properties of an element or compound are inherent to a single atom or molecule, while most, but not all, physical properties have meaning for only a collection of atoms or molecules.

Pure Substances

MATTER MADE UP OF A SINGLE ELEMENT OR COMPOUND IS KNOWN AS A SUBSTANCE.

We can touch and feel the world around us, and because of this we believe that our world has substance. In chemistry, however, **substance** takes on a more precise definition. Here, a **substance** is matter of a single kind — that is, composed of a single **element** or **compound** — which cannot be separated into simpler materials by any physical process.

A SAMPLE OF AN ELEMENT IS COMPOSED OF MANY IDENTICAL ATOMS OF THAT ELEMENT.

An "element" was first defined by Antoine Lavoisier, a French chemist born in Paris in 1743, as a substance that cannot be decomposed by chemical reaction into any simpler substance. (Lavoisier was executed by French revolutionaries in 1794, but not before he wrote the first modern chemistry textbook.) This decomposition cannot occur because each element is made up of a different type of atom. For example, a block of the element iron consists of many iron atoms and no atoms of other elements. Modern scientists realize that we cannot convert atoms of one element into atoms of another element using chemical reactions. We cannot, for example, convert lead into gold using chemical reactions, as much as we might like to.

There are 109 elements. Each one is a pure substance with different physical and chemical properties.

EACH ELEMENT IS REPRESENTED BY AN ATOMIC SYMBOL OF ONE OR TWO LETTERS.

The atomic symbols for some elements are easy enough to remember, since they are simply the first letter of the elements name in English. Examples include carbon (C), nitrogen (N), oxygen (O), sulfur (S), and phosphorus (P). Many of the less obvious element names are derived from Latin. Sodium — the element responsible for the orange color of old-fashioned street lights — has the atomic symbol Na, from its Latin name natrium (two letters are used to distinguish it from N for nitrogen). Some elements were named by classical scholars for their properties. For example, argon is named after the Greek word for inert or unreactive: *argos*. Argon is one of the least reactive of the 109 elements.

SYMBOLS AND LATIN NAMES OF ELEMENTS

ELEMENT	SYMBOL	LATIN NAME
Sodium	Na	Natrium
Potassium	K	Kalium
Antimony	Sb	Stibium
Copper	Cu	Cuprum
Gold	Au	Aurum
Silver	Ag	Argentum
Iron	Fe	Ferrum
Lead	Pb	Plumbum
Mercury	Hg	Hydragyrum
Tin	Sn	Stannum

ELEMENTS ARE ARRANGED INTO GROUPS AND PERIODS IN THE PERIODIC TABLE.

In any chemistry classroom you will see a chart known as the periodic table. The periodic table consists of boxes, each containing a different atomic symbol, each representing a different element. Vertical columns of boxes are known as **groups**, while horizontal rows of boxes are known as **periods**. The chemical and physical properties of elements vary gradually from the top to bottom of a group, and from left to right across a period. The arrangement of elements in the periodic table allows chemists to remember the relationships between the properties of different elements.

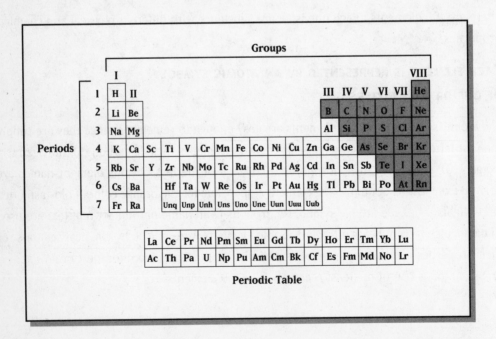

Periodic Table

In Chapter 4, we will investigate the organization of the periodic table in depth. For now, we will quickly become acquainted with its basic features.

Most of the elements in the periodic table are metals.

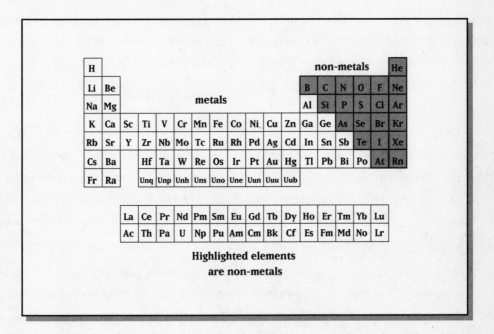

Some of the properties common to most metals are listed below. Metals are:

- lustrous — they have a shiny appearance
- ductile — they can be pulled into wires
- malleable — they can be hammered into sheets
- conductors — they conduct heat and electricity

All metals are solids at room temperature except mercury (Hg), which is a liquid. No metals are gases. Metallic properties of elements (such as malleability and conductivity) increase as one moves from right to left and from top to bottom over the periodic table.

THE REST OF THE ELEMENTS IN THE PERIODIC TABLE ARE NON-METALS.

The small portion of elements in the upper right of the periodic table display few metallic properties and their properties vary more than those of metals. These non-metals exist as gases and solids, except for bromine (Br), which is a liquid.

ELEMENTS IN THE PERIODIC TABLE HAVE A RANGE OF PROPERTIES. ELEMENTS WITHIN A GROUP HAVE SIMILAR PROPERTIES.

To grasp the variety represented in the periodic table we need only contrast the properties of elements in groups at the extreme right and at the extreme left of the table. At the extreme left of the periodic table are the Group I elements, known as the **alkali metals.** Alkali metals are soft, silvery, solid metals that react with water to produce hydrogen gas. The ferocity of reactions vary: lithium gently fizzes, while cesium reacts with violence.

$$\text{lithium + water} \rightarrow \text{lithium hydroxide + water}$$

$$\text{cesium + water} \rightarrow \text{cesium hydroxide + water}$$

The melting points of alkali metals are low and decrease as you move down the group from lithium, which melts at 180°C, to cesium, which melts just above room temperature at 28°C. Francium is so reactive that it has never been isolated in visible quantities. Elements such as francium are stored under oil (away from air and moisture), and are too reactive to occur naturally in their uncombined states.

At the other end of the periodic table in Group VIII are the **noble gases**, the most common of which is argon. Noble gases live in something like monastic isolation — they are unbound to each other or any other elements. These elements are highly unreactive. Just to the left of the noble gases are the halogens (Group VII). Fluorine, at the top of Group VII, is an almost colorless gas, chlorine is a yellow-green gas, bromine is a brown-red liquid, and iodine is a purple-black solid. All members of the halogen group are non-metals.

A SUBSTANCE MADE UP OF ATOMS OF TWO OR MORE DIFFERENT ELEMENTS, COMBINED IN A SPECIFIC AND UNIFORM RATIO, IS KNOWN AS A COMPOUND.

In a compound, the combination of elements is cemented by **chemical bonding**. Two simple types of compounds are **ionic solids** and **molecules**, which are held together by ionic and covalent bonding, respectively. For now, we will focus on the different ways that the two types of compounds can be described. (Later, in Chapter 5, we will discuss the distinction between ionic and covalent bonds.) Molecules are described by their molecular formula and ionic solids by their formula unit.

Molecules consist of definite discrete groups of bonded atoms. They are described by their **molecular formula**, which contains the atomic symbols for the atoms in the molecule together with numbers in subscript that indicate the number of atoms of that element in the molecule.

For example, H_2SO_4 is the molecular formula for sulfuric acid. The formula shows that each molecule contains 2 hydrogen (H) atoms, 1 sulfur (S) atom and 4 oxygen (O) atoms.

The formula unit of an ionic compound represents the relative amount of each ion in the compound. The formula unit of the common salt found in the ocean, in our bodies, and on the dinner table is NaCl, which represents sodium and chlorine in a 1:1 ratio. Titanium dioxide, used as a white pigment in paints and cosmetics, has the formula unit TiO_2 and contains two atoms of oxygen for every one of titanium.

Mixtures: Mix It Up!

MIXTURES ARE COMBINATIONS OF PURE SUBSTANCES. THERE ARE BOTH HOMOGENEOUS AND HETEROGENEOUS MIXTURES. A HOMOGENEOUS MIXTURE HAS A UNIFORM COMPOSITION THROUGHOUT THE SAMPLE. THE COMPOSITION OF A HETEROGENEOUS MIXTURE DIFFERS THROUGHOUT THE SAMPLE.

You are already familiar with the idea of mixtures. Mixed drinks, for example, contain a variety of liquors. Such cocktails may be homogeneous or heterogeneous. The cocktail of vodka and tomato juice known as a Bloody Mary is an example of a **homogeneous mixture**, because it is the same throughout. A cocktail known as a Brain (or, more descriptively, as a Bloody Brain) is an example of a **heterogeneous mixture**. This cocktail consists of strawberry schnapps, grenadine, and Irish cream. The thick, creamy, brown Irish cream forms a spongy brain-like clump in the red liquors — giving the drink its name. The cocktail is heterogenous because the mixture of fluids in the cocktail is not the same at every point in the liquid.

Mixtures can be separated into the pure substances that make them up — either elements or compounds — by physical methods.

FILTRATION AND DISTILLATION ARE TWO EXAMPLES OF PHYSICAL PROCESSES USED TO SEPARATE MIXTURES.

Filtration is used to separate heterogeneous mixtures of solids and liquids. Sand and sea water can be separated by filtration. The mixture is poured through a filter that allows sea water but not sand to pass through, thus separating the solids and the liquids.

Sea water itself is a homogeneous mixture of salt and water. The salt can be separated from the water by **distillation**. In this process, sea water is heated to 100°C (the boiling point of water). The steam is then cooled and collected (we say that it is distilled) to produce pure water. The salt remains in the original container.

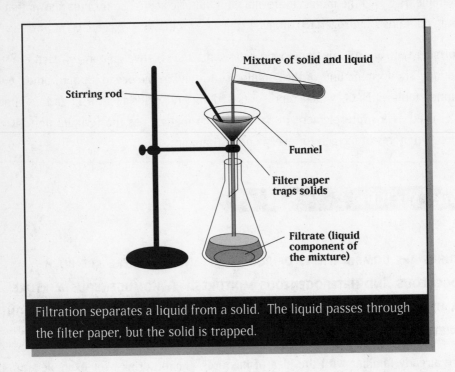

Filtration separates a liquid from a solid. The liquid passes through the filter paper, but the solid is trapped.

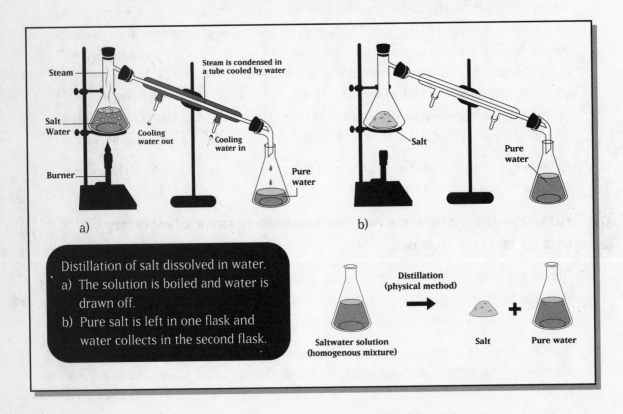

Distillation of salt dissolved in water.
a) The solution is boiled and water is drawn off.
b) Pure salt is left in one flask and water collects in the second flask.

KEY TERMS

atomic symbol: One or two letters used to denote an element.

chemical property: A description of the way that matter behaves in chemical change.

compound: A substance of two or more elements combined in a specific and uniform ratio.

element: A pure substance that cannot be decomposed by a chemical change. A sample of an element is composed of many identical atoms.

extensive properties: The physical properties of matter that are dependent on the amount of matter.

formula unit: A description of the ratio of elements in an ionic compound.

gas: Fluid matter that always fills its container and is compressible.

group: A vertical column in the periodic table.

heterogeneous mixture: A mixture in which the composition varies within the sample.

homogeneous mixture: A mixture in which the composition does not vary within the sample.

intensive properties: The physical properties of matter that are independent of the amount of matter.

liquid: Fluid matter that takes the shape of the part of its container it fills and is not easily compressed.

mixture: A combination of pure substances.

molecular formula: A description of the number of atoms of each element in a molecule.

molecule: A definite, discrete group of bonded atoms.

period: A horizontal row in the periodic table.

periodic table: A chart that arranges all the known elements into a useful form for chemists.

physical properties: The properties of matter that are observable without changing its chemical properties.

solid: Matter that is not compressible and has a shape independent of its container.

THRILLS, CHILLS AND DRILLS

True or False

1. Water spills everywhere, and yet solid ice can be packed into a snowball. Therefore, solids are more compressible than liquids.

2. The heating of ice causes it to melt into water, and the heating of water eventually leads to its boiling into steam.

3. It is observed in historic buildings that the glass at the bottom of windows is thicker than that at the top, even though the window panes were the same thickness throughout when they were first installed. This phenomenon tells us that glass is a liquid.

4. Beryllium — used in the construction of missiles and satellites — melts at 840° C and boils at 2470° C. At 2000° C, beryllium is a solid.

5. Alcohol boils at 78° C. Therefore, chicken in white wine sauce cooked at 90° C will have as much alcohol as the wine used to make it.

6. That milk sours is a physical property.

7. It is a physical property of sulfur, in eggs, that it turns silver spoons black.

8. Extensive physical properties are those that can be observed without changing the chemical nature of the matter and that depend on the amount of matter present.

9. When sugar is dissolved in a glass of water, the solution is clear and transparent. Therefore, the sugar-water solution is a pure substance.

10. Water (H_2O) is not a pure substance because it can be separated into hydrogen gas (H_2) and oxygen gas (O_2) by electrolysis.

11. The symbol for potassium is K.

12. The period in which an element is found in the periodic table is defined by the vertical column that it occupies.

13. Aluminum (Al), the most abundant element in the crust of the earth, is in Group V.

14. The elements carbon, nitrogen, phosphorus, and sulfur (which are all essential for life) are non-metals.

15. The formula unit for sodium chloride is NaCl.

16. The individual components in a homogeneous mixture remain physically separated and can be seen as separate components.

17. Distillation is a good way to separate salt from water.

18. Filtration is a good way to separate pebbles from water

Multiple Choice

1. Which of the following is not a state of matter? (More than one may be correct.)
   a) solid
   b) gas
   c) compound
   d) molecule
   e) liquid

2. Dr. Vat Apund is trying to determine whether or not his laboratory demonstration was successful. He anticipated the onset of a chemical reaction, but he can't remember what the signs of chemical changes are. Which of the following is *not* necessarily evidence of a chemical reaction having occurred?
   a) a change in compound composition
   b) a change in density of the compound present
   c) the spontaneous generation of an insoluble solid from a liquid at constant temperature
   d) a change in color of a compound at constant temperature

3. Which of the following does not constitute a chemical reaction?
   a) rusting of iron
   b) souring of milk
   c) boiling of liquid air
   d) burning of coal

4. Elements are classified according to certain properties. Which of an element's properties are always inherent – even in a single particle (as opposed to a collection of particles)?
   a) Chemical properties are inherent in a single particle.
   b) Physical properties are inherent in a single particle.
   c) Both types of properties are inherent in a single particle.
   d) Neither type of properties are inherent in a single particle.

5. Several polyamines are responsible for the smell when flesh rots. The production of polyamines by rotting meat is an example of

    a) a chemical reaction

    b) a physical process

    c) a process disfavored by free energy calculations

6. A sample of matter that exhibits uniform behavior during all physical changes necessarily would be

    a) an element

    b) a compound

    c) a mixture

    d) a pure substance

7. Which of the following symbols represents an element?

    a) CT

    b) Ca

    c) CA

    d) TX

8. Lithium is essential for our nervous system to function properly. The symbol for lithium is

    a) Lr

    b) Lu

    c) Li

    d) La

9. Which of the following properties is not a major characteristic of metals?

    a) luster

    b) smell

    c) ductility

    d) sonorous

10. Metallic elements are all solids at room temperature with the exception of

    a) aluminum

    b) lithium

    c) mercury

    d) calcium

11. The only non-metallic element to be a liquid at room temperature is:
    a) water
    b) oil
    c) fluorine
    d) bromine

The __(12)__ for an ionic compound and the __(13)__ for a molecular compound represent similar information.

12. a) formula unit
    b) molecular weight
    c) atomic mass

13. a) molar formula
    b) polyatomic anion formula
    c) molecular formula

14. The party-loving Ms. Eth Anol was confused as to how to classify her specialty drink, a screwdriver, which is made by mixing orange juice and vodka. To the unsuspecting observer, the glass looks as if it were just orange juice, because the vodka is not visible as a separate phase. This drink is best described as
    a) a heterogeneous mixture
    b) a homogeneous mixture
    c) a pure substance
    d) a non-alcoholic beverage

15. Ms. Eth Anol's party was raided by the police for excessive noise. In court, the prosecutor wanted to determine whether the amount of vodka present in the screwdriver punch was lethal. Even though two days elapsed before the trial, the screwdriver maintained a single phase. The police would do best to try to separate the components by
    a) filtration
    b) distillation
    c) carefully pouring off the vodka layer
    d) relying on the honesty of Ms. Eth Anol, who claims that no alcohol is present

Short Essays

1. Describe the different states of matter with respect to compressibility and shape.

2. Describe the microscopic changes that occur when an ice cube melts and is then heated into steam. Explain why these are physical (not chemical) changes.

3. Suppose you measure the mass, density, volume, color, melting point, color intensity, and boiling point of a sample of a new substance. Now, in a rush, you set aside an smaller amount of that sample for later analysis. Which of the above properties will it be necessary to measure again — and which will have remained the same? What is the name for those that need to be measured again?

4. A pure substance, A, is a solid at room temperature. When heated in an oil bath, it liquifies. After being cooled back to room temperature, the liquid cannot be solidified. What has happened?

5. Ima Student, who has been a chemistry graduate student for 10 years, is preparing characterizations of all of her thesis compounds. Unfortunately, it has been years since her experience with general chemistry, and she can't classify her observations as physical and chemical properties. Help her finish off this last step so that she may finally graduate. Explain the difference between a **physical** and a **chemical** property, and classify each of the following as appropriate:

   a. Water boils at 100°C and freezes at 0°C.

   b. Water will dissolve sugar but fails to dissolve tennis balls.

   c. Iron hinges rust when exposed to air.

   d. When sodium hydride is exposed to alcohol, hydrogen gas is released.

6. Mr. ECom Pounds is the CEO of a reputable industrial synthesis corporation. For the annual report to his shareholders, Mr. Pounds needs to divide the following into homogenous mixtures, heterogeneous, compounds, and elements. Unfortunately, an urgent golf appointment has up, and Mr. Pounds has asked you, the summer intern, to make the classification.

   a. cola soft drink

   b. chlorine water bleach

   c. sugar

   d. tap water

   e. distilled water

   f. iron powder

   g. chocolate chip ice cream

7. Mr. ECom Pounds greatest competitor, Ms. Fitt, is recruiting you away from Mr. Pounds' company. In order to receive a large signing bonus you must define the following as chemical or physical changes.

   a. combustion of natural gas

   b. bringing water to boil into steam

   c. melting iron

   d. burning of wood

   e. food digestion

   f. grinding salt

8. How many phases are there in the following mixtures, and how would you separate any mixtures you identify?

   a. sand and water

   b. salt and water

   c. sand and salt

ANSWERS

True or False

1. **False.** Solids and liquids are both incompressible.

2. **True.** Steam, ice, and water are all made up of water molecules.

3. **True.** Glass flows, and so it may be considered a liquid.

4. **False.** Substances above their melting point are either liquids or gases.

5. **False.** The sauce is cooked above the boiling point of alcohol. Most of the alcohol will boil off.

6. **False.** Chemical reactions cause milk to sour.

7. **False.** Chemical reactions between sulfur and silver cause the black color.

8. **True.** Extensive properties depend on the amount of matter; physical properties can be observed without changing the chemical properties. Therefore, extensive physical properties are as defined in the statement.

9. **False.** A pure substance is either an element or a compound.

10. **False.** Water is a pure substance. It can be separated into components by electrolysis, because electrolysis is a chemical process.

11. **True.**

12. **False.** The period of an element is defined by the horizontal row it occupies in the periodic table.

13. **False.** Aluminum is in Group III.

14. **True.**

15. **True.**

16. **False.** Homogeneous mixtures cannot be seen as separate components.

17. **True.**

18. **True.**

Multiple Choice Answers

1. (c) and (d)

2. (b) A density change is a physical change.

3. (c) Boiling is a physical change, all the others involve chemical reactions

4. (b)

5. (a)

6. (d) An element or compound remains unchanged by physical processes; a mixture does not. The term substance encompasses elements and compounds. The material may be either an element or a compound, but it must be a substance.

7. (b)

8. (c) Li

9. (b)

10. (c) Mercury is a liquid at room temperature.

11. (d) Fluorine is a gas; water is a compound; and oil is a mixture.

12. (a)

13. (c)

14. (b) The drink is not a heterogeneous mixture. It is not a pure substance, either, since it contains both ethanol and water.

15. (b) Filtration is used to separate a solid from a liquid, and homogeneous mixtures do not have layers. Distillation can be used to separate ethanol and water because of the difference in their boiling points.

Short Essay Answers

1. Solids are incompressible and do not adopt the shape of their container. Liquids are incompressible and take the shape of the part of the container they fill. Gases are compressible and fill their container.

2. Upon melting, the forces between water molecules holding them in a rigid array are overcome. In the liquid, there are still strong forces between molecules, but upon evaporating to a gas molecules break free of their interactions. These are physical changes; no chemical reactions take place.

3. Since we do not know the exact amount set aside, we will need to measure again the extensive properties: mass, volume, and color intensity.

4. Substance A has been chemically changed into a new substance.

5. The physical properties of matter can be observed without changing its chemical properties. Choices a and b are physical processes; c and d are chemical

6. a. homogeneous mixture

   b. homogeneous mixture

   c. compound

   d. homogeneous mixture
(tap water contains
carbonates and other
impurities)

   e. compound

   f. element

   g. heterogeneous mixture

7. a. chemical

   b. physical

   c. physical

   d. chemical

   e. chemical

   f. physical

8. a. 2 phases: separate by filtration

   b. 1 phase: distill off water

   c. 1 phase: dissolve salt in water; filter solution to separate sand and salty water; distill off water to leave salt.

CHAPTER

THE STRUCTURE
OF ATOMS:
AN INVESTIGATION

OVERVIEW

When we look from a distance at a sandy shoreline, the sand on the beach appears as continuous ground. When we look more closely, however, we see that the beach is made of individual grains of sand. While humans have probably noticed this phenomenon since time immemorial, ancient Greek philosophers took the observation one step further. They looked out from the beach to the sea and wondered whether water and indeed all matter is continuous, or whether it consists of discrete, minute particles which in bulk have the appearance of continuance. Thus the concept of the atom was born. The Greek philosopher Democritus of Abdera (ca. 460 - 370 B.C.), who is credited with formulating the concept, was so convinced of the prominence of atoms in the construction of matter that he proclaimed: "Nothing exists except atoms and empty space, everything else is opinion."

In this chapter, we will look at the classic experimental evidence for atoms. We will go on to look inside the atom and examine what differentiates atoms of different elements from each other. En route we will also discover that the same element can, in fact exist in different forms – which are known as isotopes. We will also find that we can explain the existence of the ions or charged versions of atoms.

CONCEPTS

DALTON'S ATOMIC HYPOTHESIS LINKS DIFFERENT ELEMENTS TO DIFFERENT TYPES OF ATOMS. TODAY, WE CAN "SEE" ATOMS.

In 1805, English schoolteacher John Dalton presented his **atomic hypothesis**, which was supported by his experiments. His hypothesis consisted of several main points:

- Atoms of a given element are identical.
- The atoms of different elements have different masses.
- A compound is a specific combination of atoms from more than one element.
- In chemical reactions, atoms are neither created or destroyed, but exchange partners to produce new substances.

Today, powerful evidence exists to support Dalton's hypothesis. We can see individual atoms using modern techniques such as one called surface tunneling microscopy.

Atoms: The Inside Story

ATOMS ARE MADE UP OF THREE TYPES OF PARTICLES: PROTONS, NEUTRONS, AND ELECTRONS.

Dalton's view of the atom is fine as far as it goes; however, it also leaves a great deal unanswered. An important question he did not answer is:

What distinguishes atoms of different elements?

The answer to this question rests within the structure of the atom itself. Looking inside the atom required intense investigation — years of gathering evidence by scientists Thompson, Rutherford and Chadwick. Their collective efforts eventually led to our modern knowledge of a triad of particles: **protons, neutrons, and electrons.**

ELECTRONS WERE DISCOVERED BY THOMPSON. THEY ARE NEGATIVELY CHARGED, LIGHT COMPONENTS OF THE ATOM.

J.J. Thompson, a physicist in Cambridge, England, provided the first clue to the structure of the atom. Around the turn of the twentieth century Thompson designed a glass chamber —

capped at either end with metal plates — and filled it with a small amount of gas. When he ran electricity between the two metal plates, he saw a beam of light emitted from a position close to the "cathode" (the negatively-charged plate). The beam of light was designated a cathode ray.

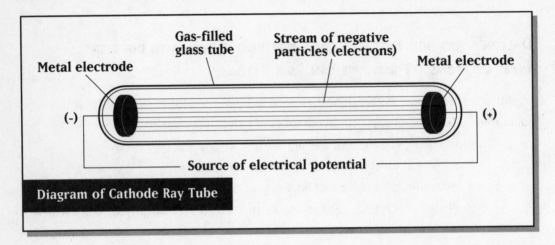

Metal electrode

Gas-filled glass tube

Stream of negative particles (electrons)

Metal electrode

(-)

(+)

Source of electrical potential

Diagram of Cathode Ray Tube

We now know that this light is caused by a stream of particles known as **electrons** (represented e⁻). The particles are attracted towards a positive plate. Because positive and negative charges attract one another, we know that electrons are negatively-charged. When the same effect was observed to be independent of the type of metal used in the plate, Thompson deduced that the electron is in all matter. In other words, the electron is a constituent of all atoms. His understanding of electrons and his glass chamber invention presaged a ubiquity of another sort: electrons in a tube similar to Thompson's produce the images on our television screens.

In 1909, American Robert Mullikan, at the University of Chicago, demonstrated that the charge of an electron is -1.6×10^{-19}C (Coulomb — the unit of electric charge), which we call a **unit** of negative charge. Electrons have a mass of 9.1×10^{-31}kg.

THE ATOM CONTAINS POSITIVELY-CHARGED PROTONS. A PROTON IS MORE THAN 1800 TIMES HEAVIER THAN ELECTRON AND HAS A UNIT OF POSITIVE CHARGE.

Armed with a single fact — the existence of the negatively-charged electron — and our everyday experience, we can deduce even more about the atom. Because matter is electrically neutral, we can guess that the atom itself is electrically neutral. If this is true, there must be positive particles in the atom that exactly balance the negatively-charged electrons. The positive particles in the atom are called **protons**. A proton has a mass of 1.67262×10^{-27} kg. While still very light, the proton is more than 1800 times heavier than an electron. It has a unit positive charge.

THE NUCLEAR MODEL OF THE ATOM WAS PROPOSED BY RUTHERFORD ON THE BASIS OF THE RUTHERFORD, GEIGER, MARSDEN EXPERIMENT.

The nature of protons in the atom was investigated by the famous scientist Ernest Rutherford (1871 - 1937) and his two students, Hans Geiger and Ernst Marsden. Rutherford was born on a farm in New Zealand and did much of his work in Cambridge, England after obtaining a scholarship to study there.

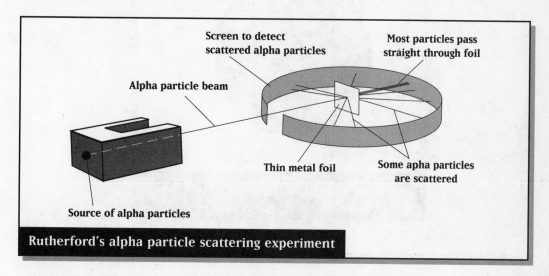

Rutherford's alpha particle scattering experiment

Rutherford knew that he could create positively-charged "alpha particles" from the element radium. He fired the **alpha** particles at a thin film of gold — one or two atoms thick. Though most of the particles passed straight through the film, to Rutherford's immense surprise, one in twenty thousand was deflected at an angle of more than 90°. It was almost "as if you fired a fifteen inch shell at a piece of tissue paper and it had come back and hit you," he said.

The nuclear atom was proposed by Rutherford to explain these observations. Rutherford suggested that most of the mass, and all of the positive charge, in the atom is concentrated in a tiny lump: the atomic nucleus. Surrounding the nucleus is empty space and electrons, which orbit the nucleus in much the same way that planets orbit the sun in the solar system.

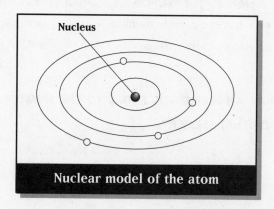

Nuclear model of the atom

Since most of the atom is empty space, most alpha particles pass straight through the gold foil. But the positively-charged alpha particles that hit a nucleus are repelled by its positive charge at a large angle, in much the same way that one billiard ball would bounce of another.

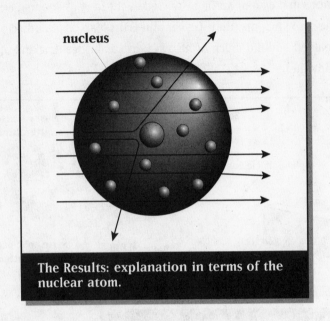

The Results: explanation in terms of the nuclear atom.

ELEMENTS ARE DISTINGUISHED BY THEIR ATOMIC NUMBER (Z), WHICH IS THE NUMBER OF PROTONS IN THEIR NUCLEI.

After Rutherford's discoveries, it was not long before Henry Moseley measured the number of protons in an atom, which has become known as the **atomic number (Z)** of an element. The atomic number strictly defines the type of atom, that is, the type of element an atom belongs to. Atoms with different atomic numbers belong to different elements. Atoms with the same atomic number belong to the same element.

Remember the question generated by Dalton's atomic hypothesis at the beginning of this chapter? What distinguishes atoms of different elements? The answer is that atoms of the same element are identical because they have the same number of protons, a number different from all other elements. For example, an atom of carbon always has the atomic number 6, nitrogen always has the atomic number 7, and oxygen always has the atomic number 8. These figures mean that the elements have 6, 7, or 8 protons in the nuclei of their respective atoms.

THE ATOMIC NUMBER OF AN ELEMENT IS EQUAL TO THE NUMBER OF ELECTRONS IN A NEUTRAL ATOM OF THAT ELEMENT.

Since the atom is neutral, and since electrons and protons both have unit charge, *and* since those unit charges are of an opposite sign, the number of protons must equal the number of electrons. Therefore, the atomic number indirectly tells us the number of electrons in an atom. For example, we noted above that carbon had an atomic number of 6. This means that a carbon atom has 6 protons in its nucleus, orbited by 6 electrons.

A THIRD PARTICLE, THE NEUTRON, WAS DISCOVERED IN THE ATOM BY CHADWICK. NEUTRONS ARE UNCHARGED, WEIGH THE SAME AS PROTONS, AND ARE FOUND IN THE NUCLEUS OF ATOMS.

A third particle — **the neutron** — was subsequently discovered in the atom by British physicist James Chadwick. The neutron has a mass of 1.67496×10^{-27} kg, almost the same as that of the proton. Like the proton, the neutron resides in the nucleus. However, unlike a proton, a neutron is uncharged. The neutron glues the protons together in the nucleus.

PARTICLE	RELATIVE MASS	RELATIVE CHARGE
electron	1	1-
proton	1836	1+
neutron	1839	none

THE ATOMIC MASS OF AN ELEMENT IS THE SUM OF THE MASSES OF THE PARTICLES IN THE NUCLEUS OF AN ATOM OF THE ELEMENT.

Atoms are made up of protons, neutrons and electrons. But because protons and neutrons are much heavier than electrons, the mass of an atom — its **atomic mass** — can be approximated by calculating the combined mass of the protons and neutrons that constitute it and ignoring the mass of electrons. (If we wanted to find the mass of a group of bowling balls and M & Ms, we could simply measure the bowling balls.) We report the **atomic mass (A)** of an element in the unit **amu**. One amu is defined as $1/12$ the mass of an atom of carbon-12 (this notation is explained below) and is approximately equal to the mass of a proton or a neutron. The atomic mass of an atom, therefore, is numerically equal to the number of protons and neutrons in the nucleus of the atom.

$$A = Z + \text{number of neutrons}$$

For example, carbon has an atomic number (Z) of 6. It also, most commonly, has 6 neutrons. The atomic mass of the most common form of carbon is therefore 6 + 6 = 12 amu.

Isotopes of an element have different atomic masses.

While atoms of an element have a fixed atomic number, they may have different atomic masses because the number of neutrons in an atom may vary. If two atoms of the same element have a different number of neutrons, then those types of atoms are known as **isotopes** of the element. For example, carbon exists as two isotopes: one with an atomic mass of 12, and another with an atomic mass of 14. Chemists often refer to isotopes using simply the element name followed by the atomic mass of the isotope. For example, "carbon-14" refers to an isotope of carbon with an atomic mass of 14; "carbon-12" refers to the isotope of carbon with an atomic mass of 12. Isotopes may also be represented by writing the symbol of an element superscripted with its atomic mass and subscripted with its atomic number. For example, carbon-14 is represented by $^{14}_{6}C$.

We can find the number of neutrons in any isotope by rearranging our equation:

$$A = Z + \text{number of neutrons}$$

Therefore, the number of neutrons = A - Z.

For example, since for all isotopes of carbon Z = 6, the number of neutrons in an atom of carbon-14 is

$$A - Z$$
$$14 - 6 = 8$$

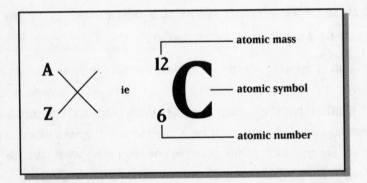

Symbol	Number of Protons	Number of Electrons	Number of Neutrons
$^{12}_{6}C$	6	6	6
$^{13}_{6}C$	6	6	7
$^{14}_{6}C$	6	6	8

EACH ELEMENT HAS A UNIQUE ATOMIC WEIGHT.

On earth, the isotopes of a given element exist in ratios that have been discovered experimentally. For example, not only do we know that chlorine exists as two isotopes, chlorine-35 and chlorine-37, we also know for every 75.8 atoms of chlorine-35, there are 24.2 atoms of chlorine-37. It is useful to define a property which takes into account this relative abundance of isotopes and allows us to use one number for the average atomic mass of a sample of chlorine. This property is an element's **atomic weight.** The atomic weight is simply the average of the atomic masses of the isotopes of an element weighted according to the isotopes' relative abundance.

For example, chlorine exists in two isotopes with atomic masses 34.97amu and 36.96amu in relative abundance of 75.8 percent and 24.3 percent, respectively.

Therefore, the atomic weight of chlorine atoms = (0.758 x 34.97amu) + (0.242 x 36.96amu) = 35.5amu.

Ions of an element are formed by the gain or loss of electrons.

Atoms are electrically neutral, but they can be made into charged particles called ions. A positively-charged ion is called a **cation**; a negatively-charged ion is called an **anion**. The existence of both cations and anions is explained in terms of the loss and gain of electrons — not by a change in the number of protons in the nucleus. (Remember, the number of protons in an element — the atomic number — is always the same.)

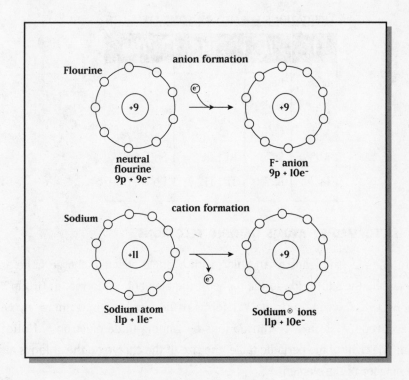

Ions are represented by the elemental symbol with the size and sign of the charge superscripted.

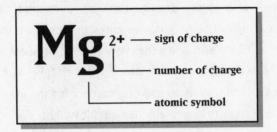

 CATIONS ARE FORMED BY THE LOSS OF ELECTRONS FROM AN ATOM.

The loss of one electron leads to a cation with a single positive charge. Sodium cations, for example are represented as Na^+. The loss of two electrons leads to a "two-plus" or **divalent** cation. Magnesium forms a divalent cation, Mg^{2+}. Similarly, aluminum forms the "three-plus," or **trivalent**, cation Al^{3+}. If you study the following table and compare it to the periodic table you will notice that the charge on the cations is the same as the group number of the element in the periodic table. In general, **the maximum, and sometimes only, charge number of cations of an element is equal to the group number of the element in the periodic table.** Cations are formed most readily by atoms at the left and bottom of the periodic table. Therefore, Group I elements generally form cations most easily, and cesium forms cations most easily of the Group I elements. (Francium is too unstable to consider.)

THE CATIONS FORMED BY SOME ELEMENTS

I	II	III	IV
Li^+	Be^{2+}		
Na^+	Mg^{2+}	Al^{3+}	
K^+	Ca^{2+}	Ga^{3+}	
Rb^+	Sr^{2+}	In^+, In^{3+}	Sn^{2+}, Sn^{4+}
Cs^+	Ba^{2+}	Tl^+, Tl^{3+}	Pb^{2+}, Pb^{4+}

 ANIONS ARE FORMED BY ATOMS GAINING ELECTRONS.

The gain of one electron leads to an anion with a single negative charge. The anions are named by adding the suffix **-ide** to the name of the element. Chlorine, in Group VII, forms chloride ions, Cl^-. Oxygen, in Group VI, forms oxide ions O^{2-} by gaining two electrons. Nitrogen, in Group V, forms N^{3-} nitride ions by gaining three electrons. Notice that **for elements on the right of the periodic table, the size of the charge on the anion is eight minus the group number of the element.**

SOME ANIONS FORMED BY SOME ELEMENTS*

IV	V	VI	VII
C^{4-}, C_2^{2-} Carbide	N^{3-} Nitride	O^{2-} Oxide	F^- Flouride
			Cl^- Chloride
			Br^- Bromide
			I^- Iodide

* Note that the arrangement of this table corresponds to the location of the elements
  in the periodic table, and not the charges of anions.

POLYATOMIC IONS ARE CHARGED MOLECULES.

In Chapter One, we discussed the existence of molecules, which are atoms combined in a specific ratio, and are building blocks of compounds. Molecules, like atoms, can be electrically charged. Charged molecules are known as **molecular ions** or **polyatomic ions.** An example of a polyatomic cation is NH_4^+, the ammonium ion. Examples of anions include SO_4^{2-} (the sulfate ion), PO_4^{2-} (the phosphate ion), and CO_3^{2-} (the carbonate ion). Note that the neutral version of a polyatomic ion need not exist. For example, though NH_4^+ exists, NH_4 does not. When polyatomic ions appear more than once in a formula unit, we subscript the ion with the number of times it appears. For example, barium nitrate contains two nitrate ions per barium atom. We write the formula unit for barium nitrate as $Ba(NO_3)_2$.

KEY TERMS

anion: A negatively-charged ion.

atom: The smallest particle with the chemical properties of an element. Atoms are made up of protons, neutrons, and electrons.

atomic mass: The mass of an atom, measured in amu.

atomic number (Z): The number of protons in the nucleus of an atom. Elements are defined by their atomic numbers.

atomic weight: The average atomic mass of an element. Takes into account the relative abundance of each of its isotopes.

cation: A positively-charged ion.

electrons: Light, negatively-charged particles that orbit the nucleus of an atom.

ion: Charged particles formed by the loss or gain of electrons from atoms.

isotopes: Elements with the same atomic numbers, but different atomic masses. They have the same number of protons, but different number of neutrons.

neutrons: Heavy, uncharged particles in the nuclei of atoms.

nucleus: The center of an atom. The nucleus of an atom contains protons and neutrons.

polyatomic ion: A molecule that has lost or gained electrons and therefore has a charge.

protons: Heavy, positively-charged particles in the nuclei of atoms.

THRILLS, CHILLS AND DRILLS

True or False

1. Dalton's theory states that atoms must combine in fixed ratios to form new compounds, but it does not predict the existence of even the most basic of molecules, such as water.

2. Cathode rays are streams of electrons flowing from the cathode toward the anode in a gas-discharge tube.

3. The charges on protons, electrons, and neutrons are +1, -1, and 0, respectively.

4. The charge-to-mass ratios for the electron and the proton are 1.7588×10^8 C/g and 9.5791×10^4 C/g, respectively. This means that the electron is more highly charged than the proton.

5. Alpha particles in Rutherford's gold leaf experiment bounce back because of electrostatic repulsion between the alpha particles and the gold atom nuclei.

6. The nuclei of atoms are held together by electrostatic attractions between the positive protons and the negative neutrons.

7. If the atomic mass of germanium-70 is 69.9244 amu, then an atom of germanium-70 has a mass in grams equal to 69.9244 times the mass of 1 amu in grams.

8. Atoms of the same element can have different atomic numbers.

9. Atoms having different numbers of protons are known as isotopes of an element.

10. Isotopes of an element have startlingly different chemical properties.

11. The atomic weight is an average number that takes into account all known isotopes of an element.

12. Carbon-13 has 7 neutrons per atom.

13. The existence of element isotopes supports Dalton's atomic hypothesis unconditionally.

14. The atomic weight defines an element.

15. When sodium metal and chlorine are allowed to react, they form the common table salt, NaCl (sodium chloride). In this reaction, an electron is transferred from sodium to chlorine. The resulting sodium ion would attract a positively-charged alpha particle.

16. Cations are positively-charged.

17. Like charges repel, and opposite charges attract. Therefore, when placed in an electric field, a cation will be attracted to the positively-charged plate.

18. The neutral version of a polyatomic ion must exist.

Multiple Choice

1. Which of the following is not a property of standard-issue cathode rays?
   a) They travel in straight lines from the cathode to the anode.
   b) They undergo deflection parallel to an applied-electrostatic field toward the negative electrode.
   c) They can cause the ionization of gas molecules.
   d) They provide evidence for the existence of the subatomic particle known as the electron.

2. The α -particles (alpha particles) used by Rutherford in his gold leaf experiments were actually helium +2 cations. This means that they were composed of
   a) 2 protons, 2 neutrons, and 2 electrons
   b) 2 protons and 2 electrons
   c) a gas that makes your voice high-pitched
   d) 2 protons and 2 neutrons
   e) 2 neutrons and 2 electrons

3. Rutherford's model of the nuclear atom suggests that all of the positive charge of an atom is located in the nucleus. If this is true, what is most responsible for keeping the electrons as a part of the atom?
   a) they aren't a part of the atom, but rather matter exists as a "sea of electrons"
   b) fear
   c) they aren't a part of the atom, but rather constantly exchanged with the environment
   d) electrostatic attraction between electrons and the nucleus
   e) gravitational attraction between electrons and the nucleus

4. The atomic number of an element is equal to
    a) the number of protons in an atom of the element
    b) the number of neutrons in an atom of the element
    c) the number of electrons in an atom of the element
    d) a and c
    e) a and b

5. The number of electrons in a neutral atom is equal to
    a) the number of neutrons in the nucleus
    b) the atomic mass
    c) the atomic weight
    d) the number of protons in the nucleus
    e) none of the above

6. We know that carbon-12 has 6 protons and 6 neutrons, so we would expect that its atomic weight should be approximately 12.000. However, carbon is reported to have an atomic weight of 12.011 amu. Account for this discrepancy.
    a) Carbon atoms of different masses exist.
    b) The atom's electrons contribute the remaining 0.011 amu.
    c) There is an insignificant statistical variation in atomic mass.
    d) Atomic mass is relative to the velocity of atomic motion, so faster moving carbon atoms have higher masses, thereby raising the average mass.

7. When an atom loses an electron, what is the charge on the resulting particle, and what is the resulting particle called?
    a) It is called an anion with a charge of 1-.
    b) It is called a cation with a charge dependent on the initial charge of the atom.
    c) It is called a cation with a charge of 1+.
    d) It is called an anion with a charge dependent on the initial charge of the atom.
    e) It is called an anion with a charge of 1+.

8. Chlorine exists as chloride ions in sodium chloride. The charge of chloride ions is
    a) +1
    b) -1
    c) +3
    d) -3
    e) +2

9. State the number of nitrogen (N) atoms and nitrate (NO_3^-) ions in 3 molecules of ammonium nitrate (NH_4NO_3).

    a) 6 nitrogen atoms, 3 nitrate ions

    b) 3 nitrogen atoms, 6 nitrate ions

    c) 1 nitrogen atoms, 4 nitrate ions

    d) 2 nitrogen atoms, 2 nitrate ions

10. In a cation, the atomic number of an atom is

    a) greater than the number of electrons in the atom

    b) unrelated to the number of electrons in an atom

    c) equal to the atomic mass of the atom

    d) equal to half the atomic mass of the atom

    e) less than the number of electrons in the atom

11. Barium is in Group II of the periodic table. We expect barium to form ions with a charge of

    a) 2+

    b) 6+

    c) 10+

    d) 3+

    e) 1+

12. Given that sodium forms 1+ ions and iodine forms 1- ions, and that sodium iodide is electrically neutral, a reasonable formula for sodium iodide is

    a) NaI_2

    b) NaI

    c) Na_2I

    d) Na_3I_2

    e) $NaCl$

13. Since magnesium forms 2+ ions and oxygen forms 2- ions, a reasonable formula unit for magnesium oxide is

    a) Mg_2O_2

    b) Mg_2O

    c) MgO_2

    d) MgO

    e) MgN

14. Ammonium hydroxide can be considered to be a combination of NH_4^+ ions and OH^- ions. Since ammonium hydroxide is a neutral compound, the ratio of these ions must be

    a) 1:1

    b) 4:1

    c) 1:4

    d) ¼:1

    e) 1: ¼

15. Which of the following statements is true for monatomic, but not polyatomic ions?

    a) They can have either positive or negative charge.

    b) They have a charge of one or more.

    c) They are made of atoms

    d) The neutral species corresponding to the ion must exist.

    e) All of the above.

Short Essay

1. Dalton's atomic hypothesis states that all atoms of a given element are identical. Is this true?

2. Technetium (Tc, Z = 43) was the first element to be produced artificially. Mr. Syn Thesis was trying to use this element in the last step of his graduate project, only to be befuddled by the presence of two isotopes.

    a. Describe to the confused chemist what constitutes an isotope.

    b. The major isotope of Tc has mass of 97 amu. How many neutrons are present in an atom of this isotope of Tc?

    c. A second isotope contains 52 neutrons. What is its mass number?

    d. If the isotope in b) occurs with 67 percent frequency, and only two isotopes exist, what is the reported atomic weight of technetium?

3. The two naturally occurring isotopes of copper, ^{63}Cu and ^{65}Cu, have masses of 62.9296 and 64.9278 amu respectively. The atomic mass of copper is reported to be 63.546 amu. Calculate the percentage of each isotope in a representative piece of copper.

4. The ions formed by some elements can display recognizable trends. Write down the main ions formed by:

    a. Li, Na, K, Rb, Cs

    b. Be, Mg, Ca, Ba

    c. N, O, F

    d. What trends do you notice between the charge number and the group number of the element in the periodic table?

ANSWERS

True or False Answers

1. **True**. Dalton's theory tells us that some atoms combine, but it is silent as to which atoms.

2. **True**.

3. **True**.

4. **False**. A proton and an electron have charges of equal size and opposite sign. The difference in charge mass ratios reflects the larger mass of the proton.

5. **True**. Both alpha particles and the nuclei are positively-charged

6. **False**. Protons are positive; neutrons are neutral. There is no electrostatic attraction. The nucleus is cemented by a strong force called a nuclear force.

7. **True**.

8. **False**. The atomic number (number of protons) of an element is always the same.

9. **False**. Isotopes have different numbers of neutrons, but the same number of protons.

10. **False**. Isotopes of an element have almost identical chemical properties.

11. **True**.

12. **True**.

13. **False**. Dalton's hypothesis says atoms of the same element are perfectly identical. Isotopes are not identical.

14. **True**.

15. **True**.

16. **True**.

17. **False**. Cations are positively-charged and will be repelled by a positive plate.

18. **False**. Unlike an atomic ion, the neutral version of a polyatomic ion need not exist.

Multiple Choice Answers

1. (b)

2. (d) Helium has an atomic number of 2 and an atomic mass of 4. The neutral atom has two protons, two neutrons. and two electrons. The two-plus cation, therefore has two protons, two neutrons, but no electrons.

3. (d)

4. (d) The atomic number is defined as the number of protons in an element, but this number is also equal to the number of electrons.

5. (d) The number of protons and electrons are equal in a neutral atom.

6. (a) Carbon has several isotopes.

7. (c)

8. (b) Chlorine is a halogen (Group VII) element. The charge of its ion is 8 - 7 = 1, which by definition has lost electrons.

9. (b)

10. (a) The atomic number is equal to the number of protons. In a cation, the number of electrons is always less than the atomic number.

11. (a) Cations are formed with a charge equal to the group number of the element.

12. (b) NaI is the only electrically neutral combination of Na^+ and I^- ions listed.

13. (d)

14. (a) The ions have equal and opposite charges. They should be combined in a 1:1 ratio to produce a neutral compound.

15. (d)

Short Essay Answers

1. No. Atoms of the same element may be isotopes. Isotopes are not identical because the number of neutrons vary. This section of Dalton's hypothesis does not hold true.

2. a. Isotopes of an element have the same atomic number but different atomic masses, because isotopes have a different number of neutrons.

   b. number of neutrons = atomic mass - atomic number = 97 - 43 = 54

   c. atomic mass = number of neutrons + atomic number = 52 + 43 = 95

   d. [67 / 100 x 97amu] + [(100 - 67) / 100 x 95] = 96.33.

3. [(y / 100) x 62.9296] + [(100 - y) / 100 x 64.9278]. If we solve for y, we get 63.546.

4. a. all +1

   b. all +2

   c. N^{-3}, O^{-2}, F^-

   d. The charge number of a cation is equal to the group number of the element in the periodic table. The charge number of an anion is equal to eight minus the group number.

CHAPTER

CHEMICAL CHANGE

OVERVIEW

At its heart, chemistry is about change. But chemical changes are not confined to the world of labs, beakers and flasks, and bubbling green liquids. In fact, countless phenomena that we encounter every day are the result of chemical changes. Hair is dyed and bleached. Beer is brewed and grapes are fermented to make wine. Rocket fuels burn and carry us into space. Leaves turn from green to brilliant reds and yellows in autumn. All of these processes rely on chemical change.

How do we recognize the signs of chemical change? And more important to chemists, how do we understand these changes and represent them?

In this chapter we focus on writing equations that represent chemical reactions. We will learn that writing the equations correctly requires "balancing" them so the number of atoms remains the same. Finally, we will learn the simple steps that allows to balance chemical equations.

CONCEPTS

CHEMICAL REACTIONS ARE OFTEN VISIBLE. HOWEVER, IN SOME CASES THE ONLY SIGN OF REACTION IS A CHANGE IN TEMPERATURE.

We can presume that a chemical reaction is occurring when we observe one or more of the following changes:

- The evolution of heat, possibly with a flame.

- The formation of a solid.

- The formation of gas bubbles, but not bubbles due simply to boiling.

- A change in color.

For example, when methane burns in air, the chemical reaction (known as combustion) results in a flame. When solutions of sodium dichromate and lead sulfate are mixed, a yellow solid is produced due to a chemical reaction. When zinc metal is added to HCl (hydrochloric acid), the new solution fizzes. When clothes are bleached, they change color.

In some cases, however, the sole indication that a reaction is occurring is a change in temperature. Temperature changes occur as a result of reactions giving off or taking in heat. Some reactions that produce heat are utilized in hot packs that are used in winter to keep hands and feet warm. Other reactions that take in heat, lowering the temperature, are used in cold packs that athletes apply to injuries to prevent their swelling up.

Representing and Understanding Chemical Change

CHEMICAL REACTIONS INVOLVE THE REARRANGMENT OF ATOMS. ATOMS OF AN ELEMENT ARE NEITHER CREATED NOR DESTROYED IN THE COURSE OF A CHEMICAL REACTION, BUT RECONFIGURED INTO NEW COMPOUNDS. A BALANCED EQUATION REPRESENTS THIS RECONFIGURATION.

Underlying the observable signs of chemical change are chemical reactions. For example, the blue flame associated with burning methane in air is a result of the chemical reaction between CH_4 (methane) and O_2 (oxygen). Chemical reactions are represented using chemical equations. To understand chemical equations, consider an analogy between the language of chemistry and everyday English:

We can compare an atom of an element to a letter of the alphabet, and compounds to words. In English, we can change the order of letters in a word to make a new word or words. For example, we can rearrange the letters in the word **aloof** to make two words: **a fool.** If we represent our transformation of one set of words into another set of words using an arrow, we can write:

$$aloof \rightarrow a + fool$$

The rearrangement of "aloof" into "a fool" is an example of an anagram. Notice that a property of anagrams is that all the letters in the first word are used in its anagram. No more, no less.

In exactly the same way, chemical equations represent rearrangements of elements (letters) from one set of compounds (words) into another set of compounds (new words). For example, the chemical reaction that occurs when solid calcium carbonate is heated and turns into solid calcium oxide and carbon dioxide gas is represented by the following equation.

$$CaCO_3(s) \rightarrow CaO(s) + CO_2(g)$$

The compound on the left ($CaCO_3$) is the **reactant**; the compounds on the right (CaO and CO_2) are **products**. The letter in parenthesis following the element or compound represents the **physical states** of the reactants and products.

SYMBOL	STATE
(s)	solid
(l)	liquid
(g)	gas
(aq)	dissolved in water (in aqueous solution)

Notice that (as in an anagram) we utilize the same number of atoms of each element (each letter) on each side of the arrow.

Knowing the reactants and products of a chemical reaction enables us to write a chemical equation. For example, if we were told aluminum reacts with oxygen to produce aluminum oxide, we could write down the equation:

$$Al(s) + O_2 (g) \rightarrow Al_2O_3 (s)$$

This equation is **unbalanced**, as we can see from the table below.

Left-hand side: reactants   ### Right-hand side: products

TYPE OF ATOM	#	SOURCE	TYPE OF ATOM	#	SOURCE
Al	1	Al	Al	2	Al_2O_3
O	2	O_2	O	3	Al_2O_3

The number of aluminum atoms on the right-hand side is greater than the number on the left-hand side. The number of oxygen atoms on the right-hand side is greater than the number of oxygen atoms on the left-hand side. (To continue our analogy, the products are not anagrams of the reactants.)

CHEMICAL EQUATIONS ARE BALANCED BY CHOOSING APPROPRIATE STOICHIOMETRIC COEFFICIENTS.

We can **balance** a chemical equation (make it into an anagram) by choosing coefficients for each item in the equation. The coefficients are chosen such that the total number of atoms of each element is equal on both sides of the equation. These coefficients are known as **stoichiometric coefficients**.

There is no single correct method for balancing all chemical equations, but you should use the guidelines on the next page to help you get started. With these rules in mind, practice until you feel comfortable.

Guidelines

- Write an unbalanced equation for a reaction

- Set the coefficient of the most complicated molecule to 1, whether that molecule is a reactant or product.

- Attempt to balance the elements. Begin with those elements in the simplest molecule and proceed toward the most complicated molecule, until the equation is balanced in all elements.

- Check that the equation is balanced by tabulating the quantity of each element and showing that it is the same on both sides of the equation.

As an example of how to use these guidelines to balance an equation, consider again the equation:

$$Al(s) + O_2(g) \rightarrow Al_2O_3(s)$$

The most complicated molecule is Al_2O_3. We set its coefficient to one. The simplest species is Al on the left-hand side. Since there are two aluminum atoms on the right-hand side, we can balance the equation in terms of aluminum atoms by setting the coefficient of Al on the left-hand side to 2. Doing this gives us:

$$2Al(s) + O_2(g) \rightarrow Al_2O_3(s)$$

This new equation is balanced in terms of aluminum atoms, but not oxygen atoms. Al_2O_3, on the right-hand side, contains three oxygen atoms. On the other side of the equation, the only oxygen-containing species is O_2, which contains two oxygen atoms. We need to find the stochiometric coefficient (x) that allows the number of O's on the left-hand side to be the same as the number on the right-hand side

$$x(2O) = 3O$$

x = 3O/2O. Canceling the O's, x = $^3/_2$.

The balanced equation is:

$$2Al(s) + {}^3/_2\, O_2(g) \rightarrow Al_2O_3(s)$$

Though this is a balanced equation, it is desirable to have all the coefficients as whole numbers. We can achieve this by multiplying all coefficients by 2.

Therefore, our final balanced equation is:

$$4Al(s) + 3O_2(g) \rightarrow 2Al_2O_3(s)$$

We can check our work by showing that there are an equal number of atoms of each element on the left-hand side and the right-hand side of the equation. See the table below.

<u>**Left-hand side: reactants**</u>   <u>**Right-hand side: products**</u>

TYPE OF ATOM	#	SOURCE	TYPE OF ATOM	#	SOURCE
Al	4(1) = 4	Al	Al	2(2) = 4	Al_2O_3
O	3(2) = 6	O_2	O	2(3) = 6	Al_2O_3

We can **never** balance a chemical equation by changing the subscripts of a formula. If we did, our equation would then involve a different chemical species; even though we could balance the number of atoms, we would be describing a wholly different transformation. For example, trying to balance the above equation as...

$$Al_2(s) + O_3(g) \rightarrow Al_2O_3(s)$$

...would be wrong.

Here is an equation that represents the reaction used to power the reuseable space shuttle rockets.

$$Al(s) + NH_4ClO_4(s) \rightarrow Al_2O_3(s) + AlCl_3(s) + NO(g) + H_2O(g)$$

At first glance, this equation looks quite difficult to balance, but it isn't if you follow the guidelines.

The most complicated molecule is NH_4ClO_4, so we set its coefficient to one. The nitrogen atoms are balanced: ther is one nitrogen atom on the left and also one on the right. The next element to balance is hydrogen. On the left-hand side, there are four hydrogen atoms; on the right-hand side, there are two hydrogen atoms per H_2O molecule, and no others. Setting the H_2O coefficient to two balances the hydrogen atoms.

$$Al(s) + NH_4ClO_4(s) \rightarrow Al_2O_3(s) + AlCl_3(s) + NO(g) + 2H_2O(g)$$

Next, look at the chlorine atoms. There is one in NH_4ClO_4, and three on the right-hand side in $AlCl_3$. We balance the chlorine atoms by putting the coefficient 1/3 before $AlCl_3$.

$$Al(s) + NH_4ClO_4(s) \rightarrow Al_2O_3(s) + 1/3\ AlCl_3(s) + NO(g) + 2H_2O(g)$$

To balance the oxygen atoms is a little more complicated. There are four oxygen atoms on the left-hand side. On the right-hand side there are three oxygen atoms in Al_2O_3, two in

$2H_2O$, and one in NO. Since nitrogen and hydrogen are already balanced, we leave H_2O and NO alone and balance the oxygen atoms by changing the coefficient of Al_2O_3.

$$4O = 2O \text{ (from } 2H_2O) + 1O \text{ (from NO)} + nO \text{ (from } Al_2O_3)$$

Solving for n, we see Al_2O_3 must provide 1O. The coefficient of Al_2O_3 is therefore 1/3.

$$Al(s) + NH_4ClO_4(s) \rightarrow 1/3\ Al_2O_3(s) + 1/3\ AlCl_3(s) + NO(g) + 2H_2O\ (g)$$

Finally we need to balance aluminum atoms. The left-hand side has 1Al; the right-hand side has 1Al. Therefore, the equation is balanced.

$$A(s) + NH_4ClO_4(s) \rightarrow 1/3\ Al_2O_3(s) + 1/3\ AlCl_3(s) + NO(g) + 2H_2O(g)$$

Multiplying the whole equation by 3 produces whole number coefficients.

$$3Al(s) + 3NH_4ClO_4(s) \rightarrow Al_2O_3(s) + AlCl_3(s) + 3NO(g) + 6H_2O(g)$$

If you check this equation, you will see that there are an equal number of aluminum, nitrogen, hydrogen, chlorine, and oxygen atoms on each side.

Left-hand side: reactants   **Right-hand side: products**

TYPE OF ATOM	#	SOURCE	TYPE OF ATOM	#	SOURCE
Al	3	Al	Al	3	Al_2O_3, $AlCl_3$
N	3	NH_4ClO_4	N	3	NO
H	12	NH_4ClO_4	H	12	H_2O
Cl	3	NH_4ClO_4	Cl	3	$AlCl_3$
O	12	NH_4ClO_4	O	12	Al_2O_3, NO, H_2O

KEY TERMS

balanced equation: An equation in which the number of atoms of a given type is equal in the products and reactants. Equations are balanced by the choice of stoichiometric coefficients.

chemical equation: A representation of the rearrangement of atoms that occurs in a chemical reaction.

chemical reaction: The transformation of one substance into another.

products: Chemical species on the right-hand side of a chemical equation.

reactants: Chemical species on the left-hand side of a chemical equation.

stoichiometric coefficients: Numbers that precede chemical formulae in chemical equations. Equations are balanced by the choice of correct stoichiometric coefficients.

THRILLS, CHILLS AND DRILLS

True or False

1. The substances present before a chemical reaction occurs are called the products.

2. The clues that a chemical reaction has occurred are always visible.

3. Matter is neither created nor destroyed in chemical reactions.

4. To denote that a substance is dissolved in water we write (aq) after its formula.

5. The total number of atoms present before and after a chemical reaction is constant.

6. The total number of a atoms of a given element is constant before and after a chemical reaction.

7. The total amount of each compound is the same before and after a chemical reaction.

8. If two molecules of oxygen gas (O_2) combine with one molecule of hydrogen gas to form water (H_2O) vapor, an **unbalanced** chemical equation is:

$$H_2(g) + O_2(g) \rightarrow H_2O(g)$$

9. A **balanced** chemical equation for the process described in Question 8 is:

$$H_2(g) + O_2(g) \rightarrow H_2O_2(g)$$

10. A stoichiometric coefficient can be a subscript in a formula.

11. Chemical equations can be balanced by choosing the correct stoichiometric coefficients.

12. Chemical equations cannot be balanced by changing the subscripts in a formula within the equation.

13. A **balanced** equation for the process described in Question 8 is:

$$H_2(g) + O_2(g) \rightarrow 2H_2O(g)$$

14. $FeO_2 + C \rightarrow Fe + CO_2$ is a balanced chemical equation.

CHAPTER 3: CHEMICAL CHANGE

Multiple Choice

1. Which of the following is definitely not the sign of a chemical reaction?
    a) bubbles due to boiling
    b) the evolution of heat
    c) a change of color
    d) a change of melting point

2. Cold packs rely on reactions that
    a) produce heat
    b) take in heat
    c) neither a nor b
    d) are not spontaneous

3. A chemical equation represents the conversion of
    a) reactants to products
    b) products to reactants
    c) lead to gold
    d) solids to liquids

4. $H_2O(s) \rightarrow H_2O(l)$ is an example of
    a) a balanced chemical reaction
    b) an unbalanced chemical reaction
    c) physical change
    d) boiling

5. When white phosphorus [$P_4(s)$] is heated in the presence of oxygen gas (O_2), the oxide P_4O_{10} is formed. A balanced equation for this process is
    a) $P_4 + O_2 \rightarrow P_4O_2$
    b) $P_4 + 5O_2 \rightarrow P_4O_{10}$
    c) $4P + O_{10} \rightarrow P_4O_{10}$
    d) none of the above

6. In a chemical equation, the total number of atoms in the reactants and products are
    a) the same
    b) different
    c) the answer depends on the reaction

7. In a chemical reaction, the total number of molecules are necessarily

   a) the same

   b) different

   c) the answer depends on the reaction

8. In a chemical reaction, the mass of the reactants and products is necessarily

   a) the same

   b) different

   c) the answer depends on the reaction

Short Essays

1. When elemental lithium (Li) reacts with chlorine gas (Cl_2), lithium chloride is formed (LiCl).

   a. Write an unbalanced equation for this reaction.

   b. Balance the equation.

2. Write unbalanced equations for the processes described:

   a. Sodium metal reacts with water to produce hydrogen gas and sodium hydroxide (NaOH) in aqueous solution.

   b. Aluminum, when heated in the presence of oxygen gas, forms a solid oxide (Al_2O_3).

   c. Calcium sulfate ($CaSO_4$) decomposes into solid calcium oxide (CaO) and sulfur dioxide (SO_2) gas.

   d. Zinc metal reacts with copper sulfate ($CuSO_4$) solution to form zinc sulfate ($ZnSO_4$) solution and copper metal.

   e. Silicon for the computer chip industry is made by the reaction of SiO_2(s) (sand) and elemental carbon. The reaction produces pure silicon and carbon monoxide.

3. Balance the equations that you wrote for Question 2.

4. Balance the following chemical equations.

a. $Sr + HNO_3 \rightarrow Sr(NO_3)_2 + H_2$

b. $NaClO_3 \rightarrow NaCl + O_2$

c. $Pb(NO_3)_2 + KI \rightarrow PbI_2 + KNO_3$

d. $Ba(NO_3)_2 + NH_4IO_3 \rightarrow Ba(IO_3)_2 + NH_4NO_3$

e. $HF + SiO_2 \rightarrow SiF_4 + H_2O$

5. Balance the following chemical equations.

a. $Na_2S_2O_3 + H_2O_2 \rightarrow Na_2S_3O_6 + Na_2SO_4 + H_2O$

b. $Li_2O + H_2O \rightarrow LiOH$

c. $Na_2O_2 + H_2O + CO_2 \rightarrow NaHCO_3 + O_2$

d. $Cu_2S + S_8 \rightarrow CuS$

6. Balance the following chemical equations.

a. $CuSO_4 + KI \rightarrow CuI + I_2 + K_2SO_4$

b. $Al + H_2SO_4 \rightarrow Al_2(SO_4)_3 + H_2$

c. $C_6H_6 + H_2 \rightarrow C_6H_{12}$

d. $PBr_3 + H_2O \rightarrow H_2PO_2 + HBr$

7. Balance the following chemical equations.

a. $O_2 \rightarrow O_3$

b. $AsI_3 \rightarrow As + I_2$

c. $Na_4P_2O_7 + AgNO_3 \rightarrow Ag_4P_2O_7 + NaNO_3$

d. $Na_2S_5 + O_2 \rightarrow Na_2S_2O_3 + S_2$

e. $K_2S_2O_3 + Cl_2 + H_2O \rightarrow KHSO_4 + HCl$

8. Balance the following chemical equations.

   a. $NO + O_2 \rightarrow NO_2$

   b. $B_2O_3 + C \rightarrow B_4C_3 + CO_2$

   c. $CO_2 + H_2O \rightarrow C_6H_{12}O_6 + O_2$

   d. $Li_2SO_3 + HBr \rightarrow LiBr + SO_2 + H_2O$

ANSWERS

True or False Answers

1. **False.**

2. **False.** Sometimes the only clue is a change in temperature.

3. **True.** Reactions simply rearrange matter.

4. **True.**

5. **True.** Reactions simply rearrange atoms.

6. **True.** Atoms are rearranged, not interchanged.

7. **False.** The amount of a compound may change in the course of a chemical reaction.

8. **True.**

9. **False.** The equations in Question 8 and Question 9 are different.

10. **False.**

11. **True.** This method is the only possible one in balancing chemical equations

12. **True.**

13. **True.**

14. **True.**

Multiple Choice Answers

1. (a) Boiling is a physical change. Signs of physical change alone do not signify chemical change.

2. (b) Cold packs cool by removing heat from their surroundings.

3. (a)

4. (c) Both sides of the equation are chemically identical, so the process cannot represent a chemical change. The conversion of ice to liquid water is an example of a physical change.

5. (b)

6. (a) Atoms are neither created or destroyed in a chemical reaction.

7. (c) Molecules are not necessarily conserved in a chemical reaction.

8. (a) There is the same amount of matter in the reactants and products, so they must have the same mass.

Short Essay Answers

1. **a.** $Li(s) + Cl_2(g) \rightarrow LiCl(s)$

    b. $2Li(s) + Cl_2(g) \rightarrow 2LiCl(s)$

2. **a.** $Na(s) + H_2O(l) \rightarrow NaOH(aq) + H_2(g)$

    b. $Al(s) + O_2(g) \rightarrow Al_2O_3(s)$

    c. $CaSO_4(s) \rightarrow CaO(s) + SO_2(g)$

    d. $Zn(s) + CuSO_4(aq) \rightarrow ZnSO_4(aq) + Cu(s)$

    e. $SiO_2 + C \rightarrow CO + Si$

3. **a.** $2Na(s) + 2H_2O(l) \rightarrow 2NaOH(aq) + H_2(g)$

    b. $4Al(s) + 3O_2(g) \rightarrow 2Al_2O_3(s)$

    c. $CaSO_4(s) \rightarrow CaO(s) + SO_3(g)$

    d. $Zn(s) + CuSO_4(aq) \rightarrow ZnSO_4(aq) + Cu(s)$

    e. $SiO_2 + 2C \rightarrow 2CO + Si$

4. **a.** $Sr + 2HNO_2 \rightarrow Sr(NO_3)_2 + H_2$

    b. $2NaClO_2 \rightarrow 2NaCl + 3O_2$

    c. $Pb(NO_3)_2 + 2KI \rightarrow PbI_2 + 2KNO_3$

    d. $Ba(NO_3)_2 + 2\,NH_4IO_3 \rightarrow Ba(IO_3)_2 + 2NH_4NO_3.$

    e. $4HF + SiO_2 \rightarrow 2SiF_4 + H_2O$

5. **a.** $2Na_2S_2O_3 + H_2O_2 \rightarrow Na_2S_3O_6 + Na_2SO_4 + H_2O$

    b. $Li_2O + H_2O \rightarrow 2LiOH$

    c. $2Na_2O_2 + 2H_2O + 4CO2 \rightarrow 4NaHCO_3 + O_2$

    d. $8Cu_2S + S_8 \rightarrow 16CuS$

6. **a.** $2CuSO_4 + 4KI \rightarrow 2CuI + I_2 + 2K_2SO_4$

    b. $2Al + 3H_2SO_2 \rightarrow Al_2(SO_4)_3 + 3H_2$

    c. $C_6H_6 + 3H_2 \rightarrow C_6H_{12}$

    e. $PBr_3 + 3H_2O \rightarrow H_3PO_3 + 3HBr$

7. **a.** $3O_2 \rightarrow 2O_3$

    b. $2AsI_3 \rightarrow 2As + 3I_2$

    c. $Na_4P_2O_2 + 4AgNO_3 \rightarrow Ag_4P_2O_7 + 4NaNO_3$

    d. $2Na_2S_5 + 3O_2 \rightarrow 2Na_2S_2O_3 + 3S_2$

    e. $K_2S_2O_3 + 4Cl_2 + 5H_2O \rightarrow 2KHSO_4 + 8HCl$

8. **a.** $2NO + O_2 \rightarrow 2NO_2$

    b. $2B_2O_3 + 6C \rightarrow B_4C_3 + 3CO_2$

    c. $6CO_2 + 6H_2O \rightarrow C_6H_{12}O_6 + 6O_2$

    d. $Li_2SO_3 + 2HBr \rightarrow 2LiBr + SO_2 + H_2O$

CHAPTER

ELECTRONIC STRUCTURE
AND THE
PERIODIC TABLE

OVERVIEW

In this chapter we consider the arrangement of elements in the periodic table (which we met in Chapter 1) in greater detail. We see that elements are placed in groups at intervals of atomic numbers, and that elements in the same group have similar properties.

We will find that the similarity in elemental properties at intervals of atomic number can be explained by the arrangement of electrons around the nuclei of atoms – the electronic structure of atoms. The chapter focuses on conceptualizing material that is generally considered difficult in a clear way. This chapter is worth studying extra throughly, because the electronic structure of atoms – which we will describe – forms the basis of explanations for many phenomena throughout chemistry.

In the first part of this chapter, we will examine the electronic structure of atoms in detail. We will see that each electron of an atom can be described by four labels (called quantum numbers). We will introduce rules for the values the labels may take. We will show that by using a simple recipe we can predict how electrons will arrange themselves around the nucleus of the atom, and even what their relative energies will be.

In the second part of the chapter we will see that the electronic structure of atoms that we have described is a powerful tool for understanding physical properties of matter such as atomic radii, ionization energies, and electron affininties.

CONCEPTS

Organizing the Elements in the Periodic Table

FIRST DEVISED BY MENDELEEV, THE PERIODIC TABLE ORGANIZES ELEMENTS ON THE BASIS OF TRENDS IN THEIR PHYSICAL AND CHEMICAL PROPERTIES.

The periodic table is the most general and useful organization of the chemical elements. It was designed by Dmitri Mendeleev, a Russian chemist who was also a keen solitaire player. Supposedly, Mendeleev wrote the elements and all their known properties out on separate cards, which he then organized into the periodic table. He then placed the elements into his table on the basis of trends in their known chemical and physical properties. The periodic table is particularly impressive because Mendeleev was playing chemical solitaire with an incomplete deck. In his day, not all the elements were known, and the properties of some of them were incorrectly assigned.

EACH BOX IN THE PERIODIC TABLE CONTAINS INFORMATION ABOUT A CHEMICAL ELEMENT.

We all know how to read the symbols and numbers on playing cards, but how does one read the boxes in the periodic table? At the center of each box is the atomic symbol of the element. Above the atomic symbol is its atomic number. Below the atomic symbol is the atomic weight of the element. Recall from Chapter 1 that vertical columns of boxes are known as **groups**, while horizontal rows are referred to as **periods**.

A representative box in the periodic table.

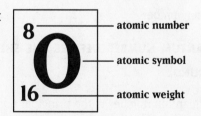

— atomic number

— atomic symbol

— atomic weight

Elements in the same group of the periodic table have similar physical and chemical properties. We will consider some of these in more detail at the end of this chapter.

ELEMENTS WITHIN A GROUP DISPLAY PERIODIC ATOMIC NUMBERS.

Elements are placed in the same group at regular and defined intervals of atomic numbers. Specifically, elements that are in the same group display atomic numbers at intervals of 8, 8,

18, 18 and 32. For example, in Group VII, fluorine has an atomic number of 9. Chlorine has an atomic number of 17, which is 9 (the atomic number of fluorine) plus 8 (the interval). Bromine has an atomic number of 17 + 8 = 35. Iodine has an atomic number of 35 + 18 = 53.

What is the significance of the periodic variation of atomic properties with atomic number? Recall (from Chapter 2) that the atomic number represents the number of protons in the nucleus, and therefore the number of electrons in a neutral atom. The arrangement of different numbers of electrons around an atom's nucleus can account for the periodic (regular) variation in atomic properties with respect to atomic numbers. In the next section, we will discuss the electronic structure of atoms with an eye to explaining the electronic basis of the periodic table.

Electronic Structure: A Visit to the Theater

The atom is a like a theater. Electrons are organized in seats, or **orbitals**, around the nuclear stage, and their seating plan is the key to the most interesting properties of atoms. We will first describe the layout of this theater, especially the places where electrons can sit. We shall see that, with a few simple rules, we can predict which orbitals (or seats) will be most likely occupied by electrons.

FOUR QUANTUM NUMBERS DEFINE THE STATE OF AN ELECTRON.

In a theater, there are various kind of seats — the orchestra, private boxes, the balcony, etc. Within each of these areas, your exact seat will be defined by a row letter and a seat number. Similarly, the seats offered to electrons are defined by four quantum numbers: the **principal quantum number**, the **azimuthal quantum number**, the **magnetic quantum number**, and the **magnetic spin quantum number**.

THE PRINCIPAL QUANTUM NUMBER DEFINES THE SHELL IN WHICH AN ELECTRON IS FOUND.

The most important quantum number is the principal quantum number (n). The value of n corresponds to a shell, and n can take all **integer** values from 1 up — that is, n can be 1,2,3, etc. In our theater analogy, the principle quantum number represents the region in which a seat is located. More specifically, n = 1 is quite close to the nuclear stage; n = 2 is slightly further from the stage; n = 4 might be the parking lot. Different shells can hold different numbers of electrons. As in many theaters, there are few seats for electrons to occupy near the nuclear stage and more electron seats further away.

shell, principal quantum number (n)	1	2	3	4
number of electrons in the nth shell	2	8	18	32

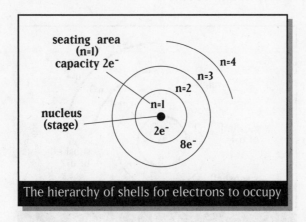

The hierarchy of shells for electrons to occupy

SUBSHELLS ARE DEFINED BY THE AZIMUTHAL QUANTUM NUMBER (l).

In the same way that the regions of a theater are divided into rows of seats, each shell is divided into subshells. A subshell is defined by its azimuthal quantum number (l). For a principal quantum number n, the azimuthal quantum number can take values from zero to n-1. For example, when n = 1, l can only take the value zero. For n = 2, l can take the values 0 and 1. For n = 3, l can take the values 0, 1, and 2.

Different subshells have different values of $-l$. Historically, though somewhat confusingly, these are also assigned a letter. A table correlating the relationship between values of l and the type of subshell is given below.

l	SUBSHELL
0	s
1	p
2	d
3	f

Recall that l may take n -1 integer values from 0 to infinity. Thus, if n = 1, l can only be zero. Using the table above, we see that an n = 1 shell contains an s subshell. Similarly, if n = 2 then l can be 0 or 1. We see that the n = 2 shell contains s and p subshells. If n = 3 then l can be 0, 1 and 2. And n = 3 contains s, p, and d subshells.

shells (principal quantum number)	1	2	3
subshells	s	s,p	s,p,d

We designate a subshell in a given principal quantum shell using the number of the principal quantum shell and the letter of the subshell. In other words, ls is the *s* subshell in the n = 1 shell, and 2*p* refers to the *p* subshell in the n = 2 shell.

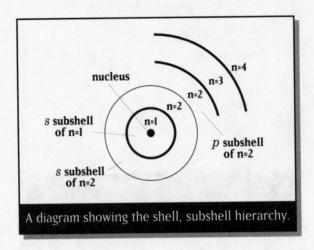

A diagram showing the shell, subshell hierarchy.

THE MAGNETIC QUANTUM NUMBER (m_l) DEFINES THE ORBITAL OF AN ELECTRON.

Each subshell (or row) is divided into **orbitals** (or seats). An orbital is defined by the **magnetic quantum number, m_l.** For an azimuthal quantum number l (row), m_l (the seat number) can take all integer values (including zero) from l to $-l$. Therefore, m_l always has $2l + 1$ different possible values. Each value of m_l corresponds to a different **orbital** (seat) For example, the s subshell, $l = 0$, has only one value for m_l — zero — and there is only one s orbital (seat) per s subshell (row). The p subshells (rows) have $l = 1$; therefore, m_l can take the values +1, 0, and -1. There are then three *p* orbitals (seats) per *p* subshell (row).

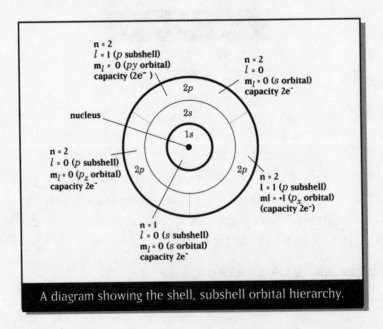

A diagram showing the shell, subshell orbital hierarchy.

Orbitals in the same subshell of a given shell have the same energy. The second seat on the left of the center aisle is essentially the same as the second seat from the right of the aisle. We say they are **degenerate**. The second seat from the right in the first row of the balcony is not the same as the corresponding seat on the floor. For example, a 2p orbital is degenerate with other 2p orbitals. Orbitals in different shells are not degenerate, even if they are in the same type of subshell. For example, though 2p and 3p orbitals are both in p subshells they are not degenerate, because the orbitals are in different shells.

Orbitals (seats) are often represented by chemists as boxes. For example an s orbital is represented by a single box, a subshell of p orbitals by three boxes:

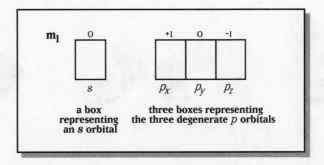

EACH ORBITAL OF AN ATOM DEFINES THE MOTION OF THE ELECTRONS THAT OCCUPY IT.

Electrons, unlike theater patrons, do not really sit observing the nucleus. Instead, they move around the nucleus in orbitals. These orbitals have a variety of shapes. An s orbital is spherical; p orbitals are shaped like dumbbells; p and d orbitals are shown below:

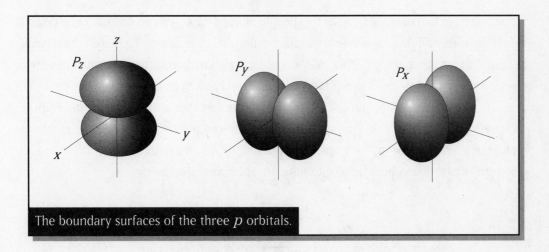

The boundary surfaces of the three p orbitals.

The five d orbitals.

ELECTRONS IN AN ORBITAL HAVE A QUANTUM MECHANICAL PROPERTY WE CALL SPIN. ELECTRONS OCCUPY ORBITALS IN ACCORDANCE WITH THE PAULI EXCLUSION PRINCIPLE.

It turns out that two electrons, unlike two people at the theater, can occupy the same orbital (or seat)! There is, however, a rule about the circumstances under which two electrons may be found in the same orbital. The rule is the Pauli exclusion principle, which states: **two electrons may occupy the same orbital only if they have opposite spins.** The quantum property called spin has no obvious physical counterpart, but is labelled as either up or down – represented ↑ or ↓. (The spin of an electron can also be labeled by the quantum number m_s. Spin-up has $m_s = +1/2$; spin-down has $m_s = -1/2$). We represent the idea that two electrons occupy the same orbital, with different spins as shown below.

ELECTRON ENERGIES IN AN ATOM ARE QUANTIZED.

Our theater analogy is useful for helping us describe the labeling of electrons in the atom, but what exactly do these labels correspond to? It turns out that the energy of an electron can only take certain values in the atom; we say that energy is **quantized**. Steps on a staircase are quantized — each step corresponds to a specific height and we cannot stand between steps. In the same way, each set of quantum numbers corresponds to a specific energy level. We might, in contrast to a staircase, consider a ramp; on a ramp we could attain all the heights between the stairs. Heights on a ramp, therefore, are **not** quantized.

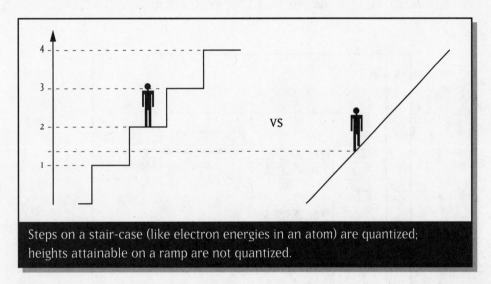

Steps on a stair-case (like electron energies in an atom) are quantized; heights attainable on a ramp are not quantized.

FOR HYDROGEN-LIKE ATOMS WITH A SINGLE ELECTRON, THE PRINCIPAL QUANTUM NUMBER OF AN ORBITAL DEFINES ITS ENERGY.

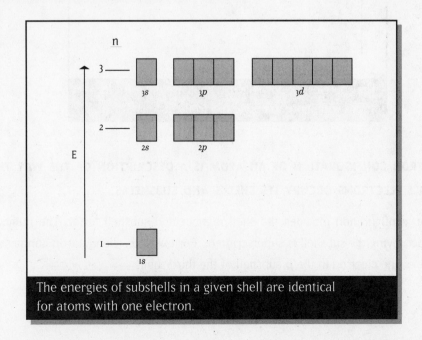

The energies of subshells in a given shell are identical for atoms with one electron.

For example, an electron in a 2s orbital is at the same energy level as an electron in a 2p orbital. However, an electron in a 2p orbital is lower in energy than any electron in the 3s, 3p, or 3d orbitals — which are all degenerate.

In contrast, in atoms with many electrons, this rule does not hold true. In these cases, different subshells within a given shell have different energies.

A 2s electron, for example, is lower in energy than a 2p electron. In general, the order of orbital energies is in a multiple-electron atom is:

1s, 2s, 2p, 3s, 3p, 4s, 3d, 4p, 5s, 4d, 5p, 6s, 4f, 5d, 6p, 7s, 5f, 6d, 7p.

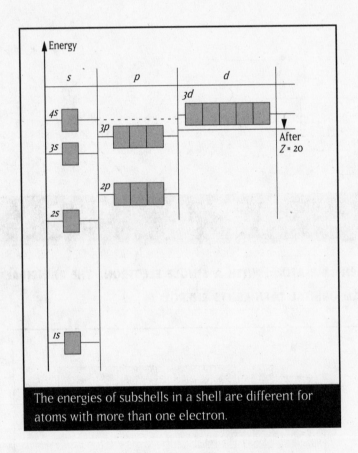

The energies of subshells in a shell are different for atoms with more than one electron.

THE ELECTRON CONFIGURATION OF AN ATOM IS A DESCRIPTION OF THE WAY THAT THE ATOM'S ELECTRONS OCCUPY ITS SHELLS AND SUBSHELLS.

An electron configuration includes the shell number and subshell letter. The number of electrons occupying the subshell is superscripted. For example, the electron configuration $3p^1$ describes one electron in the p subshell of the third shell.

VAULT
REPORTS™
www.vaultreports.com

THE BUILDING-UP PRINCIPLE IS USED TO DETERMINE THE ELECTRON CONFIGURATION OF MANY ELECTRON ATOMS.

To find the electron configuration of an atom with an atomic number Z, we use a set of rules known as the **building-up principle:**

- ◆ Place Z electrons into the orbitals.

- ◆ Fill the lowest energy orbital first. No more than two electrons occupy a single orbital.

- ◆ If more than one orbital of a subshell is available, add electrons with parallel spins to different orbitals in that subshell. This is called **Hund's first rule.**

This sounds more complicated than it really is. Let's start by determining the electron configuration for the elements hydrogen through sodium.

Hydrogen has one electron which enters the shell with n = 1; the only subshell is s. Therefore, the electron configuration of hydrogen is $1s^1$.

1s

Helium has two electrons. Using the building-up principle, we put in one electron as we did with hydrogen. There is space for one more electron in n = 1, so the second electron must go there. It must enter the s subshell, since this is the only subshell in n = 1. The s subshell contains a single orbital – which the second electron must enter. Since two electrons are in a single orbital, the spin of the second electron must be paired with that of the first, according to the **Pauli exclusion principle.** Note that it is the relative spins that are important. We can assign the single electron in hydrogen either spin (up or down), but when we add a second electron, it must be the opposite spin of the first. The electron configuration of Helium is $1s^2$.

1s

Lithium has three electrons. The third electron must enter n = 2. This shell, n = 2, contains an s and a p subshell. The s subshell is lower in energy than the p subshell, so the electron preferentially to occupies the s subshell. The electron configuration of lithium is $1s^2 2s^1$.

  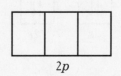

1s   2s   2p

We may rewrite $1s^2 2s^1$ as [He] $2s^1$, in which [He] is shorthand for the electron configuration of a helium atom. The electrons in a completed shell – such as those represented by [He] – are described as **core**. Those shells that are only partially full of electrons are known as **valence shells**. In the case of lithium, the shell with n = 2 is the valence shell. Electrons that occupy valence shells are known as **valence electrons**. The electron in the $2s$ subshell of lithium is an example of a valence electron.

Beryllium has four electrons. Its electron configuration is $1s^2 2s^2$, or [He] $2s^2$.

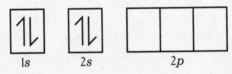

Boron has five electrons. The fifth electron enters a $2p$ orbital. Boron's electron configuration is [He] $2s^2 2p^1$.

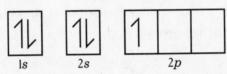

Carbon has six electrons. The sixth electron enters a $2p$ orbital different from the fifth electron, and its spin is unpaired. This is the first element in the periodic table for which we invoke Hund's first rule. The electron configuration of carbon is [He] $2s^2 2p^2$

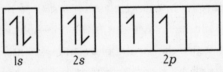

Nitrogen has seven electrons. Using Hund's rule, we know that the seventh electron enters the third $2p$ orbital, which is vacant.

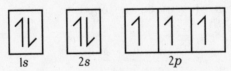

Oxygen has eight electrons. The eighth electron enters one of the occupied $2p$ orbitals, and the Pauli exclusion principle tells us that this electron is spin-paired with the electron in that orbital.

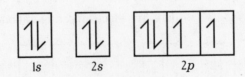

Fluorine has nine electrons. The ninth electron enters a second occupied 2p orbital. The electron configuration of fluorine is [He] $2s^2 2p^5$:

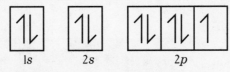

Neon has ten electrons. Its electron configuration is $1s^2 2s^2 2p^6$. All the orbitals in n = 2 are now filled to capacity with electrons.

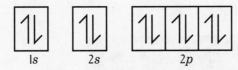

Sodium's eleventh electron enters the n = 3 shell in the s subshell. Its electron configuration is [Ne] $3s^1$.

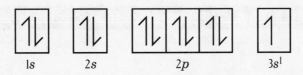

Linking electronic structure to the periodic table

All the elements in a given group of the periodic table have the same number of valence electrons in the same type of subshell. As we descend down the table through a group, we increase the highest principle quantum shell in which valence electrons occur.

For example, the elements lithium and sodium are in the same group of the periodic table. Notice the that electron configurations of lithium, [He] $2s^1$ and sodium, [Ne] $3s^1$ both have a single valence electron in an s subshell. The principal quantum shell in which the valence electrons are found increases by one (from n = 2 to n = 3) as we descend through the group from lithium to sodium.

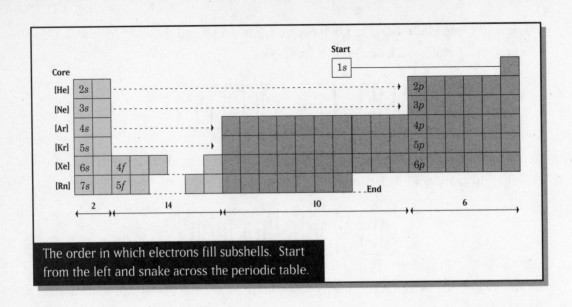

The order in which electrons fill subshells. Start from the left and snake across the periodic table.

Periodic Variation in Physical Properties and Electronic Structure

Now we can consider the periodic trends in the physical properties of atoms: atomic radii, ionization energy and electron affinity. These trends can be explained by using what we have learned about the electronic structure of atoms.

THE ATOMIC RADIUS OF AN ATOM IS HALF THE DISTANCE BETWEEN "NEAREST NEIGHBORS" IN A SOLID SAMPLE OF THE ELEMENT.

For example, in solid bromine the smallest distance between two atoms is measured as 228 pm (1 picometer = 10^{-12}m). The atomic radius of potassium is therefore 114 pm.

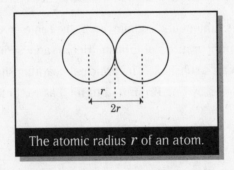

The atomic radius r of an atom.

THE ATOMIC RADIUS INCREASES AS WE MOVE DOWN A GROUP, AND IT DECREASES AS WE GO ACROSS A PERIOD OF THE PERIODIC TABLE. THESE TRENDS CAN BE EXPLAINED BY THE ELECTRONIC STRUCTURES OF ATOMS.

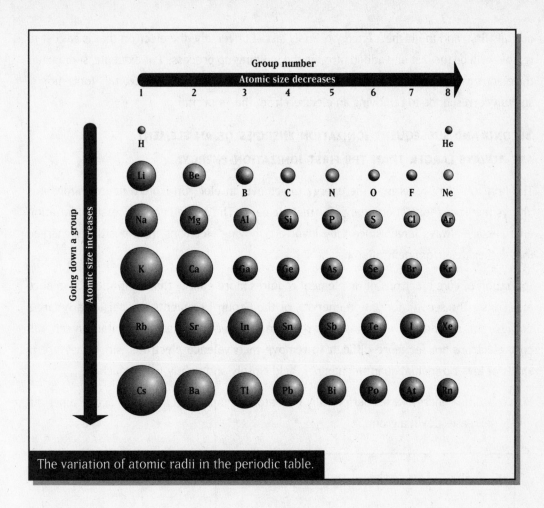

The variation of atomic radii in the periodic table.

The increase in radii as we move down a group is a result of the valence electrons (which define the outer limit of the atom) being in shells of increasing principle quantum numbers. Shells with larger principal quantum numbers are further away from the nucleus. The decrease in radii across a period is a result of increasing attraction between electrons and increasing nuclear charge. The increased attraction pulls the electrons towards the nucleus, shrinking the radii of the atoms.

Ionization is the process of removing an electron from an atom. There is an energy cost associated with this process that is known as the ionization energy.

The first ionization energy is the energy required for the process:

$$X(g) \rightarrow X^+(g) + e^-(g)$$

We have seen that electrons in an atom occupy orbitals of different energy. Which electron is removed first in ionization? To answer this question, recall how we used the building-up principle to arrive at the electron configuration of an element. We filled the lowest energy orbitals first, and the highest energy orbitals last. Conversely, the electron that is easiest to remove will be the last one added through the building-up process. For example, sodium has the electron configuration [Ne] $3s^1$. The last electron added is in the $3s$ orbital. Ionization of sodium corresponds to removing an electron from the $3s$ orbital.

SECOND AND SUBSEQUENT IONIZATION ENERGIES OF AN ELEMENT ARE ALWAYS LARGER THAN THE FIRST IONIZATION ENERGY.

The first ionization energy — the energy to remove an electron from a neutral atom — is always the lowest ionization energy for that element. The second and successive ionization energies are always larger since they involve removing electrons from positively charged ions rather than from neutral atoms.

Ionization of core electrons of an element requires more energy than ionization of valence electrons. The second ionization energies of the Group I elements are particularly large, because this second ionization involves removing an electron in a core orbital. In general, **core electrons are far more difficult to remove than valence electrons**, since they are in shells of lower principal quantum number, held closely and tightly to the nucleus.

First ionization energy varies periodically with atomic number. It increases across a period, and it decreases down a group.

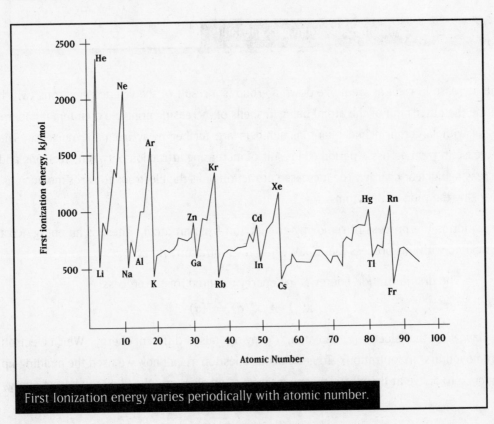

First Ionization energy varies periodically with atomic number.

We can understand the trends in first ionization energy in terms of atomic radii. Going across a period, atomic radii decrease; electrons in the atom are brought nearer the nucleus, where they attracted more strongly to its positive charge and become more difficult to remove. Going down a group, the outer electron occupies an orbital in a shell with a larger principal quantum number, further away from the nucleus. Because the electron is further away from the nucleus, the nuclear attraction is less, and the electron is easier to remove.

THE CATIONS FORMED BY AN ELEMENT CAN BE UNDERSTOOD IN TERMS OF ITS IONIZATION ENERGIES.

Core electrons are much more difficult to remove than valence electrons. Therefore, the maximum charge number of an ion results from the loss of all the valence, but none of the core, electrons. The Group I metals form I+ ions by losing their outer s electron. The Group II metals loose two electrons in the same way and form 2+ ions. Group III elements lose three electrons. Note that the ionization of valence electrons leads to cations with the same electron configurations as the noble gas (Group VIII) that directly precedes the element in atomic number. For example, aluminum loses three electrons to form Al^{3+} ions with the electron configuration Al[Ne].

THE ELECTRON AFFINITY OF AN ATOM OR ION IS A MEASURE OF THE FEASIBILITY OF THE PROCESS THROUGH WHICH IT GAINS AN ELECTRON. ELECTRON AFFINITY IS GREATEST AT THE TOP RIGHT OF THE PERIODIC TABLE.

Electron affinity involves the process converse to ionization energy:

$$X(g) + e^-(g) \rightarrow X^-(g)$$

An atom or ion has a high electron affinity if this process is favorable. Electron affinities increase towards the upper right of the periodic table and are largest for chlorine and fluorine. For fluorine and chlorine, the electron gained by the atom is placed in an orbital close to the highly positively-charged nucleus, a favorable process. For these elements, a single electron fills the last place in the valence shell. Adding another electron would be an unfavorable process, because the electron would be added in a new shell further away from the nucleus and would be repulsed by the negative charge already present. The high electron affinity of fluorine and the low electron affinity of fluoride (F^-) accounts for the fact that F^{2-} is never found in ionic compounds.

KEY TERMS

atomic radii: Half the distance between the nearest atoms in a solid sample of an element.

Azimuthal quantum number (l): This number takes values from zero to n - l. The value of l defines which subshell an electron occupies.

building-up principle: A method of finding the electron configuration of an atom or monatomic ion.

degenerate orbitals: Orbitals of equal energy.

electron affinity: A measure of the energy necessary to add an electron to a gaseous atom to form an anion.

electron configuration: A description of the way in which electrons are organized in an atom or monatomic ion.

Hund's first rule: If more than one orbital of a subshell is available, add electrons with parallel spins to different orbitals in that subshell.

ionization: The process of removing an electron from an atom or ion.

ionization energy: The energy associated with ionization.

Magnetic quantum number (m_l): The magnetic quantum number has $2l + 1$ values from $+l$ to -l. The magnetic quantum number defines the orbital an electron occupies.

Magnetic spin quantum number (m_s): The magnetic spin number may take the value $+1/2$ or $-1/2$.

orbital: A region around the nucleus in which electrons are free to move. Each orbital can hold up to two electrons but must obey the Pauli exclusion principle.

Pauli exclusion principle: No two electrons may occupy the same orbital unless they have opposite spins.

principal quantum number (n): The principal quantum number can take values from 1 to infinity. It defines the shell of an atom in which an electron is found.

quantized: A description of the discrete values the energy of an electron in an atom may take.

quantum number: The quantum number defines the state of a particle. The four quantum numbers of an electron define its state.

shell: The orbitals in an atom or monatomic ion with the same value of n.

subshell: Degenerate orbitals with the same value of n and l.

valence electrons: Electrons that occupy the valence shell.

valence shell: The outermost shell of electrons in an atom or monatomic ion.

THRILLS, CHILLS AND DRILLS

True or False

1. Elements in the periodic table in the same group occur at periodic atomic number.

2. The quantum numbers of an electron in an atom defines its state.

3. The principal quantum number of an electron defines its spin state.

4. For an electron with n = 1, l can take any value.

5. An electron with l = 1 will be in an p subshell.

6. For principal quantum number n = 2, the azimuthal quantum number can take on values l = 0, 1. These represent one s and three p orbitals. As such, this n = 2 level has four orbitals.

7. The shape of an orbital is defined mainly by the quantum number l.

8. Three p orbitals in a subshell of a given shell are degenerate.

9. The s orbital is shaped like a dumbbell centered on the nucleus.

10. The Pauli exclusion principle suggests that two electrons can occupy the same orbital with the same spin.

11. The Pauli exclusion principle can be restated as: No two electrons can have the same set of quantum numbers n, l, m_l, and m_s.

12. The energy of an electron in an atom can take any value.

13. For many electron atoms, orbitals with the same n are degenerate.

14. The building-up principle feeds electrons into the highest energy orbitals first.

15. Boron has 5 valence electrons.

16. All of the alkali metals (Group I) have a general electronic configuration of [noble gas] np^1.

17. Atomic radii increases down a group

18. First ionization energy decreases across a period.

19. The second ionization energy of calcium is greater than the first ionization energy, because it involves removing an electron from a positively-charged cation.

20. Anions, such as Cl^-, are formed by the release of an electron, resulting in a full valence shell.

21. The net charge on an ion is determined by the mass of protons present less the mass of electrons present.

22. The energy required to remove the least tightly-bound electron from a gaseous atom is known as the electron affinity of that element.

23. The atomic number gives the position of the element in the periodic table and is equal to the positive charge on the nucleus of each atom of that element.

24. The atomic number of fluorine is 9, whereas that of chlorine is 17. Therefore, we know that the chlorine atom is smaller than a fluorine atom because of the greater nuclear charge drawing the electrons closer to the nucleus.

25. When an ion is formed, it is equivalent to saying that the atom has gained or lost a certain number of electrons. As such, we must account for these electrons when writing the ion's electron configuration. Knowing this, then the electron configuration for an S^{2-} ion is $1s^2 2s^2 2p^6 3s^2 4p^6$.

26. Argon has a smaller atomic radius than sodium.

27. Ca^+ and K both have 19 electrons, but K is more easily ionized.

Multiple Choice

1. Don Quantum, a college chemistry major, has lost sight of the meaning of the important quantum numbers. Help him decide which of the quantum numbers is the principal quantum number
    a) n
    b) l
    c) m_l
    d) m_s

2. For n = 3, l can take the values
   a) 2, 1, 0, -1, -2
   b) 3, 2, 1, 0
   c) 2, 1, 0
   d) 0, -1, -2

3. How many electrons does the first principal quantum shell contain?
   a) 2
   b) 6
   c) 8
   d) 18

4. The 2p subshell contains up to
   a) 4 electrons
   b) 6 electrons
   c) 12 electrons
   d) 3 electrons

5. Orbitals are described as degenerate if they are
   a) occupied by same number of electrons
   b) in the same principal quantum shell
   c) the same energy
   d) the same shape

6. n = 2 contains
   a) 2p and 3p subshells
   b) a 2s and a 2p subshell
   c) a 2p and 2d subshell
   d) a 2s 2p and a 2d subshell

7. Hund's first rule suggest that
   a) all electrons have parallel spin
   b) electrons preferentially occupy a subshell with parallel spin
   c) electrons are always spin paired
   d) the bigger the electron, the harder it falls

8. For n = 2, in a multiple-electron atom, the relationship between the energies of the s and p orbitals is
   a) $E(s) > E(p)$
   b) $E(s) < E(p)$
   c) $E(s) = E(p)$
   d) the relationship is not general and is a function of n

9. For n = 2, in multiple-electron atoms, the 2p orbital is occupied

    a) before the 2s orbital is occupied

    b) after the 2s orbital is occupied

    c) before the 1s orbital is occupied

10. The outer, partially-occupied shell of electrons contains

    a) core electrons

    b) no electrons

    c) positrons

    d) valence electrons

11. The electron configuration of oxygen is

    a) $1s^2 2s^2 2p^4$

    b) $1s^2 2s^2 2p^6$

    c) $1s^2 2s^6$

    d) $1s^2 2p^4$

12. The electron configuration of potassium (Z = 19) is

    a) [Ne] $3s^1$

    b) [Kr] $5s^1$

    c) [He] $3s^1$

    d) [Ar] $4s^1$

13. The electron configuration of Boron is [He] $2s^2 2p^1$. To which group of the periodic table does boron belong?

    a) III

    b) IV

    c) I

    d) II

14. Aluminum is directly below boron in the same group (see Question 13). The electron configuration of aluminum is

    a) [Ne] $2s^2 2p^1$

    b) [Ne] $3s3$

    c) [Xe] $2s^2 3p^1$

    d) [Ne] $3s^2 3p^1$

15. How many unpaired electrons does an oxygen atom have?

    a) 0

    b) 2

    c) 4

    d) 6

16. Given that when filling degenerate orbitals electrons are arranged so as to minimize spin pairing, which of the following atoms or ions has the most unpaired electrons?

    a) fluorine (9 electrons)

    b) fluoride ion (10 electrons)

    c) argon (18 electrons)

    d) magnesium (12 electrons)

17. Paramagnetism is a property of atoms that increases with the number of unpaired electrons. Which of the following atoms is the most paramagnetic?

    a) barium (56 electrons)

    b) calcium (20 electrons)

    c) krypton (36 electrons)

    d) bromine (35 electrons)

18. Which of the following corresponds to the definition of an atom's ionization energy?

    a) the amount of energy released when an electron is gained by an atom

    b) the amount of energy required to add an electron to a particle

    c) the amount of energy required to remove an electron from an atom

    d) the amount of energy required to remove an electron from a particle

    e) the amount of energy released when an electron is gained by a particle

19. Which of the following isoelectronic ions has the smallest radius?

    a) S^{2-}

    b) K^+

    c) Cl^-

    d) Ca^{2+}

20. Professor Sizedoz Matter is having trouble arranging the halogenic acids by their sizes. Although he knows that the size of these acids follows the same trend as the size of the halogen, he can't figure out the proper order. Can you arrange them in order of increasing size for him?

    a) HBr, HF, HCl, HI

    b) HCl, HF, HI, HBr

    c) HF, HCl, HBr, HI

    d) HI, HBr, HF, HCl

21. Because you have saved him the time and expense of having to use expensive spectroscopic methods to determine the size trend Professor Matter is very pleased with you. He now has a new task for you. In the given isoelectronic series of ions, pick the ion with the smallest radius

    a) S^{2-}

    b) Cl^-

    c) Ar

    d) K^+

    e) Ca^{2+}

    f) Sc^{3+}

22. Dr. Noten Ure is trying to isolate stable compounds of Neon. Which neutral element does Dr. Ure describe as having the electron configuration [Ne] $3s^2$, $3p^5$, $4s^1$?

    a) neon

    b) potassium

    c) sodium

    d) nitrogen

    e) argon

Short Essays

1. Arsenic, a deadly poison commonly used by mystery authors because of its odorless nature, occurs in Group V of the periodic table. Please answer the following questions about As (Z = 33) for Ms. Kneed Aclue, whose mystery deadline is rapidly approaching.

    a. How many electrons are in the third principal shell (n = 3)?

    b. How many p subshells are occupied in neutral arsenic?

2. Consider the following elements: beryllium (Be), oxygen (O), fluorine (F), sulfur (S), potassium (K), and krypton (Kr). Based upon general periodic trends, predict which one has

    a. the lowest ionization energy

    b. the largest size

    c. the highest electron affinity

    d. the highest third ionization energy

3. Ionization energies are typically measured in a unit known as the electron-volt (eV). Suppose that an element has values for its first through sixth ionization energies as follows: 7.0, 12.5, 21.2, 68.8, 79.2, 92.5 eV. Explain the relatively large jump between the third and fourth ionization energies. What does this data indicate about the atom's electronic structure? In which family of the periodic table would the element most likely belong?

4. News Flash! New data from the Galaxy Rover suddenly indicates that the element organization on a new planet in the Gamma Quadrant is startlingly different than on Earth! The rules there are that:

    1) Principal Quantum Number, $n = 1, 2, ...$ (as on Earth)

    2) Angular Momentum Quantum Number, $l = 0, 1, 2, ..., n - 1$ (as on Earth)

    3) Magnetic Quantum Number, $m = 0, 1, 2, ..., l$ (that is, only positive integers up to and including l are allowed)

    4) Spin Quantum Number, $s = -1, 0, +1$ (that is, three allowed values of spin)

a. Write the electronic configuration of the element with atomic number 9 in the periodic table.

b. Assuming that no electrons can have identical quantum numbers, what is the maximum number of electrons that can populate a given orbital?

ANSWERS

True or False Answers

1. **True.**

2. **True.** The state of an electron in an atom is define by four quantum numbers: n, l, m_l, m_s.

3. **False.** n defines the shell, m_s defines spin.

4. **False.** l can take values from 0 to n - 1, i.e. for n = l, l = 0 only.

5. **True.**

6. **True.**

7. **True.** l defines the 3-D shape of an orbital.

8. **True.**

9. **False.** The p orbital is shaped like a dumbbell. The s orbital is spherical.

10. **False.** The Pauli exclusion principle says two electrons can occupy the same orbital only if they have opposing spins.

11. **True.** Electrons in the same orbital have the same n, l, and m_l values, but the Pauli exclusion principle says they must have different spins, i.e., different values of m_s.

12. **False.** The energy of electrons in atoms is quantized.

13. **False.** Orbitals with the same n value, but different l value, have different energies in an atom with more than one electron.

14. **False.**

15. **True.** Boron has 5e⁻, but only 3 valence e⁻.

16. **True.** Group I atoms have e⁻ configurations of [noble gas]ns¹.

17. **True.**

18. **False.** First ionization energy increases across a period.

19. **True.**

20. **False.**

21. **False.** Anions are formed by the gain of e⁻.

22. **False.** The process described is the ionization energy.

23. **True.**

24. **True.**

25. **True.**

26. **True.** Argon and sodium are in the same period. Argon is to the right of sodium and atomic radius decreases across a period.

27. **True.** Calcium has more protons in its nucleus attracting the electrons (holding them from being ionized). Therefore potassium is more easily ionized

Multiple Choice Answers

1. (a) n is the principal quantum number.

2. (c) l takes the values from zero to n -l.

3. (a) If n = 1, l = 0, ml orbitals = $2l + 1$ = 1. One orbital may contain up to two electrons.

4. (b) 6 electrons. The $2p$ subshell contains three $2p$ orbitals. Each orbital may contain 2 electrons.

5. (c) the same energy.

6. (b) n = 2 contains a $2s$ and a $2p$ subshell. For n = 2, l can take the values 0 and 1 corresponding to an s and a p subshell.

7. (b) Electrons preferentially occupy a subshell with parallel spin.

8. (b) $E(s) < E(p)$.

9. (b) After the $2s$ orbital is occupied, according to the building-up principle.

10. (d) valence electrons

11. (a) $1s^2 2s^2 2p^4$

12. (d) $[Ar] 4s^1$

13. (a) 3

14. (d) $[Ne] 3s^2 3p^1$

15. (b) 2

16. (a) fluorine (9 electrons) has two unpaired electrons.

17. (d) bromine (35 electrons)

18. (c) the amount of energy required to remove an electron from an atom.

19. (d) Ca^{2+}

20. (c) HF, HCl, HBr, HI. Atomic size decreases down a group.

21. (e) Ca^{2+}

22. (b) potassium

Short Essay Answers

1. **a.** 18

   b. Three p subshells are occupied.

2. **a.** K   **b.** K   **c.** F   **d.** Be

3. The first three ionizations reflect the removal of valence electrons. Removing the fourth electron involves breaking into the core electrons. The element is in Group III.

4. **a.** $1s^3 2s^3 2p^3$

   b. 3

CHAPTER

THE TIES THAT BIND:

CHEMICAL BONDING

OVERVIEW

Yes, the world is made from only the hundred or so elements you see in the periodic table. How can this small number of elements account for the staggering diversity of colors, textures, shapes, smells, and tastes we sense? Think for a minute about our alphabet. It has only 26 letters and yet combinations of these letters — words — manage to convey (quite literally) all we have to say to each other. In a similar way, the combination of elements accounts for the diversity we see, smell, and taste around us. In the last few chapters we have learned the 'alphabet' of chemistry — the symbols, electron configurations and properties of elements. In the same way that we once learned words, we shall see how to assemble the elements into compounds.

In this chapter, we'll learn about the chemical bonding that holds atoms (letters) together in molecules and ionic solids (words). In particular, we will look at two different types of bonding: ionic and covalent. We will see that different combinations of elements form different sorts of bonds, but that the goal of all atoms in bonding in any sort of bond is the same, to get a noble gas electron configuration (Chapter 4). We will also introduce the concept of resonance, and show that it accounts for properties of molecules which are difficult to explain otherwise.

CONCEPTS

**THE ELECTRONEGATIVITY OF AN ELEMENT TELLS US ABOUT ITS ABILITY TO
ATTRACT AND HOLD ON TO ELECTRONS IN A CHEMICAL ENVIRONMENT.**

Valence electrons — not core electrons — play the critical roles in chemical bonding. Chemical bonding involves the nuclei of an element fighting for their shares of valence electrons and, as a result, forming relationships with other elements. For some combinations of elements, chemical bonding creates one dominant element and one submissive element. In these combinations, one element loses an electrons, while the other gains electrons. In other pairs, two atoms share valence electrons equally. But how can we assess which pairs of elements form a dominant-submissive relationship and which pairs of elements share valence electrons?

Linus Pauling developed the concept of electronegativity for assessing the dominance of a particular element in a compound. Electronegativity, χ, is a measure of an atom's ability to attract and hold onto electrons in a chemical compound. Pauling defined electronegativity as:

$$1/2 \ (IE + EA) \qquad IE = \text{Ionization energy, } EA = \text{electron affinity}$$

Elements that have a high IE (do not easily lose electrons) and a high EA (easily gain electrons) will tend to form negatively-charged anions. This makes sense, because such elements gain electrons easily but do not lose them easily. The atoms of these elements have high electronegativities. Elements with high electronegativities — such as fluorine, chlorine, or oxygen — will almost invariably be the dominant partner in the fight for electrons between two atoms.

In contrast, elements that have a low IE (easily lose electrons) and a low EA (do not easily gain electrons) will tend to form positively-charged cations. Think about why: if such elements lose electrons easily but do not gain them, they will have fewer electrons and be positively charged. The atoms of such elements have low electronegativities and are described as **electropositive**. Electropositive elements, metals such as sodium or cesium, are always submissive in the battle for valence electrons as they have no real interest in holding onto them.

ELECTRONEGATIVITIES OF THE MAIN-GROUP ELEMENTS

			H			
			2.1			
Li	Be	B	C	N	O	F
1.0	1.5	2.0	2.5	3.0	3.5	4.0
Na	Mg	Al	Si	P	S	Cl
0.9	1.2	1.5	1.8	2.1	2.5	3.0
K	Ca	Ga	Ge	As	Se	Br
0.8	1.0	1.6	1.8	2.0	2.4	2.8
Rb	Sr	In	Sn	Sb	Te	I
0.8	1.0	1.7	1.8	1.9	2.1	2.5
Cs	Ba	Tl	Pb	Bi	Po	At
0.7	0.9	1.8	1.8	1.9	2.0	2.2

THE DIFFERENCE IN THE ELECTRONEGATIVITY OF TWO ATOMS TELLS US ABOUT WHAT TYPE OF BOND THEY WILL FORM.

If a dominant and a submissive element are paired, then the difference in electronegativity between elements is large (usually greater than 2). The pairing of these elements leads to the formation of **ionic** bonds in which the electronegative (dominant) element takes all the electrons it wants from the electropositive (submissive) element. If two dominant elements are paired, then the difference in electronegativity will be small (less than 1). This type of pairing leads to a sharing of electrons in the form of **covalent bonds**.

Note that metals are more electropositive and non-metals more electronegative. Metals form ionic bonds with non-metals, and non-metals form covalent bonds with other non-metals. Metals, however, do not usually form classical, covalent bonds with other metals. Because of the ease of ionization of metals, they exist as ions, with a noble gas core electron configuration surrounded by a sea of valence electrons from all the metal atoms in the solid. Sodium metal, for example, exists as Na^+ cations in a sea of electrons which we consider to be spread out or **delocalized** throughout the sample.

Next we consider ionic and covalent bonding in detail.

Ionic Bonding: Master and Servant

IONIC BONDS ARE CEMENTED BY THE ATTRACTION BETWEEN OPPOSITELY-CHARGED IONS.

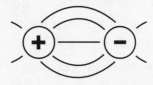

The ions in an ionic bond arise from transfer of valence electrons from electropositive elements to electronegative elements. Elements then attain complete shells of electrons in the formation of ionic bonds. The electropositive element attains a complete shell by emptying its valence shell. By gaining these electrons, the electronegative element completes its valence shell.

For example, the ionic compound sodium chloride is formed from the elements sodium ([Ne] $3s^1$) and chlorine ([Ne] $3s^23p^5$). The transfer of a single valence $3s$ electron from sodium (electropositive) to chlorine (electronegative) leads to noble gas electron configurations for both atoms. Na^+ has a [Ne] core of electrons; Cl^- has an [Ar] core. As in this example, electropositive elements are usually metals, and electronegative elements are usually non-metals.

VALENCE ELECTRONS ARE CONVENIENTLY REPRESENTED BY USING ELECTRON DOT DIAGRAMS.

To draw an electron dot structure for an atom, we write its atomic symbol and put a dot next to this symbol to represent each valence electron. (Remember: the number of valence electrons is the same as the group number.)

For example, a sodium atom has an electron dot structure, with a single dot next to the symbol Na. Chlorine atoms have electron dot structures, with seven dots around the symbol Cl.

For the ionic solid sodium chloride, the dot diagram has eight dots around Cl^- and none around Na^+.

We can say that both ions have **completed their octets, since each atom has eight electrons in its outer shell.**

$$\text{Na} \quad \cdot \ddot{\underset{\cdot\cdot}{\text{Cl}}} : \quad \longrightarrow \quad \text{Na}^{\oplus} \quad : \ddot{\underset{\cdot\cdot}{\text{Cl}}}^{\ominus} :$$

THE FORMATION OF IONS IN AN IONIC SOLID IS DRIVEN BY THE TENDENCY OF ELEMENTS TO ATTAIN NOBLE GAS ELECTRON CONFIGURATIONS.

We introduced the idea of the ionic bond in terms of a dominant element stealing electrons from a submissive element, but the actual exchange is more subtle than this. The submissive element only gives away enough electrons to leave it with a noble gas core electron configuration, and the dominant element only gains enough electrons to acquire a noble gas electron configuration. In terms of electron configuration, the dominant and submissive elements are both satisfied by their interaction in the ionic bond.

Here are some more examples that demonstrate how the atoms in an ionic solid attain noble gas configurations:

In magnesium oxide, the electropositive metal magnesium completes its octet by losing two electrons. Oxygen, the electronegative non-metal, completes its octet by gaining these two electrons.

$$\text{Mg} : \overset{\curvearrowright}{\underset{\curvearrowright}{}} \ddot{\underset{\cdot\cdot}{\text{O}}} : \quad \longrightarrow \quad \text{Mg}^{2\oplus} \quad : \ddot{\underset{\cdot\cdot}{\text{O}}}^{2\ominus} :$$

In magnesium chloride, magnesium needs to lose two electrons to complete its octet, yet a single chlorine atom only needs one electron to complete its octet. Two chlorine atoms are therefore required for every magnesium atom; as a result, the formula is $MgCl_2$.

$$: \ddot{\underset{\cdot\cdot}{\text{Cl}}} \cdot \overset{\curvearrowleft}{} \cdot \text{Mg} \cdot \overset{\curvearrowright}{} \cdot \ddot{\underset{\cdot\cdot}{\text{Cl}}} : \quad \longrightarrow \quad : \ddot{\underset{\cdot\cdot}{\text{Cl}}}^{\ominus} : \quad \text{Mg}^{2\oplus} \quad : \ddot{\underset{\cdot\cdot}{\text{Cl}}}^{\ominus} :$$

WE CAN ARRIVE AT THE FORMULA UNIT FOR AN IONIC COMPOUND BY BALANCING THE CHARGES OF THE ANION AND CATION.

For example, in aluminum oxide, aluminum completes its octet by forming 3+ ions. Oxygen completes its octet by forming 2- ions. We can balance the charges by combining two aluminum ions (with a combined charge of 6+) and three oxygen atoms (with a combined charge of 6-). The difference between the charges is zero, so the neutral ionic compound has the formula unit Al_2O_3. This formula works because the octet of both atoms being combined is satisfied in formation of the ions.

We have considered ionic compounds formed by metals in the main groups: Groups I, II and III. Metals in other regions of the periodic table — the transition metals, or lanthanides and actinides — have more complex behavior that we will not consider here.

Covalent Bonds: Sharing, Caring Atoms

COVALENT BONDS RESULT FROM ATOMS SHARING ELECTRONS TO COMPLETE THEIR OCTET.

Covalent bonds result from the sharing of pairs of electrons between atoms. The atoms in a covalent bond are held together by the attraction of the nuclei of both atoms to the same electrons.

In covalent bonds, electrons are shared between atoms' nuclei in such a way that each atom attains a noble gas electron configuration. Each atom fills its partially filled valence shell with shared electrons.

Hydrogen $1s^1$, with one electron, needs only one more electron to attain a noble gas electron configuration $1s^2$ (the electron configuration of helium). We say hydrogen follows a duet rule. Atoms of most elements require a total of 8 electrons in their valence shell to attain a noble gas electron configuration, and this attribute is the basis of the octet rule.

Octet rule: Atoms complete their octets by sharing electrons.

Here are some examples of how to use the octet or duet rule:

Consider the formation of a H_2 molecule from two atoms of hydrogen. Each H atom has a single electron. The two atoms share their electrons so that each electron is owned by both atoms. Each atom needs two electrons to satisfy the duet rule, and "joint ownership" of a pair of electrons allows both hydrogen atoms to satisfy their "duet" using only two electrons in total. The shared pair of electrons is known as a **bonding electron pair** and constitutes a **covalent bond**. This bond is represented by a line between the bonded atoms in the **Lewis structure** of H_2.

$$\cdot H \quad \cdot H \longrightarrow H \odot\odot H$$
(electron dot)

representations of an H_2 molecule

$$H-H$$
(Lewis structure)

THE LEWIS STRUCTURES OF HOMONUCLEAR DIATOMICS CAN BE FOUND
USING THE OCTET RULE

When two atoms are bonded together in a discrete molecule, we call the molecule a diatomic. When the two bonded atoms belong to the same element, we call it a homonuclear diatomic. Homonuclear diatomic molecules form **covalent** bonds because the difference in electronegativity of the two atoms involved is zero.

Fluorine has seven valence electrons. In F_2, the total number of valence electrons is fourteen. Forming a single covalent bond leads to each atom having eight electrons, satisfying of the octet rule for both atoms. There are twelve non-bonding valence electrons ($14 - 2 = 12$), and these electrons are grouped into pairs, known as **lone pairs**. From the twelve electrons we get six pairs of electrons; the lone pairs are distributed equally between the two identical fluorine atoms, three lone pairs per atom.

The lone pairs on the two fluorine atoms repel each other, weakening the bond between the two atoms.

An oxygen atom has six valence electrons. In O_2, the total number of valence electrons is twelve. Forming one covalent bond between oxygen atoms leads to each atom having seven valence electrons, which is not enough to complete an octet. In this case, the octet for both atoms can be satisfied by the sharing of a second pair of electrons — forming a second bond. The O_2 molecule is represented by its Lewis structure, with each line representing a single covalent bond in the **double bond**. Double bonds hold atoms together more tightly than single bonds.

Nitrogen has five valence electrons. Two nitrogen atoms, each providing three pairs of electrons, give a total of six electrons that can form three covalent bonds with both atoms satisfying their octet. The N_2 molecule is represented by a Lewis structure with a **triple bond** between atoms and a single lone pair on each atom.

Triple bonds hold atoms together more tightly than either single or double bonds.

THE LEWIS STRUCTURES FOR ANY COVALENTLY BONDED SPECIES CAN BE FOUND USING A SIMPLE SET OF RULES.

You can arrive at Lewis structures in any way that satisfies the octet requirements of each atom involved. The following rules provide a framework to help you find Lewis structures in a systematic way.

- Obtain the total number of valence electrons from all the atoms involved in a molecule. (This is the single most important thing to do. In this step, do not think of electrons as belonging to individual atoms, but find the total number of valence electrons in the molecule.)

- Use one pair of electrons to form bonds between all the connected atoms.

- Arrange the rest of the electrons to form multiple bonds or lone pairs such that the octets of all atoms are satisfied.

Consider, for example, H_2O. Oxygen is in Group VI and provides six valence electrons. Each hydrogen atom provides one electron. The total number of electrons is eight.

Using a pair of electrons for each bond we arrive at:

The duet for hydrogen is satisfied, but only four electrons surround oxygen. Adding the other four electrons as two lone pairs to oxygen satisfies the octet of oxygen.

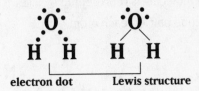

electron dot   **Lewis structure**

Now think about NH_3. Nitrogen is in Group V and provides five valence electrons. Each of three hydrogen atom provides a single electron. The total number of electrons is $5 + 3 = 8$. Using a pair of electrons for each bond, we arrive at :

The duets for the hydrogen atoms are satisfied, but only six electrons surround nitrogen. Adding the final two electrons as a lone pair to nitrogen satisfies its octet.

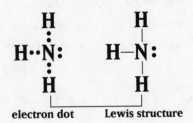

electron dot   **Lewis structure**

Finding the Lewis Structure of Polyatomic Ions

You can find the Lewis structures of polyatomic ions (defined in Chapter 2) using methods similar to those you have used with neutral molecules. The only difference is in the way we find the number of valence electrons in the polyatomic ion.

To calculate the number of valence electrons in a polyatomic ion, we first calculate the number of valence electrons for a hypothetical neutral compound. Then, to arrive the number of electrons in an anion we **add** the charge number of the anion to the number of valence electrons. To arrive at the number of electrons in a cation, we **subtract** the charge number of the cation from the number of electrons.

Let's find the Lewis structure of the polyatomic cation NO^+. Consider the neutral compound NO (in this case the neutral molecule does exist, but in general it need not). Nitrogen has five valence electrons; oxygen has six. The total number in the neutral compound is eleven. In formal terms NO^+ is merely NO that has lost one electron. Therefore, the total number of electrons for the ion is 11 - 1 = 10. We place one pair of electrons between the atoms. This leaves eight electrons, or four pairs. The octets of both atoms can be satisfied by a triple bond between the atoms and a lone pair on each atom.

$$\left[:N \equiv O: \right]^{\oplus}$$

Resonance Structures

RESONANCE STRUCTURES ARE DIFFERENT ARRANGEMENTS OF THE SAME VALENCE ELECTRONS AROUND THE SAME NUCLEI. THE NUCLEI HAVE THE SAME CONNECTIVITY IN EACH STRUCTURE. THE OBSERVED PROPERTIES OF THE MOLECULE IS A BLEND OF THE VARIOUS RESONANCE STRUCTURES.

We will consider NO_3^- as an example of finding the Lewis structure of polyatomic anions, because the solution we arrive at forces us to consider another important concept — **resonance**. NO_3^- has 5 + 3(6) + 1 = 24 valence electrons. To connect the atoms, we need three pairs (six electrons), which leaves 18 electrons to arrange.

Symbol of atom or e⁻	N	O	e⁻
Number of units (1)	1	3	1
Number of e⁻ per unit (2)	5	6	1
Number of e⁻ contributed (1) x (2)	5	18	1	24

Total number of e⁻

We could put six electrons on each of the three oxygen atoms; in combination with the two electrons each oxygen atom shares with nitrogen, these six atoms would complete the oxygen atoms' octet. To satisfy the nitrogen atom octet, however, we need to form a double bond between an oxygen atom and a nitrogen.

Yet we can draw three structures which satisfy the octet requirements of both types of atoms:

Which Lewis structure is correct? All of them! These Lewis structures for NO_3^- represent **resonance structures**, and the actual structure is a blend of all three. If we were describing snowboarding, we might say it is like skiing and also like skateboarding. In the same way, we say that the actual molecule is like all the resonance structures, but not adequately represented by any one of them alone. Resonance structures have different arrangements of electrons around the same atoms, but the arrangement of the nuclei does not change in resonance structures. Therefore, you need to consider all possible permutations of electron arrangements.

The resonance structures of NO_3^- are all the same energy. We say that they are **degenerate** and that all represent the observed properties of NO_3^- equally well. Each of the N-O bonds is the same length and strength, consistent with the real structure being an equal blend of the three resonance structures.

For some other molecules, resonance structures are not degenerate. For example, CO_2 has the following three resonance structures:

$$:\ddot{O}\!-\!C\!\equiv\!O: \longleftrightarrow \ddot{O}\!=\!C\!=\!\ddot{O} \longleftrightarrow :O\!\equiv\!C\!-\!\ddot{O}:$$

The middle resonance structure has the lowest energy and best represents the observed properties of CO_2. We know this because the CO_2 bonds that chemists observe have the same length and strength. This is indicated by the middle structure, but not by the two structures flanking it.

Exceptions to the Octet Rule

The octet rule has exceptions. Atoms may have incomplete or expanded octets.

For all its utility, the octet rule does not account for some classic exceptions. These exceptions tricky, but they also appear on chemistry exams everywhere. The first exception relates to incomplete octets.

ONE POSSIBLE EXCEPTION TO THE OCTET RULE IS A MOLECULE WITH AN INCOMPLETE OCTET. SUCH A MOLECULE HAS AN ATOM WITH LESS THAN EIGHT ELECTRONS IN ITS VALENCE SHELL.

The classic example of this phenomenon is BF_3. The following resonance structures can be drawn for BF_3 in which each atom has a complete octet:

However, the resonance structure that most accurately represents the observed properties of BF_3 is one in which boron (B) with only six electrons in its valence shell:

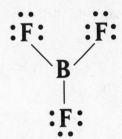

Comparing these resonance structures, we see that the one that best represents the properties of BF_3 gives fluorine a greater share of electrons. In the first three resonance structures, one fluorine atom has to share a second pair of electrons in covalent bonding. But we know that fluorine is highly electronegative and therefore keeps a tight hold on its electrons. The accurate resonance structure reflects the electronegativity of fluorine by keeping the electrons localized on fluorine as a lone pair.

ANOTHER CLASSIC EXCEPTION TO THE OCTET RULE IS OCTET EXPANSION.

This exception applies to compounds with atoms in the third period. These atoms are able to accommodate more than eight electrons in their valence shell. One example of octet expansion is the molecule SF_4. Sulfur has six valence electrons; each fluorine atom has seven valence electrons. The total number of electrons is $6 + 4(7) = 34$ electrons. Forming four covalent bonds between sulfur and fluorine uses 8 electrons — leaving 26 electrons. Each fluorine atom takes six more electrons to complete its octet, for a total of $4(6) = 24$ electrons. This leaves ten electrons localized on sulfur. This is called an expanded octet for the sulfur atom.

Polar Covalent Bonds

POLAR COVALENT BONDS CAN BE DESCRIBED AS A BLEND OF TWO RESONANCE STRUCTURES:

Some molecules, such as HCl, have bonds that are neither ionic or covalent, but somewhere in between. We can think of these bonds — called **polar covalent** bonds — as two extreme resonance structures. In one resonance structure, the bonding pair of electrons is shared equally between the two atoms; in the other, the bonding pair is transferred completely to the more electronegative element. The greater the difference in electro-negativity between the two elements, the more the second resonance structure will contribute to the observed structure of the molecule.

$$H\!-\!\ddot{\underset{\cdot\cdot}{Cl}}\!: \quad \longleftrightarrow \quad H^{\oplus} \quad :\!\ddot{\underset{\cdot\cdot}{Cl}}\!:^{\ominus}$$

The atoms in a polar covalent bond actually share electrons unequally, such that one atom (H) has a slight deficiency of electrons, and therefore has a slight, or "partial" positive charge (represented as δ^+). The other atom (Cl) has an excess of electrons and has a slight, or "partial" negative charge (represented as δ^-).

$$\delta^+ \, H\!-\!\!-\!\!-\!\! Cl \; \delta^-$$

Bonds with one positive and one negative end have a dipole, represented by an arrow from the positive to negative center.

$$\delta^+ \, H\!-\!\!-\!\!-\!\!-\!\! Cl \; \delta^-$$

Key Terms

bonding electrons: Valence electrons of an atom that are involved in a covalent bond.

covalent bonds: The type of chemical bonds in which elements share electrons.

dipole: The property of covalently bonded molecules with slight, or "partial" positive ends and "partial" negative ends. The electric imbalance is caused by an unequal sharing of electrons.

electron dot structure: A representation of the valence electrons in an atom or molecule.

electronegativity: A measure of the ability of elements to attract and hold on to electrons in a chemical bond.

ionic bonds: The type of chemical bonds in which elements are held together by the electrostatic attraction between their oppositely-charged ions. In these bonds, one element gains an electron or electrons, while another loses an electron or electrons.

Lewis structures: Diagrams in which each covalent bond between two atoms is represented by a line between their atomic symbols.

lone pair electrons: Pairs of electrons in the valence shell that are uninvolved in chemical bonding.

octet: An atom with eight electrons in its valence shell is said to have completed its octet.

octet rule: When combining chemically, atoms try to complete their octets.

resonance structures: Lewis structures that have the same arrangement of atoms' nuclei, but different arrangements of their valence electrons.

THRILLS, CHILLS AND DRILLS

True or False

1. Electronegativity is defined as $\frac{1}{2}(IE + EA)$.

2. Electronegative elements form cations easily.

3. Electronegative elements form anions easily.

4. O_2 is ionically bonded.

5. Electropositivity is a measure of an atom's potential to gain a positron.

6. In general, bonds formed between metals and non-metals tend to be ionic whereas those formed between non-metals and non-metals tend to be covalent.

7. $BaCl_2$ is an ionic compound.

8. Given that iron can form the Fe^{3+} ion and that chlorine can form the Cl^- ion, the compound combining these two ion types would be Fe_3Cl.

9. In $BaBr_2$, the barium 2+ ion has the an electron configuration that can be represented simply as: [Xe].

10. Sodium and oxygen can bond to form Na_2O.

11. Potassium and fluorine form a covalent compound in which the bonding has no ionic character.

12. The formation of ionic bonds leads to a noble gas electron configuration for both elements involved.

13. Bonding always occurs due to the interaction of core electrons with nuclei.

14. Covalent bonds are cemented by the attraction of two nuclei to the same valence electron pair.

15. The octet rule states that elements share electrons to complete their octets in covalent bonds.

16. Diatomic molecules include F_2 from Group VII, O_2 from Group VI, and N_2 from Group V.

17. Multiple lone pairs between fluorine atoms in F_2 increase the strength of the bond between the two atoms.

18 The O_2 molecule contains a double bond.

19. NH_4^+ has eight valence electrons.

20. The total number of electrons in all resonance structures of a given molecule is the same.

21. Nuclei of atoms can be connected differently in different resonance structures.

22. All bonds are either purely ionic or covalent.

23. The compound BCl_3 is only theoretical. It cannot exist because it cannot form a stable octet.

Multiple Choice

1. Electronegative elements have a combination of
   a) low IE and high EA
   b) high IE and low EA
   c) low IE and high EA
   d) high IE and high EA

2. Electric dipoles exist when electrons are unequally shared by atoms in a covalent bond. Roughly speaking, the strength of a dipole increases with increased difference in electronegativity between the two atoms. Which of the following four bonds has the largest dipole?
   a) H - O
   b) H - F
   c) O - C
   d) N - C

3. Ionic bonds result from
   a) attractive magnetic forces between cations and anions
   b) repulsive magnetic forces between cations and anions
   c) attractive electrical forces between cations and anions
   d) repulsive electric forces between cations and anions

4. Which element most likely forms an ionic bond with calcium?
   a) Mg
   b) Al
   c) Br
   d) Li

5. In a neutral calcium bromide compound, how many atoms of bromide do you expect to find for each atom of calcium?

    a) 0.5

    b) 1

    c) 2

    d) 4

6. From the most likely charges on ions, decide which of the following compounds does not exist.

    a) $CaCl_2$

    b) MgO

    c) He_2S

    d) MgF_2

7. Ca^{2+} and PO_4^{2-} bond to form

    a) $CaPO_4$

    b) $Ca_3(PO_4)_2$

    c) $Ca_2(PO_4)_3$

    d) $Ca(PO_4)_5$

8. Covalent bonds result from

    a) attractive forces between nuclei and electrons

    b) repulsive forces between nuclei and electrons

    c) attractive magnetic forces between nuclei and electrons

    d) attractive electric forces between different nuclei

9. Ms. Iwanna Share is a 4th year graduate student investigating the property of coordinate covalent bonding. This kind of covalent bond occurs when an atom in the molecule donates both of the electrons required for the covalent bond. In order to further her research, she has asked you (as the resident undergrad) to determine which of the following molecules demonstrates coordinate covalent bonding.

    a) BF_3NH_3

    b) H_2SO_4

    c) $BeCl_2$

    d) NH_3

10. The number of valence electrons in SO_3 is

    a) 12

    b) 18

    c) 24

    d) 40

11. How many valence electrons are shown in the electron dot structure for an oxygen atom?

    a) 2

    b) 4

    c) 6

    d) 16

12. Diatomic oxygen forms which type of covalent bond?

    a) single

    b) double

    c) triple

    d quadruple

13. Water molecules are held together by

    a) non polar covalent bonds

    b) polar covalent bonds

    c) resonance structures

    d) ionic bonds

14. For homonuclear diatomics, the difference in electronegativity between bonded atoms is

    a) 1

    b) 2

    c) >2

    d) 0

15. Which of the following molecules is stable according to the octet and duet rules?

    a) H_2S

    b) H_3

    c) NH_4

    d) NH_5

16. What is the correct Lewis structure for $SiCl_4$?

    a) Cl-Cl-Si-Cl-Cl

    b) Cl-Cl-Si=Cl-Cl

    c) 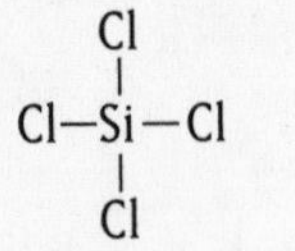
$$\begin{array}{c} \text{Cl} \\ | \\ \text{Cl}-\text{Si}-\text{Cl} \\ | \\ \text{Cl} \end{array}$$

    d) Cl-Cl=Si=Cl-Cl

17. In the formation of chemical bonds, elements generally

   a) fill valence shells

   b) obtain a noble gas electron configuration

   c) have no valence electrons

   d) decrease the entropy of the universe

   e) all of the above

18. Which of the following bonds would you expect to be most polar?

   a) B-F

   b) B-O

   c) B-N

   d) B-C

19. Which of the following compounds include atoms with an incomplete octet (or duets in the case of hydrogen)?

   a) NH_3

   b) BF_3NH_3

   c) H_2SO_4

   d) $BeCl_2$

20. Sulfur hexafluoride is used as a gaseous insulator in high-voltage electrical equipment. Which of the following is not a property of sulfur hexafluoride?

   a) Sulfur is surrounded by 12 valence electrons in the compound.

   b) The sulfur fluorine bond is polar.

   c) It is an example of sulfur octet expansion.

   d) The molar ratio of S to F is 2 to 6.

Short Essays

1. Mr. Am Iplus is confused about the relationship between ionization energy, electron affinity, and electronegativity. Can you explain to him low ionization energies and low electron affinities are correlated with low electronegativities?

2. Coroner Sul Fates has brought a mystery to you. A list of three compounds (Na_2SO_4, Na_2SO_3, and SO_2) was left near the site of a recent homicide, along with a message saying that the murder was accomplished by exposing the victim to large concentrations of the compound with the shortest S-O bond length.

   a. Draw the structures of each of the compounds (including any resonance structures).

   b. Knowing that a single bond is longer than a double bond, identify the cause of death and put the coroner's mind to rest.

3. Instead of giving you the questions he promised you, Dr. Resin Ate has stumped you on his final exam with theoretical questions. Can you overcome his plan to fail you? His research deals primarily with electron location and mobilization, so he asks you questions about resonance.

   a. What is the need for a concept of resonance?

   b. Does any one resonance structure describe a molecule?

   c. Draw the structures for NO, NO_2^-, and NO_3^-, including any resonance structures.

4. Benzene (C_6H_6) consists of a six-membered ring of carbon atoms with one hydrogen atom bonded to each.

   a. Write Lewis structures for benzene, including all resonance structures. (The resonance of the benzene ring is responsible for its remarkable stability.)

   b. An important observation supporting the need for resonance structures is that there are only three different distinct dicholorobenzene ($C_6H_4Cl_2$) molecules in which two chlorine molecules replace two hydrogens. Draw these three structures.

   c. How does your answer to part b) support the concept of resonance?

5. On a clear day, the white chalk cliffs of Dover along the English Coast can be seen from France, 24 miles away. The cliffs are composed of calcium carbonate ($CaCO_3$).

   a. Draw Lewis structures (including any resonance structures) of the carbonate ion.

   b. Classify all the bonds in calcium carbonate as ionic or covalent.

ANSWERS

True or False Answers

1. **True.**

2. **False.** Electronegative elements form anions easily because they have high electron affinity and high ionization energies.

3. **True.**

4. **False.** O_2 is a homonuclear diatomic molecule. It is covalently bonded because the difference in electronegativity of the two oxygen atoms involved is zero.

5. **False.** Electropositive elements have low electronegativities and tend to lose electrons to form cations.

6. **True.** The difference in electronegativity between a metal and a nonmetal tends to be large, and so the bonds formed between such elements will be ionic. On the other hand, the difference in electronegativity between two nonmetals tends to be small and so two nonmetals will form a covalent bond.

7. **True.** Chlorine, $[Ne]3s^23p^5$, is electronegative and barium, $[Xe]6s^2$, is electropositive. The transfer of one 3s valence electron from barium to each chlorine atom leads to noble gas configurations for both atoms.

8. **False.** Iron ($[Ar]4s^23d^6$) and chlorine ($[Ne]3s^23p^5$) would form an $FeCl_3$ molecule. Iron would transfer three electrons, two 4s electrons and one 3d electron, to form the Fe^{3+} cation ($[Ar]3d^5$). Each chlorine atom would gain one electron, forming a Cl- ion, for a total charge of 3-.

9. **True.** The electron configuration of Ba is $[Xe]6s^2$. Hence, the Ba^{2+} atom can be represented as just [Xe].

10. **True.** Sodium, $[Ne]3s^1$ needs to lose one electron to gain a noble gas configuration and oxygen, $[He]2s^22p^4$, needs to gain two electrons to gain a noble gas configuration. Two Na atoms will combine with one O atom to form Na_2O.

11. **False.** Fluorine has a high electronegativity and potassium has a low electronegativity; the large difference in electronegativity means that these two atoms will form an ionic bond. The transfer of one 4s electron from K to F leads to the formation of KF.

12. **True.**

13. **False.** Core electrons are not involved in chemical bonding. Valence electrons are the key to bonding.

14. **True.**

15. **True.**

16. **True.**

17. **False.** The lone pairs on the two fluorine atoms repel each other and this weakens the bond between the two atoms.

18. **True.** O_2 has 12 valence electrons. The formation of one covalent bond between oxygen atoms leads to each atom having seven valence electrons. If the two oxygen atoms share a second pair of electrons, the octet rule will be satisfied for both atoms. Therefore, O_2 contains a double bond.

19. **True.** Nitrogen has 5 valence electrons and each H has 1 valence electron. NH_4 has 9 valence electrons, and the loss of one of these leads to the formation of NH_4^+, with 8 valence electrons.

20. **True.**

21. **False.** Resonance structures are different arrangements of the same valence electrons around the same nuclei. The nuclei have the same connectivity in each structure.

22. **False.** Polar covalent bonds are partially covalent and partially ionic in nature.

23. **False.** In the BCl_3 molecule, B has an incomplete octet. This exception to the octet rule is due to the high electronegativity of Cl.

Multiple Choice Answers

1. (d) Electronegativity is defined as $1/2(IE + EA)$.

2. (b) The difference in electronegativity between hyrogen and fluorine is 1.9.

3. (c) The opposite charges of cations and anions attract.

4. (c) Br has the highest electronegativity of the atoms listed and will therefore be most likely to form an ionic bond with Ca.

5. (c) Calcuim, $[Ar]4s^2$, needs to lose 2 electrons to have a noble gas configuration, while bromine, $[Ar]4s^24p5$, needs to gain one electron. Therefore, two bromine atoms will each gain a 4s valence electron from calcium, thereby forming $CaBr_2$.

6. (c) Helium is a noble gas with a complete duet. It does not like to form ions.

7. (a) The resulting molecule, $CaPO_4$, is neutral.

8. (a) The atoms in a covalent bond are held together by the attraction of the nuclei of both atoms to the same electrons.

9. (b) The nitrogen atom contributes both electrons to the covalent bond formed between nitrogen and boron.

10. (a) Sulfur, $[Ne]3s^23p^4$, has 6 valence electrons and each oxygen atom, $[He]2s^22p^4$, has 6 valence electrons, for a total of 24.

11. (c) The oxygen atom has the electron configuration $[He]2s^22p^4$.

12. (b) O_2 has 12 valence electrons. If the two oxygen atoms shared only one pair of electrons, they each would have 7 valence electrons. If the two oxygen atoms share a second pair of electrons, the octet rule will be satisfied for both atoms. O_2 contains a double bond.

13. (b) The bonds between hydrogen and oxygen in water can be thought of as two extreme resonance structures. In one resonance structure, the bonding pair of electrons is shared equally between the two atoms, while in the other, the bonding pair is transferred completely to the more electronegative element, oxygen.

14. (d) Homonuclear diatomic molecules contain two atoms of the same element. Thus there is no difference in electronegativity between the two atoms.

15. (a) Sulfer has 6 valence electrons, while each hydrogen atom has 1. Sulfer can share one pair of electrons with each hydrogen atom. In H_2S, the duet rule will be satisfied for H and the octet rule will be satisfied for S.

16. (c) In Lewis dot symbols, Si, $[Ne]3s^23p^2$, can be drawn with 4 dots around it and Cl, $[Ne]3s^23p^5$, can be drawn with 7 dots around it. Each of the four valence electrons of Si can be shared by a Cl atom, thus satisfying the octet rule for all atoms. Hence, the Lewis structure is $SiCl_4$.

17. (b) All elements aspire to obtain a noble gas configuration and when forming bonds, will gain or lose electrons to do so.

18. (a) Fluorine is more electronegative than oxygen, nitrogen or carbon. B-F will be the most polar because it will have the largest difference in electronegativity between the atoms involved.

19. (d) The electron configuration of beryllium is $[He]2s^2$. The electron configuration of chlorine is $[Ne]3s^23p^5$. Be can share one pair of electrons with each chlorine atom. This satisfies the octet rule for Cl, but leaves Be with only 4 valence electrons. There is no way to satisfy the octet rule for Be in this molecule.

20. (d) The molar ratio of S to F is 1 to 6. Each of sulfer's 6 valence electrons forms a covalent bond with one fluorine atom.

Short Essay Answers

1. Electronegativity is defined as 1/2 (IE +EA). If both EA and IE are low, then the sum is a Jlow number and the electronegativity is low. We understand electronegativity as the ability of an atom to attract, and hold onto electrons in a chemical reaction. If the EA is low it is hard to attract electrons. If IE is low it is hard to keep hold of electrons.

2. **b.** The shortest bond will have the most double bond character. All but SO_2 have resonance structures where the SO bond is represented as a single bond. SO_2 thus contains the S-O bond with the most double bond character. As such it has the shortest strongest S-O bond. The cause of death was exposure to SO_2.

3. **a.** We need to envoke resonance to explain properties that are not readily explained by any one Lewis structure.

   b. No one Lewis structure, but a hybrid of all Lewis structures for a molecule explains its properties.

4. **c.** If we did not envoke resonance there would be more physically distinct observable molecules (known as isomers).

5. **b.** C-O bond is polar covalent. The $Ca^{2+} - CO_3^{2-}$ bond is ionic.

CHAPTER

NOMENCLATURE: WHAT'S IN A NAME?

6

OVERVIEW

We have seen how chemists describe matter in terms of atomic symbols and formulas. At times, you may have thought of chemists as aliens, speaking an undecipherable, otherworldly language. But after studying this chapter you will be able to communicate more effectively the knowledge you gain while studying chemistry. You will be able to talk like a chemist.

In this chapter we will learn a set of rules for translating the language of chemical symbols and formulae into words that at least resemble English. There are a number of conventions for naming substances which reflect their chemical root, just as our names may reflect our ethnic heritage. The chemical names of substances reflect their chemical root, but even more so than do the names of people. As we learned in Chapter 5, compounds may be classed as ionic or covalent. These compounds are named according to strict sets of rules, which we will learn.

CONCEPTS

Naming Ions

MONATOMIC CATIONS ARE NAMED FOR THE ELEMENT FROM WHICH THEY ARE DERIVED.

Some elements form only one type of cation. For these elements, cations are named by simply adding ion to the name of the element. For example, calcium only forms the cation, Ca^{2+}. This cation is called a calcium ion.

Elements that form only one type of ion are:

- Group I (I+ ions)

- Group II (2+ ions)

- aluminium (3+ ions)

- cadmium (2+ ions) and zinc (2+ ions)

Some elements, such as iron, can form a range of cations (Fe^{2+}, Fe^{3+}). When referring to cations of such elements, we need to specify their charge. We can do so by writing the charge of the ion as a Roman numeral. For example, Fe^{2+} is denoted as an iron (II) ion, while Fe^{3+} is denoted as an iron (III) ion.

MONATOMIC ANIONS ARE NAMED USING THE STEM NAME OF THE ELEMENT AND THE SUFFIX -IDE.

Monatomic anions are named by adding the suffix -**ide** to the first part (or stem) of the element name. For example, the anion of chlorine is called a chlor**ide** ion. The name is a composite of chlor – the stem of chlorine – and the suffix -**ide** .

ELEMENT	FIRST PART OF NAME (STEM)	ION
Chlorine	**Chlor**	Chloride (Cl^-)
Fluorine	**Fluor**	Fluoride (F^-)
Oxygen	**Ox**	Oxide (O^{2-})
Nitrogen	**Nitr**	Nitride (N^{3-})
Sulfur	**Sulf**	Sulfide (S^{2-})

Naming Binary Compounds

Binary compounds are composed of only two elements. First we will see how to name binary ionic compounds formed by a metal and a non-metal, then we will turn to naming binary compounds formed by two non-metals.

The names of simple binary ionic compounds made up of monatomic ions can be derived using a single simple rule.

TO NAME BINARY IONIC COMPOUNDS, WRITE THE NAME OF THE CATION FOLLOWED BY THE NAME OF THE ANION.

Consider the following compounds as examples:

a) NaCl   **b)** CaO   **c)** $MgCl_2$ **d)** $AlCl_3$

a) The element that forms the cation is sodium. The element that forms the anion is chlorine. Therefore, the compound is named sodium chloride.

b) The element that forms the cation is calcium. The element that forms the anion is oxygen. The compound is named calcium oxide.

c) The element that forms the cation is magnesium. The element that forms the anions is chlorine. The compound is named magnesium chloride.

d) The element that forms the cation is aluminum. The element that forms the anions is chlorine. The compound is named aluminum chloride.

Notice that in each of these examples the elements involved can each form only one type of ion. However, we have seen that some elements can form cations with a range of different charges. When these elements are part of a compound, we need to specify the cation involved.

TO NAME COMPOUNDS INVOLVING ELEMENTS THAT CAN FORM A RANGE OF CATIONS, WRITE THE NAME OF THE CATION INCLUDING THE ROMAN NUMERALS THAT DEFINE ITS CHARGE FOLLOWED BY THE NAME OF THE ANION.

To name compounds involving elements that can form a range of cations, we need to first determine the cation involved in the compound. As you know, ionic compounds are neutral overall, and so the total charges of the cations and anions in the formula unit must exactly balance. Since the non-metals form only one type of anion, we can find the negative charge in the formula unit by adding together the charges on each anion. The charge of the cation must be equal to the sum of the known charges of the anions.

Let's name these compounds containing metal ions of unknown charge:

a) CuCl   **b)** Fe_2O_3 **c)** HgO

a) In CuCl, the chloride ion has a charge of 1-:

$$x + (-1) = 0, \text{ where } (x) \text{ is the charge of the copper ion}$$

$$x = +1$$

The name of the compound is copper (I) chloride.

b) In Fe_2O_3, each oxide ion has a charge of 2-. Three oxygen atoms have a combined charge of $3x(-2) = -6$.

$$x + (6-) = 0, \text{ where } (x) \text{ is the charge of two iron ions}$$

$$x = 6+$$

Since there are two iron atoms per formula unit, the charge per iron atom is $6+/2 = 3+$.

The compound is named iron (III) oxide.

c) In HgO, the oxide ion has a charge of 2-.

$$x + (2-) = 0, \text{ where } (x) \text{ is the charge of the mercury cation}$$

$$x = 2+$$

The compound is named mercury (II) oxide.

BINARY COMPOUNDS CONTAINING ONLY NON-METALS ARE NAMED ACCORDING TO THE FOLLOWING SET OF RULES.

1) The first element in the formula is named first, using the full element name.

2) The second element is named as if it were an anion.

3) Prefixes are used to denote the number of atoms of each element in the molecular formula.

4) The prefix **mono**- can be used for the second, but not the first, element.

The table on the next page shows the prefixes and the numbers they represent.

PREFIX	NUMBER INDICATED
mono-	1
di-	2
tri-	3
tetra-	4
penta-	5
hexa-	6

To illustrate these rules, let's look at the following compounds:

a) NO   **b)** BCl_3 **c)** SF_4 **d)** N_2O_5 **e)** CO_2 **f)** SF_6

a) The first part of the name is nitrogen (rule 1).

The second part of the name is oxide (rule 2).

Oxide is prefixed with **mono**-, but nitrogen is not prefixed (rules 3 and 4).

NO is called nitrogen monoxide.

b) The first part of the name is boron (rule 1).

The second part of the name is chloride (rule 2).

Chloride is prefixed with **tri**- (rule 3).

BCl_3 is called boron trichloride.

c) The first part of the name is sulfur (rule 1).

The second part of the name is fluoride (rule 2).

Fluoride is prefixed with **tetra**- (rule 3).

SF_4 is named sulfur tetrafluoride.

d) The first part of the name is nitrogen (rule 1).

The second part of the name is oxide (rule 2).

Nitrogen is prefixed with **di**-, and oxygen is prefixed with **penta**- (rule 3). N_2O_5 is named dinitrogen pentoxide.

e) The first part of the name is carbon (rule 1).

The second part of the name is oxide (rule 2).

Oxide is prefixed with **di**- (rule 3).

CO_2 is named carbon dioxide.

f) The first part of the name is sulfur (rule 1).

The second part of the name is fluoride (rule 2).

Flouride is prefixed with **hexa-** (rule 3).

SF_6 is named sulfur hexafluoride.

Naming Compounds Containing Polyatomic Ions

polyatomic ions are those that contain an important class of compounds that we must name. Recall that polyatomic ions, such as NH_4^+, are charged species composed of several atoms. Polyatomic ions form parts of ionic compounds. For example, Na_2SO_4 (sodium sulfate) is an ionic compound composed of sodium cations and the polyatomic SO_4^{2-} anions.

To name compounds containing polyatomic ions, we must know the names of the polyatomic ions involved.

The table below shows the formulas and names of common polyatomic ions. **You should memorize the names of these ions and their formulas.**

NAMES OF COMMON POLYATOMIC IONS

ION	NAME	ION	NAME
NH_4^+	ammonium	CO_3^{2-}	carbonate
NO_2^-	nitrite	HCO_3^-	hydrogen carbonate
NO_3^-	nitrate		(bicarbonate is the most
SO_3^{2-}	sulfite		commonly used name)
SO_4^{2-}	sulfate	ClO^-	hypochlorite
HSO_4^-	hydrogen sulfate	ClO_2^-	chlorite
	(bisulfate is the most	ClO_3^-	chlorate
	commonly used name)	ClO_4^-	percholate
OH^-	hydroxide	$C_2H_3O_2^-$	acetate
CN^-	cyanide	MnO_4^-	permanganate
PO_4^{3-}	phosphate	$Cr_2O_7^{2-}$	dichromate
HPO_4^{2-}	hydrogen phosphate	CrO_4^{2-}	chromate
$H_2PO_4^-$	dihydrogen phosphate	O_2^{2-}	peroxide

Notice that several polyatomic anions contain an atom of one element in combination with various amounts of oxygen. Polyatomic anions containing oxygen are described by the general name **oxoanion**. When two oxoanions exist, the one with less oxygen is named with the suffix -**ite**. The ion with more oxygen atoms is given the suffix -**ate**. For example, nitrogen forms nitrite (NO_2^-) and nitrate (NO_3^-) ions.

When there are more than two oxoanions, the one with the least oxygen content is named with the prefix **hypo**- (less than), and the ion with the most oxygen content is named with the prefix **per**- (more than). For example, the oxoanions of chlorine have the following names.

ClO^- **hypochlorite**

ClO_2^- **chlorite**

ClO_3^- **chlorate**

ClO_4^- **perchlorate**

Compounds containing polyatomic ions are named in a manner similar to other ionic compounds. The name of the cation is written first and is followed by the name of anion.

How would you name these compounds containing polyatomic ions?

a) $KClO_3$ **b)** Na_2CO_3 **c)** $NaHCO_3$ **d)** NH_4Cl **e)** NH_4OH **f)** $Fe(NO_3)_3$

a) The cation is potassium. The anion is chlorate (ClO_3^-). The name of the compound is potassium chlorate.

b) The cation is sodium. The anion is carbonate (CO_3^{2-}). The name of the compound is sodium carbonate.

c) The cation is sodium. The anion is hydrogen carbonate (HCO_3^-). The name of the compound is sodium hydrogen carbonate.

d) The cation is ammonium (NH_4^+). The anion is chloride. The name of the compound is ammonium chloride.

e) The cation is ammonium. The anion is hydroxide (OH). The name of the compound is ammonium hydroxide.

f) The cation is iron. The anion is nitrate (NO_3^-). Each nitrate contributes a charge of -1 to the formula unit. Since the formula unit is neutral overall, we can figure out which iron cation is contained in this compound.

$$? + 3(1-) = 0 \text{ , where (?) is the charge of the iron ion}$$
$$? = 3+, \text{ meaning that iron (III) ion is the cation}$$

The name of the compound is iron (III) nitrate.

Naming Acids

The final class of compounds that we will learn to name are the acids.

Acids are named according to three simple rules.

IF THE ANION OF THE ACID DOES NOT CONTAIN OXYGEN ATOMS, THE ROOT NAME FOR THE ELEMENT IN THE ANION IS PREFIXED WITH HYDRO- AND SUFFIXED WITH -IC.

For example, HCl dissolves in water to give H^+ ions and Cl^- ions. It is known as **hydro-chloric** acid.

Many oxoanions are found in acids. The H^+ ions in the acid balance the negative charge of the anion, so that the acid is electrically neutral. Acids containing oxoanions are called **oxoacids**. The names of oxoacids are derived from those of the oxoanions.

WHEN THE NAME OF THE OXOANION ENDS IN -ATE, THE CORRESPONDING ACID NAME ENDS IN -IC.

For example, the sulf**ate** ion (SO_4^{2-}) is part of sulfur**ic** acid. The nitr**ate** ion (NO_3^-) is part of nitr**ic** acid.

WHEN THE NAME OF THE OXOANION ENDS IN -ITE, THE NAME OF THE CORRESPONDING ACID ENDS IN -OUS.

For example, the sulf**ite** ion (SO_3^{2-}) is found in sulfur**ous** acid, and the nitr**ite** ion is found in nitr**ous** acid (HNO_2^-).

These rules for the endings for acid names hold true even when the name of the oxoanion is prefixed with **hypo-** or **per-**. The oxoacids of chlorine give us some common examples.

ION NAME	ION	ACID	ACID NAME
perchlorate ion	ClO_4^-	$HClO_4$	perchloric acid
chlorate ion	ClO_3^-	$HClO_3$	chloric acid
chlorite ion	ClO_2^-	$HClO_2$	chlorous acid
hypochlorite ion	ClO^-	$HClO$	hypochlorous acid

KEY TERMS

oxoacid: An acid containing an oxoanion

oxoanion: An anion that contains oxygen

Prefixes and Suffixes:

-ate: When more than two oxoanions exist, the one with more oxygen takes the suffix -ate. Eg. With (NO_2^-) and (NO_3^-), (NO_3^-) is nitrate.

hypo-: When more than two oxoanions exist, the one with the least oxygen takes the prefix hypo-: Eg: With ClO^-, ClO_2^-, ClO_3^-, ClO_4^-, ClO^- is hypochlorite.

hydro- -ic: The prefix and suffix used for acids when the anion that forms the acid does not contain oxygen. Eg. The acid formed with Cl^-, HCl, is called hydrochloric acid.

-ic: The suffix used for acids formed by oxoanions with the suffix -ate: Eg.: The acid formed with the sulfate ion is called sulfuric acid.

-ite: When more than two oxoanions exist, the one with more oxygen takes the suffix -ite. Eg. With (NO_2^-) and (NO_3^-), (NO_2^-) is nitrite.

-ous: The suffix used for acids formed by oxoanions with the suffix -ite: Eg.: The acid formed with the nitrite ion is called nitrous acid.

per-: When more than two oxoanions exist, the one with the most oxygen takes the prefix per-. Eg: With ClO^-, ClO_2^-, ClO_3^-, ClO_4^-, ClO_4^- is perchlorate.

THRILLS, CHILLS AND DRILLS

True or False

1. A Ca^{2+} cation is called a calcium ion.

2. A Na^+ ion is called a sodium (I) ion.

3. A Mn^{2+} ion is called a manganese (II) ion.

4. A sulfide ion has a charge of 3-.

5. An oxide ion has a charge of 2-.

6. The F^- ion is called a flourine ion.

7. MgF_2 is named magnesium difluoride.

8. CaO is named calcium (I) oxide.

9. $PbCl_2$ is called lead chloride.

10. In TiC_4, the titanium ion has a charge of 4+.

11. In Fe_2O_3, iron has a charge of 3+.

12. N_2O_4 is called dinitrogen tetroxide.

13. SF_4 is called sulfur fluoride.

14. CO_2 is called dicarbondioxide.

15. PBr_3 is called phosphorus tribromide.

16. K_2CO_3 is called potassium carbonate.

17. MnO_2 is called manganese (II) oxide.

18. The nitrate ion can be written: NO_3^-.

19. The sulfate ion has a charge of 2-.

20. The oxoacid corresponding to sulfuric acid is H_2SO_4.

21. Nitrous acid is HNO_3.

22. Hypochlorous acid is $HClO_4$.

Multiple Choice

1. $MgCl_2$ is called
   a) magnesium dichloride.
   b) magnesium(II) chloride.
   c) magnesium (II) chlorine.
   d) magnesium chloride.

2. $AlCl_3$ is called
   a) aluminum trichloride.
   b) aluminum (III) chloride.
   c) aluminum chloride.
   d) aluminum (II) chlorate.

3. $HgCl_2$ is known as
   a) mercury dichloride.
   b) mercury (I) chloride.
   c) mercury (II) chloride.
   d) mercury (II) chlorine.

4. BF_3 is called
   a) boron (III) fluoride.
   b) boron trifluoride.
   c) boron (I) fluoride.
   d) boron (I) fluorine.

5. Fe_2O_3 is called
   a) iron (III) oxide.
   b) iron (II) oxide.
   c) iron oxide.
   d) diron trioxide.

6. $FeCl_3$ is called
   a) iron (II) chloride.
   b) iron trichloride.
   c) iron (III) chloride.
   d) iron chloride.

7. Na_3N is called
   a) sodium nitride.
   b) trisodium nitride.
   c) sodium (III) nitride.
   d) sodium (I) nitride.

8. S_2O is called
   a) silver oxide.
   b) disilver oxide.
   c) disulfur oxide.
   d) sulfur dioxide.

9. NI_3 is known as
   a) nitrogen (III) iodide.
   b) nitrogen triiodide.
   c) nitride triiodine.
   d) sodium iodide.

10. The sulfite ion is
    a) SO_4^{2-}
    b) SO_4^-
    c) SO_3^-
    d) SO_3^{2-}

11. The nitrate ion has the formula
    a) NO_2^-
    b) NO_3^{2-}
    c) NO_2^-
    d) NO^{2-}

12. The ammonium ion has the formula
    a) NH_3^+
    b) NH_4^+
    c) NH_4^-
    d) NH_3^-

13. The perchlorate ion has the formula
    a) ClO_4^-
    b) ClO_3^-
    c) ClO_2^-
    d) ClO^-

14. The chlorate ion has the formula

    a) ClO_4^-

    b) ClO_3^-

    c) ClO_2^-

    d) ClO^-

15. The chlorite ion has the formula

    a) ClO_4^-

    b) ClO_3^-

    c) ClO_2^-

    d) ClO^-

16. The phosphate ion has the formula

    a) PO_4^{2-}

    b) PO_4^{3-}

    c) PO_4^-

    d) PO_4^{4-}

17. Ammonium nitrate has the formula

    a) NH_4NO_3

    b) NH_3NO_2

    c) NH_2NO_4

    d) NH_3N_3

18. Sodium chlorite has the formula

    a) $NaClO$

    b) $NaCl$

    c) $NaClO_2$

    d) $NaClO_4$

19. H_2S dissolves in water to give an acidic solution of

    a) hydrosulfuric acid.

    b) hydrosulfurous acid.

    c) sulfurous acid.

    d) sulfuric acid.

20. HF dissolves in water to give

    a) hydrofluorous acid.

    b) hypofluororous acid.

    c) perchlorous acid.

    d) hydrogen fluoride.

21. The acetate ion has the formula $C_2H_3O_2^-$. The acid $HC_2H_3O_2$ is therefore known as

   a) acetous acid.

   b) hydroacetous acid.

   c) hydroacetic acid.

   d) acetic acid.

Short Essays

1. Calcium supplements may help prevent bones from weakening (known as osteoporosis). Many calcium supplements are largely calcium carbonate. The calcium carbonate reacts with hydrochloric acid in the stomach to produce calcium chloride, water, and carbon dioxide.

   a. Write an equation for this reaction.

   b. List any polyatomic ions involved in the reaction.

2. Sodium hydrogen carbonate is otherwise known as baking soda. The reaction of ammonia, sodium chloride, water, and carbon dioxide to produce ammonium chloride and sodium hydrogen carbonate is one commercial process by which baking soda is made. Write a balanced equation for this process.

3. The carbon dioxide that astronauts exhale is be removed from the ship's cabin through a process known as scrubbing. Lithium hydroxide is used to scrub the air free of carbon dioxide. The products of the reaction are lithium carbonate and water. Write a balanced equation for this process.

ANSWERS

True or False Answers

1. **True.**
2. **False.** Na^+ is simply called a sodium ion.
3. **True.**
4. **False.** A sulfide ion has a charge of 2-.
5. **True.**
6. **False.** The F- ion is called a flouride ion.
7. **False.** MgF_2 is named magnesium fluoride.
8. **False.** CaO is named calcium oxide.
9. **False.** $PbCl_2$ is called lead (II) chloride.
10. **True.**
11. **True.**
12. **True.**
13. **False.** SF_4 is called sulfur tetrafluoride.
14. **False.** CO_2 is called carbon dioxide.
15. **True.**
16. **True.**
17. **False.** MnO_2 is manganese (IV) oxide.
18. **True.**
19. **True.**
20. **True.**
21. **False.** Nitric acid is HNO_3
22. **False.** Perchloric acid is $HClO_4$

Multiple Choice Answers

1. (d)
2. (c)
3. (c)
4. (b)
5. (a)
6. (c)
7. (a)

8. (c)
9. (b)
10. (d)
11. (a)
12. (b)
13. (a)
14. (b)
15. (c)
16. (b)
17. (a)
18. (a)
19. (a)
20. (a)
21. (d)

Short Essay Answers

1   **a.** $CaCO_3(s) + 2HCl(aq) \rightarrow CaCl_2(aq) + H_2O + CO_2(g)$
    b. CO_3^{2-}

2. $NH_3 + NaCl + H_2O + CO_2 \rightarrow NH_4Cl + NaHCO_3$

3. $2LiOH(s) + CO_2(g) \rightarrow Li_2CO_3(s) + H_2O(l)$

CHAPTER

MOLECULES IN THREE DIMENSIONS

7

OVERVIEW

Roses are red, violets are blue, sugar is sweet — but why? Would you believe that sugar owes its sweetness to its shape? The three-dimensional shape of the glucose molecules that make up sugar are responsible for its sweet taste. The glucose molecule fits, like a hand in a glove, into the sweetness taste-receptors in our mouths. To mimic the effect of sugars, manufacturers of artificial sweetners have tried to copy the three-dimensional shape of the glucose molecule, so that those who wish to lose weight can satisfy their sweetness cravings without piling on the calories. This is just one example of why a knowledge of the shapes of molecules is important.

In Chapter 5 we introduced the concept of the bonding of elements by ionic and covalent bonds. Covalently-bonded molecules often have discrete three-dimensional shapes. Often it is the three-dimensional shape of a molecule that is responsible for many of its properties. In this chapter we consider a set of rules for finding the shapes of covalently-bonded molecules. The rules require that we know the Lewis structures of the molecules (also covered in Chapter 5), and are known as valence shell electron pair repulsion theory or VSEPR. VSEPR predicts the geometry for molecules by minimizing repulsions between valence electron pairs.

In this chapter we will learn to assign shapes to molecules with 2, 3, 4, 5 and 6 electron pairs around the central atom of a molecule.

CONCEPTS

THE MOLECULAR STRUCTURE IS DEFINED IN TERMS OF BOND ANGLES AND BOND LENGTHS.

The shape of a molecule is known as its molecular structure, which is described geometrically in terms of bond angles and bond lengths. A bond length is a measure of the distance between two chemically-bonded atoms along a straight line between their nuclei. Bond lengths are measured in picometers (pm), which are 10^{-12} meters, or in Å (1 Å = 100 pm). A bond angle is the angle between any two bonds that includes a common atom. Like all angles, it is measured in degrees.

As an example of how to assign bond angles and bond lengths, consider the formaldehyde molecule.

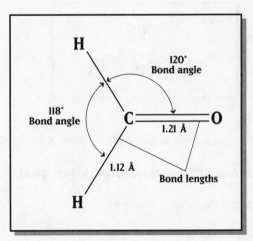

In formaldehyde, there are three bonds, one C=O and two C-H bonds. The bond lengths are shown on the diagram. There are three bond angles in formaldehyde: two bond angles and one HCH bond angle in. In general, bond angles are described in terms of the three atoms that define them.

WE CAN PREDICT THE APPROXIMATE BOND ANGLES IN SIMPLE MOLECULES USING A MODEL KNOWN AS VALENCE SHELL ELECTRON PAIR REPULSION THEORY (VSEPR).

VSEPR states that electron pairs in the valence shell of an atom will minimize their repulsion by maximizing their separation. Given the electron structure, which minimizes repulsion, we can work out the positions of atoms surrounding the central atom.   Below, we consider the geometric arrangement of electron pairs around an atom at the center of a molecule and give examples of the molecular geometries that can result from each type of electron distribution.

TWO ELECTRON PAIRS ARE BEST ARRANGED IN A LINE.

As a simple example of VSEPR in action, consider $BeCl_2$. This molecule has the Lewis structure:

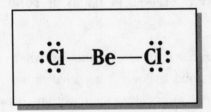

The central atom is berrylium. There are two electron pairs around the berrylium atom, one electron pair in each Be-Cl bond. To put these electron pairs as far apart as possible, we place them on opposite sides of the berrylium atom. The angle between the electron pairs is 180°.

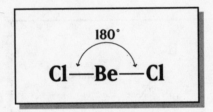

Two electron pairs surrounding a central atom always form a linear structure.

THREE ELECTRON PAIRS ARE BEST ARRANGED IN A TRIGONAL PLANE.

Next, consider BF_3, which has the Lewis structure:

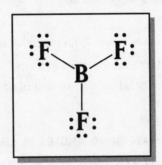

The central boron atom is surrounded by three electron pairs – one pair per B-F bond. We can achieve the maximum separation of these electron pairs putting them at an angle of 120°, in a plane. Three electron pairs around a central atom are always arranged in this structure called a **trigonal plane.**

Since each of the three electron pairs is shared between a boron and fluorine atom, the molecular structure can be drawn.

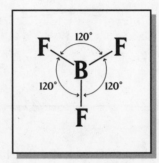

This arrangement of atoms is described as **trigonal planar**.

FOUR ELECTRON PAIRS ARE BEST ARRANGED IN A TETRAHEDRON.

Let's look at the molecule CH_4, known as methane, which has the Lewis structure:

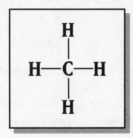

Here, the central carbon atom is surrounded by four electron pairs: one pair per C-H bond.

The angles between four electron pairs are maximized by placing them at 109.5°. With this configuration, the electron pairs describe a **tetrahedron,** and the arrangement of electron pairs is **tetrahedral.** Whenever a compound has four electron pairs around a central atom, are arranged according to tetrahedral geometry.

Since each electron pair corresponds to one C-H bond, the molecular geometry of methane (CH_4) is tetrahedral.

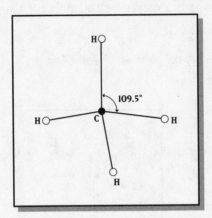

So far, we have considered the shapes of molecules that have only bonding electron pairs around the central atom.

Ammonia (NH_3) has the Lewis structure:

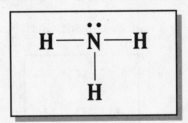

The central nitrogen atom in ammonia is surrounded by three electron pairs in NH bonds and one lone pair of electrons. Overall, there are four electron pairs associated with the nitrogen atom. We have seen that the separation of four electron pairs is maximized in a tetrahedral arrangement, but now three vertices of the tetrahedron are occupied by hydrogen atoms and one by the nitrogen lone pair.

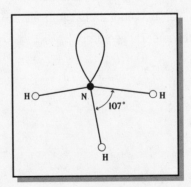

Recall that the molecular structure is defined by the position of the atoms, not by the position of electron pairs. While the electron pairs are in a tetrahedron, the arrangement of the atoms is described as **trigonal pyramidal**. However, this is not the whole story. If the electronic structure was exactly tetrahedral, we would expect the bond angles in trigonal pyramidal molecules, like ammonia, to be 109.5°.

In fact, the measured bond angle is 107°. We can explain this deviation in bond angle applying a sub-rule of VSEPR that defines a hierarchy in the repulsion between different types of electron pairs. The sub-rule states that:

- Lone pairs tend to repel other lone pairs most strongly.

- A lone pair and bonding pair repel each other with lesser ferocity.

- Bonding pairs have the least repulsion between them. Consequently, it is favorable to keep lone pairs as far apart as possible and to keep bonding and lone pairs apart, even if that means putting bonding pairs closer together. In summary, the order of electron pair repulsions is:

$$lp \cdot lp > lp \cdot bp > bp \cdot bp$$

A consequence of the hierarchy in electron pair repulsion is that molecules with lone pairs tend to have smaller bond angles than what we would predict if all electron pairs were equal.

Ammonia contains a lone electron pair and, therefore, we expect the H-N-H bond angles to be less than 109°. Notice that VSEPR predicts that the bond angle of NH_3 will be less than 109°, **but says nothing about how much less.**

As a final example of tetrahedral electron geometry, consider water, H_2O, which has the Lewis structure:

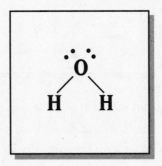

The oxygen atom is surrounded by two lone pairs and two pairs of bonding electrons in the O-H bonds. The four electron pairs form an approximately tetrahedral arrangement around the oxygen atom:

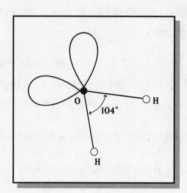

The arrangement of the atoms is described as **bent** or **V-shaped**. Since the molecule contains two lone pairs, we expect the H-O-H bond angle to be less than 109°. In fact, it has been found to be 104°.

FIVE ELECTRON PAIRS ARE BEST ARRANGED IN A TRIGONAL BIPYRAMID.

Five electron pairs are best arranged in a structure known as a **trigonal bipyramid**.

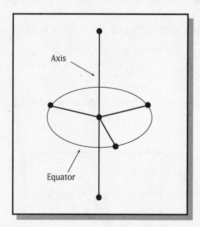

The trigonal bipyramid is unique in VSEPR in that the angles between the electron pairs are not identical. Three electron pairs lie in a plane with an angle of 120° between them. These electron pairs are described as **equatorial,** because they go around the middle of the trigonal bipyramid in much the same way that the equator goes around the middle of the earth. The other two electron pairs are at right angles to the equatorial pairs and are described as **axial**.

The simplest example of a molecule with five electron pairs is PF_5, which has the Lewis structure:

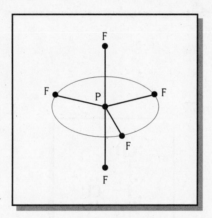

Each of the five electron pairs is accounted for by one P-F bond.

The structure of the PF_5 molecule is described as trigonal bipyramidal:

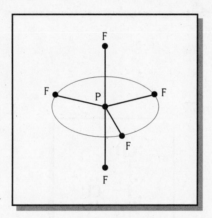

Here's another example. SF_4 has the Lewis structure:

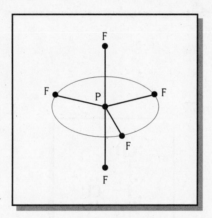

The molecule has five electron pairs that form a trigonal bipyramid. Four electron pairs are used in forming S-F bonds, and one is a lone pair. In theory we could put the lone pair in either an axial or equatorial position of the trigonal bipyramid. But as a general rule, **lone**

pairs occupy the equatorial positions in trigonal bipyramids. Putting atoms in the remaining positions gives the molecular geometry known as **see-saw**.

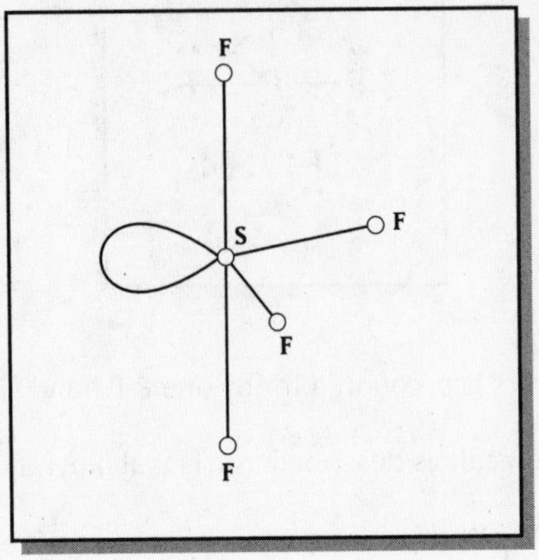

ICl_3 has the Lewis structure:

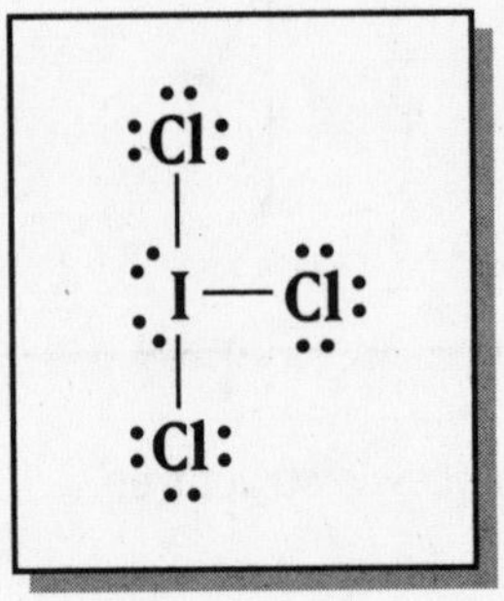

The molecule has five electron pairs, and this forms a trigonal bipyramid. Placing the two lone pairs equatorially leaves one equatorial position for the electron pair in an I-Cl bond . If we then fill the axial positions with the remaining I -Cl bond, we arrive at the structure:

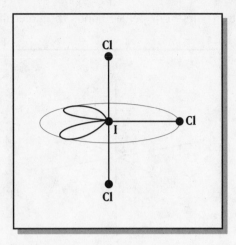

This molecular structure is known as **T-shaped.**

SIX ELECTRON PAIRS ARE ARRANGED IN AN OCTAHEDRON.

When a central atom is surrounded by six electron pairs, the maximum separation between electron pairs can be achieved through an **octahedral** arrangement.

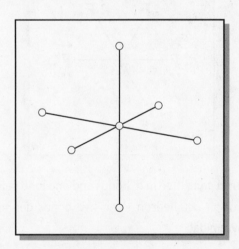

In an octahedron, the angle between electron pairs is 90°.

For example, the molecule SF_6 has the Lewis structure:

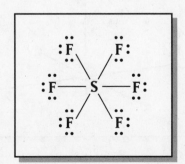

The molecule has six electron pairs – one per S-F bond. The molecular structure is octahedral:

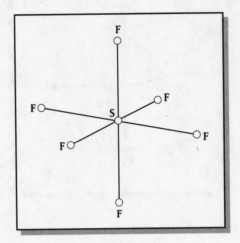

Consider another example. IF_5 has the Lewis structure:

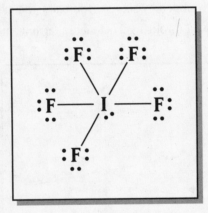

The molecule has six electron pairs: five in IF bonds and one lone pair. The six electron pairs point to the six corners of an octahedron. The five bonds define a molecular structure known as **square-based pyramidal**.

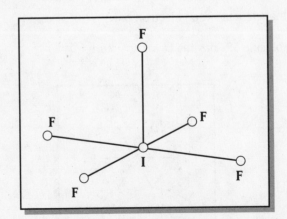

Here's a final example. XeF_4 has the Lewis structure:

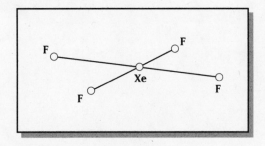

The central xenon atom of the molecule is surrounded by six valence electron pairs: four Xe-F bonds and two lone pairs. The six electron pairs point to the six corners of an octahedron; the two lone pairs maximize their separation by occupying opposite vertices of the octahedron. The four XeF bonds lie in a plane; the angle between them is 90°. This molecular structure is known as **square planar**.

In VSEPR, double bonds act as a single repulsive unit.

Consider the molecule CO_2. It has the Lewis structure:

$$\ddot{O}=C=\ddot{O}$$

CO_2 is a linear molecule, as we would expect if each of the C-O double bonds were a single bond. From this observation, we conclude that double bonds act as a single repulsive unit in VSEPR. Some people refer to a double bond as an **effective pair** in VSEPR, meaning that double bonds act effectively, as if they were a pair of electrons.

KEY TERMS

bond angle: The angle between any two bonds that includes a common atom.

bond length: The distance between two chemically-bonded atoms along a straight line between their nuclei.

molecular structure: A description of the three dimensional shape of a molecule in terms of its bond lengths and bond angles.

octahedral: The arrangement of six electron pairs predicted by VSEPR. Here, the angle between electron pairs is 90°.

tetrahedral: The arrangement of four electron pairs predicted by VSEPR. The angle between electron pairs in a tetrahedron is approximately 109°.

trigonal bipyramid: The arrangement of five elctron pairs predicted by VSEPR. The angles between electron pairs in this arrangement are either 90° or 120°.

trigonal planar: The arrangement of three electron pairs predicted by VSEPR. The angle between electron pairs in a trigonal plane is 120°.

trigonal pyramidal: The arrangement of three atoms and one lone pair predicted by VSEPR.

VSEPR: Valence Shell Electron Pair Repulsion Theory. A theory used to predict the bond angles in molecules based on the minimization of repulsion between electron pairs.

THRILLS, CHILLS AND DRILLS

True or False

1. Molecular shape can be determined solely from knowledge about atomic connectivity.

2. Valence Shell Electron Pair Repulsion (VSEPR) theory predicts that NH_3 will have a trigonal planar structure.

3. A lone pair of electrons repels other electron pairs more than a bonding pair.

4. One can predict the shape of a molecule using VSEPR.

5. In BF_3NH_3, the coordinate covalent bond between the nitrogen of NH_3 and the boron in BF_3 converts the Boron center from trigonal planar to tetrahedral.

6. Formaldehyde ($H_2C=O$) has 8 electrons surrounding the carbon atom. These 4 electron pairs suggest a tetrahedral arrangement of the molecule.

7. CO_2 has a linear arrangement of oxygen atoms about the carbon atom.

8. In formic acid, $H(OH)C=O$, the bond length of the $C=O$ bond is shorter than that of the $C-O$ bond.

9. The bond angle in water is greater than 109.5° because the two electron lone pairs attract each other — thereby making room for more repulsion among the bonding pairs.

10. PCl_5 is a trigonal bipyramidal molecule.

11. VSEPR theory is based on the idea that the structure of a molecule is determined by the interaction among pairs of electrons.

12. Potassium cyanide is an ionic molecule with K^+ and CN^- ions. The configuration at the carbon center is bent, because there are three bonds and one lone pair of electrons

13. Xenon is highly unreactive. One of the few compounds it forms is XeF_4. XeF_4 is square planar.

14. SF_4 is T-shaped.

15. ICl_3 has trigonal planar geometry.

16. SF_6 is octahedral, and all six flourine atoms are in identical arrangements.

17. A bond length is half the distance between two bonded nuclei.

18. A double bond acts as a single repulsive unit, according to VSEPR.

19. Water (H_2O) and $BeCl_2$ have similar geometries.

20. Ammonia (NH_3) and ICl_3 have similar geometries.

Multiple Choice

1. Picture the shape of PCl_3 as compared to the shape of PCl_5. Why is the Cl-P-Cl bond angle smaller in PCl_3 than in PCl_5?
   a) The lone pairs in PCl_3 provide more repulsion than the bond pairs in PCl_5.
   b) The bond pairs in PCl_5 align so as to decrease the dipole of the molecule.
   c) The statement is false; the bond angles are the same.
   d) The bonded pairs provide more electron density than the lone pairs.

2. The Cl_2 molecule is characterized by a single bond between the Cl centers. What is the organization of the electrons around the Cl center?
   a) Linear, because only two atoms are present.
   b) Tetrahedral, because there are three lone pairs.
   c) Trigonal planar, because there are three lone pairs.
   d) Square planar, because there are three lone pairs and one bonding pair.

3. Isomorphism is a term used to describe the species with the same approximate geometry about a given atom. Which of the following species is isomorphic with methane (CH_4)? (More than one of the following may be correct.)
   a) water, H_2O
   b) xenon tetrafluoride, XeF_4
   c) phosphorus pentachloride, PCl_5
   d) ethene, C_2H_6
   e) formaldehyde, $H_2C = O$
   f) sulfate, SO_4^{2-}

4. Formaldehyde, $H_2C = O$, is used as a preserving agent for biological specimens. In general, organic molecules with 2 bonds to a single oxygen and 2 other bonds to distinct atoms are known as carbonyl compounds. What is the organization of a carbonyl carbon?
   a) trigonal planar
   b) linear
   c) square planar
   d) tetrahedral

5. How many distinct fluorine positions appear in SF_6?

    a) One, because all fluorines are equal, and axial/equatorial arrangements are no different.

    b) Two, because of isotope effects.

    c) Two, because not all fluorines are equal, and axial/equatorial arrangements are different.

    d) Six, because there are six fluorine atoms.

6. In enyzme catalysis, for a compound to act as a competitive inhibitor of another it is necessary that both compounds have the same approximate geometry. Heme is a portion of a protein that binds to oxygen gas (O_2) in order to transport it to the body's cells. Which of the following substances could serve as a competitive inhibitor of this transport? (More than one of the following may be correct.)

    a) CO_2, carbon dioxide

    b) H_2O, water

    c) CN^-, cyanide

    d) HCl, hydrochloric acid

    e) NH_3, ammonia

    f) HCO_3^-, bicarbonate

7. Among the structure characterizaiton in his final thesis, Mr. Howit Looks has included the following geometries. Which of the following should be corrected before he prepares to defend his work and conclusions?

    a) square planar, KrF_4

    b) linear, H_2Se

    c) trigonal planar, $AlCl_3$

    d) T-Shaped, PF_2Cl

    e) tetrahedral, NH_3

8. ICL_4^- has which of the following molecular geometries?

    a) octahedral

    b) tetrahedral

    c) trigonal planar

    d) square planar

    e) linear

9. NH_3 is trigonal pyramidal. It follows that NH_4^+

    a) is square planar

    b) is tetrahedral

    c) is octahedral

    d) does not exist

    e) is trigonal bipyramidal

10. XeF_2 has which of the following geometries?

   a) trigonal bipyramidal

   b) trigonal planar

   c) T-shaped

   d) linear

   e) bent

11. CCl_4 was used in dry cleaning for years before it was discovered to cause cancer. The geometry of CCl_4 is

   a) tetrahedral

   b) square planar

   c) linear

   d) bent

   e) none of the above

12. Sulfur dioxide (SO_2) is one of the gases associated with the production of acid rain that corrodes buildings and poisons lakes. The geometry of SO_2 is

   a) linear

   b) bent

   c) trigonal Planar

   d) T-shaped

   e) trigonal pyramidal

13. O_3 (ozone) is responsible for the protective ozone layer that shields us from harmful ultraviolet rays. The geometry of ozone is

   a) linear

   b) bent

   c) T-shaped

   d) trigonal planar

   e) trigonal pyramidal

14. Ether, $(CH_3)_2O$, was one of the first known anesthetics. The C-O-C bond angle predicted by VSEPR is

   a) 90°

   b) 180°

   c) 120°

   d) 109°

   e) none of the above

15. Chloroform was used as an early anesthetic. Doctors even used to take it to parties to amuse their friends – before it started killing their patients. It was taken by parties by early doctors to amuse their friends, before it killed several patients. The structure of chloroform, $CHCl_3$, is

   a) bent
   b) square planar
   c) T-shaped
   d) trigonal planar
   e) trigonal bipyramidal

16. In ether, $(CH_3)2O$, the geometry surrounding the carbon atom is approximately

   a) tetrahedral
   b) trigonal planar
   c) square planar
   d) octahedral
   e) trigonal bipyramidal

17. Nitrates form the basis of many fertilizers. The nitrate ion, NO_3^-, is quite soluble in water. The structure of the nitrate ion is

   a) tirigonal planar
   b) tetrahedral
   c) trigonal pyramidal
   d) trigonal bipyramidal
   e) linear

18. What is the geometry of SO_3?

   a) trigonal planar
   b) linear
   c) tetrahedral
   d) T-shaped
   e) bent

Short Essays

1. Mr. Isthi Sreal is testing his ideas about halo-compounds. Explain to him which of the following exist, and describe the geometries of those that do.

   a. SF_6 with an octahedral geometry

   b. XeF_4 with a tetrahedral geometry

   c. XeF_8 with an octahedral geometry

   d. PCl_3 with a trigonal planar geometry

   e. PCl_5 with a pentagonal geometry

   f. H_2O with a linear geometry

2. Given the series trigonal bipyrimidal for 5 ligands and octahedral for 6 ligands, what is the expected geometry of a 7 ligand compound with no other lone pairs? Use your knowledge of how to minimize repulsion of electron pairs to answer this question.

3. Dr. Sul Fate is inspecting the organization of the sulfate ion (SO_4^{2-}). By drawing the Lewis structure of the sulfate ion, determine the geometry at the sulfur atom.

4. SO_3 has a trigonal planar structure. Formally, SO_3^{2-} is SO_3 that has gained two electrons.

   a. Draw the Lewis structure for SO_3.

   b. Draw the electron dot structure for SO_3^{2-}.

   c. Predict the geometry of SO_3^{2-}.

Answers

True or False Answers

1. **False.** Knowledge of bond angles and bond lengths as well as atomic connectivity is needed to determine molecular shape.

2. **False.** VSEPR theory predicts that NH_3 will have a trigonal pyramidal geometry. There are three bonding pairs and one lone pair of electrons around the nitrogen atom in NH_3. The lone pair repels the bonding pairs more strongly than the bonding pairs repel each other, which pushes the bonding pairs closer together.

3. **True.** A lone pair repels another lone pair more than it repels a bonding pair. Two bonding pairs have the least repulsion between them.

4. **True.**

5. **True.** In BF_3, boron is surrounded by three bonding pairs of electrons and so its geometry is trigonal planar. In BF_3NH_3, boron is surrounded by four bonding pairs of electrons and its geometry is tetrahedral.

6. **False.** Four of the electrons around carbon are involved in single bonds, while the other four are involved in a double bond. Double bonds are treated as a single repulsive unit in VSEPR theory. The arrangement around the carbon in formaldehyde will be trigonal pyramidal.

7. **True.** The carbon in CO_2 forms a double bond with each oxygen atom. Each double bond can be treated as an effective electron pair. Two electron pairs surrounding a central atom always form a linear structure.

8. **True.** A double bond is shorter than a single bond.

9. **False.** The bond angle in water is less than 109.5 degrees (104.5 degrees, to be exact) because the two lone pairs of electrons on the oxygen atom repulse each other more strongly than they repulse the two bonding pairs and more strongly than the bonding pairs repulse each other. This pushes the bonding pairs together.

10. **True.** Each of the 5 valence electrons of P forms a covalent bond with a F atom. Five electron pairs are best arranged in a trigonal bipyramid.

11. **True.**

12. **False.** A triple bond forms between carbon and nitrogen in a cyanide ion. Like a double bond, a triple bond can be treated as an effective electron pair. Thus, in KCN, carbon is surrounded by two electron pairs, which leads to a linear arrangement around the carbon.

13. **True.** In XeF_4, four of xenon's valence electrons are involved in covalent bonds with fluorine and the other four valence electrons are arranged in two lone pairs. Six electron pairs are best arranged in an octahedron. The two lone pairs maximize their separation by occupying opposite vertices of the octahedron, and the molecular structure can therefore be described as square planar.

14. **False.** Four of sulfur's 6 valence electrons are used in forming S-F bonds, nd two are in a lone pair. The five electron pairs are best arranged in a trigonal bipyramid. The lone pair will preferentially occupy an equatorialJpositions. The resulting molecular structure is described as see-saw.

15. **False.** Iodine has 7 valence electrons. In ICl_3, three of these form covalent bonds with Cl atoms and the other four are arranged in two lone pairs, for a total of 5 electron pairs. The two lone pairs will occupy equatorial positions in a trigonal bipyramid, resulting in a T shaped molecular structure around I.

16. **True.** Each of the six valence electrons of sulfur form a covalent bond with an F atom. Six electron pairs are best arranged in an octahedron. All bond angles in an octahedron are 90 degrees.

17. **False.** A bond length is the distance between two chemically bonded atoms along a straight line between their nuclei.

18. **True.**

19. **False.** Water has a bent geometry. Two bonding pairs of electrons and two lone pairs surround the central oxygen atom. The two lone pairs repulse each other, and the resulting molecular structure is bent. $BeCl_2$, however, is linear. Each of Be's two valence electrons form a covalent bond with Cl. The two electron pairs surrounding the central Be atom form a linear structure.

20. **False.** Ammonia has a trigonal pyramidal geometry, while ICl_3 has a T shaped geometry. See answers to questions 2 and 15 in this section.

Multiple Choice Answers

1. (a) The central P in PCl_5 is surrounded by five bonding pairs of electrons and adopts a trigonal bipyramidal molecular structure. The central P in PCl_3 is surrounded by three bonding pairs of electrons and one lone pair and adopts a trigonal pyramidal molecular stucture. The lone pair of electrons in PCl_3 repels the bonding pairs more than the bonding pairs in PCl_5 repel each other.

2. (b) Each Cl atom has 7 valence electrons. One of these forms a covalent bond with the other Cl atom, and the remaining 6 valence electrons are arranged in three lone pairs. Four electron pairs are best arranged in a tetrahedron.

3. (f) Methane has tetrahedral geometry about the central carbon atom. Water has bent geometry. XeF_4 has square planar geometry. PCl_5 has trigonal bipyramidal geometry. The carbons in ethene and formaldehyde have trigonal planar geometry. Sulfate has tetrahedral geometry about the central sulfur atom.

4. (a) A double bond can be treated as an effective electron pair. Three electron pairs are best arranged in a trigonal plane.

5. (a) SF_6 has octahedral geometry about the central sulfur atom. All bond angles are 90 degrees.

6. (c) Of the compounds listed, only carbon dioxide and cyanide have linear structures. Cyanide, like O_2, contains two atoms.

7. (b) In H_2Se, the Se has two bonding pairs of electrons and two lone pairs. H_2Se has bent geometry.

8. (d) Four of iodine's valence electrons can form covalent bonds with Cl atoms. The remaining three valence electrons, along with the extra electron can form two lone pairs. This results in a square planar geometry.

9. (b) NH_3 has three bonding pairs of electrons and one lone pair arranged around the central N. NH_4^+, therefore, has four bonding pairs of electrons (and no lone pairs) around the nitrogen. NH_4^+ has tetrahedral geometry.

10. (c) The central Xe atom is surrounded by two bonding pairs of electrons and three lone pairs of electrons.

11. (a) Each of the four valence electrons of carbon forms a covalent bond with a chlorine atom. The four bonding pairs of electrons are arranged in a tetrahedral geometry.

12. (b) Sulfur forms a double bond with each oxygen atom; four of sulfur's valence electrons are in bonding pairs. The other two valance electrons are in a lone pair. The double bonds can be treated as effective electron pairs. SO_2 has bent geometry.

13. (b) The central oxygen atom forms a double bond with each of the other two oxygen atoms. The central oxygen also has a lone pair. Ozone has bent geometry.

14. (d) Two of oxygen's 6 valence electrons form covalent bonds with the carbons in ether. The other four valence electrons are arranged in two lone pairs. Hence, ether has bent geometry, and the C-O-C bond angle is slightly less than 109 degrees.

15. (e) Three of carbon's 4 valence electrons form covalent bonds with Cl atoms. The other valence electron forms a covalent bond with a H atom. The central carbon in chloroform is surrounded by four bonding pairs of electrons; the geometry is tetrahedral.

16. (a) Carbon has 4 valence electrons. Three of these are involved inbonding pairs in covalent bonds to H. The other valence electron forms a covalent bond with O. Thus, the geometry about C is tetrahedral.

17. (a) Each resonance structure of NO_3^- has nitrogen double bonded to one oxygen atom and single bonded to the other two oxygen atoms. The double bond can be treated as an effective electron pair. The three bonding electron pairs are arranged in a trigonal plane about the nitrogen atom.

18. (a) In SO_3, four of sulfur's 6 valence electrons are involved in double bonds with two of the oxygen atoms; these double bonds can be treated as effective electron pairs. The two electrons in the covalent bond between sulfur and the other oxygen atom are both donated from sulfur. Three bonding pairs of electrons are best arranged in a trigonal plane.

Multiple Choice Answers

1. **a.** Octahedral Sulfur is surrounded by 6 bonding pairs of electrons in SF_6. These are best arranged in an octahedron.

   b. Square planar Xe is surrounded by four bonding pairs of electrons and two lone pairs in XeF_4.

   c. Does not exist

   d. Trigonal pyramidal. The central P atom is surrounded by three bonding pairs of electrons and one lone pair. The electron pairs arrange in a tetrahedron, and the molecular structure is trigonal pyramidal.

   e. Trigonal bipyramidal. The central P atom is surrounded by five bonding pairs of electrons. These are best arranged in a trigonal bipyramid.

2. Pentagonal bipyramidal

3. Tetrahedral. The central S atom is surrounded by four bonding pairs, which are best arranged in a tetrahedron.

4. **c.** Trigonal pyramidal. The sulfur atom is double bonded to each oxygen atom, and hence has three effective bonding electron pairs. It also has a lone pair of electrons. This combination of electrons produces a trigonal pyramidal geometry.

CHAPTER

REACTION ACTION: WHY SOME THINGS GO "BOOM"

OVERVIEW

Why do some chemical reactions happen while others do not? In order for a chemical reaction to happen, driving force is required. The driving forces that make reactants 'want' to form products can be classed as in the table below.

DRIVING FORCES	TYPE OF REACTION
formation of a solid	precipitation reactions
formation of water	acid base reactions
transfer of electrons	redox reactions

In this chapter we will consider each type of reaction in turn. We will show that the identity of a solid in a precipitation reaction can be predicted on the basis of a simple set of rules known as "solubility" rules. In fact, we can even predict whether or not a solid is likey to form using these rules. We will also show that acids and bases undergo neutralization reactions, and that an acid always requires a base to function as an acid.

In a section devoted to reactions involving electron transfer (called redox reactions), we will show that the reduction of one species is accompanied by the oxidation of another. We will show that we can assign oxidation numbers to compounds on the basis of a simple set of rules, and that these rules allow us to identify and balance redox reactions effectively. Finally we will see that we can predict the direction of change in redox reactions using the electrochemical series.

CONCEPTS

Precipitation Reactions

Some solids dissolve in water and are known as **soluble**; others do not dissolve and are **insoluble.** A solid dissolved in a liquid is said to be in **solution.**

Solid sodium chloride (table salt) is soluble in water. A solution of NaCl dissolved in water conducts electricity, yet pure water does not. Why? Recall that sodium chloride is made up of Na^+ ions and Cl^- ions, and that the electrostatic attraction between these ions accounts for the ionic bonds that hold sodium chloride together. Upon dissolving in water, the Na^+ and Cl^- ions separate and move around independently. A solution in which positive and negative ions circulate independently is described as a strong electrolyte. The ions in a strong electrolyte are responsible for its ability to conduct electricity.

A SOLID THAT FORMS UPON MIXING TWO SOLUTIONS IS KNOWN AS A PRECIPITATE.

Silver nitrate ($AgNO_3$) is also a strong electrolyte that forms Ag^+ ions and NO_3^- ions in solution. However, if we mix a silver nitrate solution and a sodium chloride solution, a white solid forms. A solid that forms from a solution is called a **precipitate.**

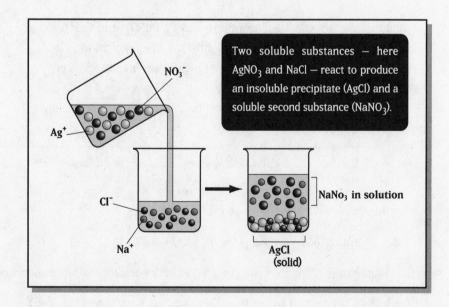

Two soluble substances — here $AgNO_3$ and NaCl — react to produce an insoluble precipitate (AgCl) and a soluble second substance ($NaNO_3$).

WE DISCOVER THE CHEMICAL IDENTITY OF ANY PRECIPITATE THAT IS FORMED THROUGH THE MIXTURE OF TWO ELECTROLYTIC SOLUTIONS.

What is the precipitate? To find its chemical identity, we must use a combination of deductive reasoning and knowledge of chemical concepts.

If we dissolve silver nitrate and sodium chloride together, we know that there are potentially four ions in the mixture: Na^+, Cl^-, Ag^+, and NO_3^-. The precipitate is a combination of these ions. The ions can be combined in four different cation-anion pairs: NaCl, $AgNO_3$, $NaNO_3$, and AgCl. We can rule out NaCl and $AgNO_3$; they are **totally** soluble and are the strong electrolytes with which we began. The precipitate is therefore either $NaNO_3$ or AgCl. To decide between these two, we need to know how soluble these ionic compounds are. It turns out that there is a set of rules — summarized in the table below — for assessing the solubility of ionic compounds. We see that **all** nitrates are soluble, whereas silver chloride is insoluble. We can therefore say with certainty that the precipitate is the insoluble compound silver chloride (AgCl). When an ion or compound is dissolved we say it is aqueous. These dissolved substances are denoted with (aq). For example, dissolved Na^+ is represented as $Na^+(aq)$. When a precipitate is formed, it is denoted with an (s) for solid.

GENERAL RULES FOR SOLUBILITY OF IONIC COMPOUNDS (SALTS) IN WATER AT 25 C

1. Nitrate (NO_3^-) salts are usually soluble.
2. Salts of Na^+, K^+, and NH_4^+ are usually soluble.
3. Chloride salts are usually soluble. Notable exceptions are AgCl, $PbCl_2$, and Hg_2Cl_2.
4. Most sulfate salts are soluble. Exceptions: $BaSO_4$, $PbSO_4$, and $CaSO_4$.
5. Hydroxide (OH^-) compounds are only slightly soluble.* Exceptions: NaOH and KOH are highly soluble. $Ba(OH)_2$ and $Ca(OH)_2$ are only moderately soluble.
6. Sulfide (S^{2-}), carbonate (CO_3^{2-}), and phosphate (PO_4^{3-}) salts are usually only slightly soluble.*

---

* Such a tiny amount of substance dissolves for a slighlty soluble compound that it is not possible to detect it with the naked eye.

The equation for the process we have described is:

$$AgNO_3(aq) + NaCl(aq) \rightarrow AgCl(s) + NaNO_3(aq)$$

Since the ions are separated in solution, we can also write a complete (ionic) equation:

$$Ag^+(aq) + NO_3^-(aq) + Na^+(aq) + Cl^-(aq) \rightarrow AgCl(s) + Na^+(aq) + NO_3^-(aq)$$

Na^+ and NO_3^- are on both sides of the equation; they do not take part in chemical change and are known as **spectator ions**. We can rewrite this equation to describe only the elements involved in the change occurring. This is known as a **net ionic equation**:

$$Ag^+(aq) + Cl^-(aq) \rightarrow AgCl(s)$$

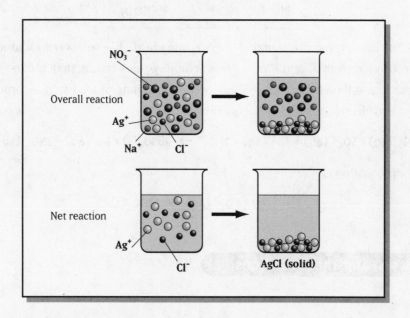

YOU CAN USE THE SAME DEDUCTIVE REASONING AND KNOWLEDGE OF SOLUBILITY TO PREDICT WHETHER A PRECIPITATE WILL FORM, AS WELL AS THE IDENTITY OF THE PRECIPITATE.

Consider this question: If we mix $KNO_3(aq)$ and $BaCl_2(aq)$, will a precipitate form?

The potential products are:

	NO_3^-	Cl^-
K^+	KNO_3	KCl
Ba^{2+}	$Ba(NO_3)_2$	$BaCl_2$

Since KNO_3 and $BaCl_2$ are initially in solution, they cannot form a precipitate. From the solubility rules, we see that Group I chlorides are soluble (so we expect KCl to stay in solution) and that all nitrates are soluble (so we expect $BaCl_2$ to stay in solution). There is, therefore, no precipitation, and no chemical change occurs. For such a process we cannot write a net ionic equation.

As another example, consider mixing $Na_2SO_4(aq)$ and $Pb(NO_3)_2(aq)$.

The potential products are:

	SO_4^{2-}	NO_3^-
Na^+	Na_2SO_4	$NaNO_3$
Pb^{2+}	$PbSO_4$	$Pb(NO_3)_2$

We know that our original compounds — Na_2SO_4 and $Pb(NO_3)_2$ — will stay in solution, so we are left to consider $NaNO_3$ and $PbSO_4$. Our solubility rules tell us that sodium nitrate is soluble, but lead sulfate is insoluble. Therefore, a precipitate of lead sulfate forms. When we mix the two electrolytes, the ionic equation is:

$$Na^+(aq) + SO_4^{2-}(aq) + Pb^{2+}(aq) + 2NO_3^- \rightarrow PbSO_4(s) + Na^+(aq) + 2NO_3^-(aq)$$

The net ionic equation is:

$$Pb^{2+}(aq) + SO_4^{2-}(aq) \rightarrow PbSO_4(s)$$

Acids, Bases, and Their Reactions

Acids figure in everyday conversation. "Acid indigestion," for example, is a common complaint. It can happen when someone eats too much and their stomach overproduces the **acid** HCl (hydrochloric acid), which normally aids digestion. Heartburn results from the excess acid backing up our esophagus — the tube the food passes through to get to our stomachs. The concentration of HCl in our stomachs can reach a level that might dissolve the stomach lining, were it not for the effect of the **base** H_2CO_3, which is found in the mucus layer in our stomach. Hydrogen carbonate ions react with and neutralize the effect of any acid that gets through the protective coating of the stomach.

Definitions of Acids and Bases

AN ACID WAS INITIALLY DEFINED BY ARRHENIUS AS A SUBSTANCE THAT PRODUCES H^+ IONS, SOMETIMES CALLED PROTONS, WHEN DISSOLVED IN WATER.

Svante August Arrhenius, who won a Nobel Prize in chemistry in 1903 for his work, gave us our initial definitions of acids and bases. An example of an acid is hydrochloric acid, which dissolves in water to produce one H^+ ion and one Cl^- ion per HCl molecule.

$$HCl(aq) \xrightarrow{H_2O} 2H^+(aq) + Cl^-(aq)$$

BASES WERE DEFINED, ALSO BY ARRHENIUS, AS SUBSTANCES THAT DISSOLVE IN WATER TO PRODUCE OH^- IONS.

An example of a base is sodium hydroxide, NaOH, which dissolves in water to produce Na^+ ions and OH^- ions.

$$NaOH(s) \xrightarrow{H_2O} Na^+(aq) + OH^-(aq)$$

Arrhenius's definitions of acids and bases, while important first steps to understanding acids and bases, are somewhat limited. A base might be more accurately defined as a substance capable of accepting protons. Since ions other than the OH^- ion can accept protons, this general definition of bases is useful.

BRØNSTED AND LOWRY DEVELOPED MODERN DEFINITIONS OF ACIDS AND BASES.

Wider definitions of acids and bases were provided by Johannes Brønsted, a Danish chemist, and Thomas Lowry, an English chemist. Brønsted and Lowry, whos lives spanned the latter half of the 19th century and the first half of the 20th century, defined acids and bases as follows:

- A Brønsted-Lowry acid is a proton donor
- A Brønsted-Lowry base is a proton acceptor

These definitions focus attention squarely on the proton as the key player in acid-base chemistry, rectifying the shortcoming of Arrhenius's conception of OH^- as the only ion characteristic of a base. The Brønsted-Lowry definition of acids and bases includes and augments Arrhenius's definitions.

You can think of the relationship between an acid and a base as similar to that between a quarterback (acid) and a receiver (base) in a game of football. The proton is the ball. A quarterback with the ball wants to throw it to a receiver. A quarterback requires a receiver to catch the ball, and the receiver requires the quarterback to throw it. In exactly the same way, Brønsted-Lowry acids require Brønsted-Lowry bases, since a proton donor must have something to accept its proton. For example, when HNO_3 dissolves in water we can write:

$$HNO_3(l) + H_2O(l) \rightarrow H_3O^+(aq) + NO_3^-(aq)$$

In this equation, HNO_3 is an acid that donates a proton to water. Water is the base that accepts a proton from nitric acid to form the **hydronium ion H_3O^+**.

Nitric acid is an example of a **strong acid**. Strong acids are completely ionized in solution; in other words, they are strong electrolytes. There are only a handful of **strong acids** – they are **HCl** (hydrochloric acid), **HBr** (hydrobromic acid), **H_2SO_4** (sulfuric acid), **HNO_3** (nitric acid), and **HI** (hydrogen iodic acid) – and they are worth memorizing.

Brønsted-Lowry bases require Brønsted-Lowry acids, since proton acceptors must have something from which to receive protons. For example, when ammonia dissolves in water, we can write:

$$NH_3(l) + H_2O(l) \rightarrow NH_4^+(aq) + OH^-(aq)$$

In this equation, ammonia is a base and water is an acid.

THE REACTION BETWEEN AN ACID AND BASE IS KNOWN AS A NEUTRALIZATION REACTION.

When an acid and a base react, they form a neutral salt and water

$$\textbf{acid + base} \rightarrow \textbf{salt + water}$$

The best known example of this reaction is the reaction of sodium hydroxide and hydrochloric acid.

$$HCl(aq) + NaOH(aq) \rightarrow NaCl(aq) + H_2O(l)$$

Since HCl is a strong acid and NaOH a strong base, we can also write an ionic equation

$$H_3O^+(aq) + Cl^-(aq) + Na^+(aq) + OH^-(aq) \rightarrow Na^+(aq) + Cl^-(aq) + 2H_2O(l)$$

The net ionic equation is:

$$H_3O^+(aq) + OH^-(aq) \rightarrow 2H_2O(aq)$$

Neutralization reactions of this sort are driven by the formation of water. The salt derives its cation from the base, and its anion is derived from the acid.

A disguised type of acid-base reaction is represented by the general equation:

$$\textbf{acid + carbonate} \rightarrow \textbf{salt + water + carbon dioxide}$$

An example of this disguised type occurs when sodium carbonate reacts with hydrochloric acid to produce sodium chloride, water, and carbon dioxide.

$$Na_2CO_3(aq) + 2HCl(aq) \rightarrow 2NaCl(aq) + H_2O(l) + CO_2(g)$$

By considering this reaction in two steps, we can reveal the acid-base reaction. First, as we would expect, there is a simple acid-base reaction, represented by the equation:

$$Na_2CO_3(aq) + 2HCl(aq) \rightarrow H_2CO_3(aq) + 2NaCl(aq)$$

The second step is to recognize that H_2CO_3 is unstable and changes into $H_2O(l)$ and $CO_2(g)$. (The driving force for this second step is the evolution of a gas CO_2.)

Anions other than carbonates display analogous behavior. Some of these are shown in the table below.

IONIC COMPOUND	GAS	EXAMPLE
Carbonate (CO_3^{2-})	CO_2	$Na_2CO_3 + 2HCl \rightarrow 2NaCl + H_2O + CO_2$
Sulfite (SO_3^{2-})	SO_2	$Na_2SO_3 + 2HCl \rightarrow 2NaCl + H_2O + SO_2$
Sulfide (S^{2-})	H_2S	$Na_2S + 2HCl \rightarrow 2NaCl + H_2S$

Redox Reactions

Consider this reaction between sodium and chlorine, which forms sodium chloride:

$$2Na(s) + Cl_2(g) \rightarrow 2NaCl(s)$$

Because Na atoms and Cl_2 molecules are electrically neutral, and because NaCl consists of Na^+ and Cl^- ions, this reaction involves the transfer of electrons from sodium atoms to chlorine atoms.

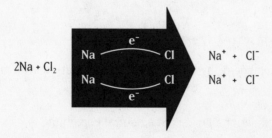

REACTIONS, LIKE THIS ONE, IN WHICH ELECTRONS ARE TRANSFERRED FROM ONE SPECIES TO ANOTHER ARE CALLED OXIDATION REDUCTION, OR REDOX, REACTIONS.

- Oxidation is the loss of electrons.

- Reduction is the gain of electrons.

In chemical reactions, oxidation of one species cannot occur without reduction of another, since in order for one species to lose electrons another species must gain them. In the example above, chlorine gained electrons and was reduced; sodium lost electrons and was oxidized.

THE OXIDATION NUMBER OF AN ELEMENT IN A COMPOUND IS THE CHARGE IT WOULD HAVE IN AN IONIC COMPOUND.

We keep track of which elements are oxidized and which are reduced in chemical processes by applying a simple set of rules, outlined below. These rules determine the **oxidation number** for each element in a compound. The oxidation number of an ion is the charge of the ion, and, in general, the oxidation number of an element in a compound represents the charge it would have if it were in an ionic compound. The same element can have a range of oxidation numbers in different compounds. The maximum oxidation number is the same as the group number of the element in the periodic table – consistent with our view of the ions an element is capable of forming.

Oxidation numbers are assigned using a set of rules.

A logical set of rules for assigning oxidation numbers is:

1) The oxidation number of an atom in a sample of an element is zero.

2) The oxidation number of an atomic ion equals the charge on the ion.

3) The oxidation number of Group I or II metals is the group number.

4) The oxidation number of fluorine is always -1.

5) The oxidation number of a group VII element in a binary compound is -1 unless it is combined with a group VII element above it in the periodic table – or unless the other element is oxygen.

6) The oxidation number of oxygen is usually -2.

7) The oxidation number of hydrogen is +1 in combination with non-metals and -1 in combination with metals.

8) The sum of the oxidation numbers in a neutral compound is 0.

9) The sum of the oxidation numbers in a polyatomic ion equals the charge on the ion.

As examples of how to use these rules, consider assigning oxidation numbers to all the atoms in the following compounds:

a) H_2O **b)** SO_2 **c)** HCl **d)** H_2SO_4 **e)** HNO_3.

a) The oxidation number of H is +1, according to rule 7. Since there are two hydrogens, they contribute +2. This means that the oxygen atom contributes -2, in accordance with rule 8 and in agreement with rule 6.

b) The oxidation number of oxygen is -2 (rule 6). There are two oxygen atoms, so they contribute 2(-2) = -4. The single sulfur atom must have an oxidation state of +4, in accordance with rule 8.

c) The oxidation state of hydrogen is +1, since chlorine is a non metal (rule 7). The oxidation state of chlorine is -1, in accordance with rule 8.

d) The oxidation state of hydrogen is +1 (rule 7). The oxidation state of oxygen is -2 (rule 6). Using rule 8, we know that the oxidation number of sulfur is x, where $x + (2(+1)) + (4(-2)) = 0$. Solving for x, we find that $x = +6$.

e) The oxidation state of hydrogen is +1 (rule 7). The oxidation state of oxygen is -2 (rule 6). The oxidation state of nitrogen (invoking rule 8) is therefore x, where $x + ((+1)) + 3((-2)) = 0$. Solving for x, we find that $x = +5$.

Now, try using these same rules to find the oxidation numbers for the atoms in these polyatomic ions.

a) BrO_3^- **b)** O_2^{2-} **c)** O_2^- **d)** O_3^- **e)** ClO_2^-

a) Oxygen usually has an oxidation number of -2 (rule 6). The three oxygen atoms contribute 3(-2) = -6 to the ion. Because of rule 9, we know that the oxidation number of bromine is x, where $x + (-6) = -1$. Solving for x, we find that $x = +5$.

b) The overall charge of the ion is -2. There are two oxygen atoms, so each must contribute an oxidation number of -1. (Reexamine rule 6. Note that it says the oxidation number of oxygen is **usually** -2.)

c) The overall charge of the ion is -1. There are two oxygen atoms, so each must contribute an oxidation number of $-1/2$.

d) The overall charge of the ion is -1. There are three oxygen atoms so each must contribute a charge of $-1/3$.

e) Oxygen atoms contribute 2(-2)= -4 (rule 6). The oxidation number of chlorine is x, where $x + (-4) = -1$. Solving for x, we find that $x = +3$.

The real utility of oxidation numbers is that we can use them to easily identify an oxidation reduction (or redox) reaction, to identify the oxidized and reduced species, and to balance redox reactions.

A CHANGE IN THE OXIDATION NUMBER OF AN ELEMENT IN THE COURSE OF A CHEMICAL REACTION IMPLIES A REDOX REACTION.

Consider the balanced equation for the process responsible for the mini-explosion that occurs when you strike a safety match:

$$2KClO_3(s) + 3S_2(s) \rightarrow 2KCl(s) + 3SO_2(g)$$

First, we assign the oxidation states to each atom in each compound. On the left-hand side, we arrive at the following oxidation numbers: $K = +1$; $Cl = +5$; $O = -2$; $S = 0$. On the right-hand side, we get: $K = +1$; $Cl = -1$; $S = +4$; $O = -2$.

We can now see that Cl is reduced from +5 to -1. Sulfur, meanwhile, is oxidized from 0 to +4.

$KClO_3$ is an oxidizing agent that oxidizes elemental sulfur to $SO_2(g)$. Elemental sulfur is a reducing agent that reduces Cl_5^+ to Cl^-.

The reaction is identified as a redox reaction.

THE GENERAL METHOD FOR BALANCING REDOX REACTIONS TAKES AS ITS PREMISE THAT THE NUMBER OF ELECTRONS LOST BY THE OXIDIZED SPECIES MUST BE EQUAL TO THE NUMBER GAINED BY THE REDUCED SPECIES.

Consider balancing the equation for the reaction between cerium +4 ions and tin +2 ions:

$$Ce^{4+}(aq) + Sn^{2+}(aq) \rightarrow Ce^{3+}(aq) + Sn^{4+}(aq)$$

Cerium +4 is reduced to cerium +3; and tin +2 is oxidized to tin +4.

We can write half-reactions which reflect these processes (e^- = electron):

$$Ce^{4+}(aq) + e^- \rightarrow Ce^{3+}(aq)$$

$$Sn^{2+}(aq) \rightarrow Sn_4(aq) + 2e^-$$

Since the number of electrons gained by Ce must be equal to the number lost by Sn, we multiply the first equation by 2:

$$2Ce^{4+}(aq) + 2e \rightarrow 2Ce^{3+}(aq)$$

$$Sn^{2+}(aq) \rightarrow Sn_4^+(aq) + 2e^-$$

Recombining the half-equations we arrive at:

$$2Ce^{4+}(aq) + 2e + Sn^{2+}(aq) \rightarrow 2Ce^{3+}(aq) + Sn^{4+}(aq) + 2e^-$$

Since the electrons appear on both sides of the equation, we can cancel them out. The final result is:

$$2Ce^{4+}(aq) + Sn^{2+}(aq) \rightarrow 2Ce^{3+}(aq) + Sn^{4+}(aq)$$

Equations in acidic or basic solution can be balanced by an extension of the method above.

Below are guidelines to balance redox reactions in acidic or basic solutions.

1. Identify the oxidizing and reducing agents

2. Write unbalanced half equations. In the case of an acidic solution, balance O and H atoms in each half-reaction using H_2O and H^+.

3. Balance the electrical charges so that they are equal on both sides of a given half-reaction.

4. Match the number of electrons in each half-reaction.

5. Recombine the half-reactions

6. If the reaction is in basic solution, add as many OH^- ions as there are H^+ ions. Combine H^+ and OH^- ions to produce H_2O molecules.

Let's look at a redox reaction in acidic solution first:

$$Cl_2(g) \rightarrow HOCl(aq) + Cl^-(aq)$$

The half-reactions are:

$$Cl_2(g) + 2e^- \rightarrow 2Cl^-(aq)$$
$$Cl_2(g) \rightarrow 2e^- + 2HOCl(aq)$$

Balance the elements involved in the half-reactions using H_2O and H^+

$$Cl_2(g) + 2H_2O(aq) \rightarrow 2e^- + 2HOCl(aq) + 2H^+(aq)$$
$$Cl_2(g) + 2e^- \rightarrow 2Cl^-(aq)$$

The electrical charges are already balanced, and the number of electrons is the same in each half-reaction. Combining the half-reactions we arrive at:

$$2Cl_2(g) + 2H_2O(aq) \rightarrow 2HOCl(aq) + 2H^+(aq) + 2Cl^-(aq)$$

Dividing by 2 on each side we come up with:

$$Cl_2(g) + H_2O(aq) \rightarrow HOCl(aq) + H^+(aq) + Cl^-(aq)$$

Notice that in this reaction, the element chlorine forms products in which the oxidation number of chlorine is above and below the oxidation number of the reactant (elemental chlorine). Such a reaction is known as a **disproportionation reaction.**

As an example of a reaction in basic solution, consider:

$$MnO_4^-(aq) + SO_3^{2-}(aq) \rightarrow MnO_2(aq) + SO_4^{2-}(aq)$$

Write two half-reactions:

$$MnO_4^-(aq) + 3e^- \rightarrow MnO_2(aq)$$

$$SO_3^{2-}(aq) \rightarrow 2e^- + SO_4^{2-}(aq)$$

Next, balance the oxygen atoms in the half-equations using H_2O:

$$MnO_4^-(aq) + 3e^- \rightarrow MnO_2(aq) + 2H_2O(l)$$

$$SO_3^{2-}(aq) + H_2O(l) \rightarrow 2e^- + SO_4^{2-}(aq)$$

Then balance the hydrogen atoms using H^+:

$$MnO_4^-(aq) + 4H^+(aq) + 3e^- \rightarrow MnO_2(aq) + 2H_2O(l)$$

$$SO_3^{2-}(aq) + H_2O(l) \rightarrow 2e^- + SO_4^{2-}(aq) + 2H^+(aq)$$

Equalize the electrons on each side of the half-equations:

$$2MnO_4^-(aq) + 8H^+(aq) + 6e^- \rightarrow 2MnO_2(aq) + 4H_2O(l)$$

$$3SO_3^{2-} + 3H_2O \rightarrow 6e^- + 3SO_4^{2-} + 6H+$$

Combine the half-equations:

$$2MnO_4^-(aq) + 3SO_3^-(aq) + 2H^+(aq) \rightarrow 2MnO_2(aq) + 3SO_4^{2-}(aq) + H_2O(l)$$

Add OH- equal in number to H+:

$$2MnO_4^-(aq) + 3SO_3^{2-}(aq) + 2H_2O(l) \rightarrow 2MnO_2(aq) + 3SO_4^{2-}(aq) + H_2O(l) + 2OH^-(aq)$$

Finally, cancel the redundant H_2O molecules.

$$2MnO_4^-(aq) + 3SO_3^-(aq) + H_2O(l) \rightarrow 2MnO_2(aq) + 3SO_4^{2-}(aq) + 2OH^-(aq)$$

REDUCTION HALF-REACTIONS

OXIDIZING AGENT			REDUCING AGENT
Strongly oxidizing agent			*Weakly reducing agent*
F_2	+ $2e^-$	$\rightarrow$	$2F^-$
$S_2O_8^{2-}$	+ $2e^-$	$\rightarrow$	$2SO_4^{2-}$
Au^+	+ e^-	$\rightarrow$	Au
Pb^{4+}	+ $2e^-$	$\rightarrow$	Pb^{2+}
Ce^{4+}	+ e^-	$\rightarrow$	Ce^{3+}
$MnO_4^- + 8H^+$	+ $5e^-$	$\rightarrow$	$Mn^{2+} + 4H_2O$
Cl_2	+ $2e^-$	$\rightarrow$	$2Cl^-$
$Cr_2O_7^{2-} + 14H^+$	+ $6e^-$	$\rightarrow$	$2Cr^{3+} + 7H_2O$
$O_2 + 4H^+$	+ $4e^-$	$\rightarrow$	$2H_2O$
Br_2	+ $2e^-$	$\rightarrow$	$2Br^-$
Ag^+	+ e^-	$\rightarrow$	Ag
Hg_2^{2+}	+ $2e^-$	$\rightarrow$	$2Hg$
Fe^{3+}	+ e^-	$\rightarrow$	Fe^{2+}
I_2	+ $2e^-$	$\rightarrow$	$2I^-$
$O_2 + 2H_2O$	+ $4e^-$	$\rightarrow$	$4OH^-$
Cu^{2+}	+ $2e^-$	$\rightarrow$	Cu
$AgCl$	+ e^-	$\rightarrow$	$Ag + Cl^-$
$2H^+$	+ $2e^-$	$\rightarrow$	H_2
Fe^{3+}	+ $3e^-$	$\rightarrow$	Fe
$O_2 + H_2O$	+ $2e^-$	$\rightarrow$	$HO_2^- + OH^-$
Pb^{2+}	+ $2e^-$	$\rightarrow$	Pb
Sn^{2+}	+ $2e^-$	$\rightarrow$	Sn
Fe^{2+}	+ $2e^-$	$\rightarrow$	Fe
Zn^{2+}	+ $2e^-$	$\rightarrow$	Zn
$2H_2O$	+ $2e^-$	$\rightarrow$	$H_2 + 2OH^-$
Al^{3+}	+ $3e^-$	$\rightarrow$	Al
Mg^{2+}	+ $2e^-$	$\rightarrow$	Mg
Na^+	+ e^-	$\rightarrow$	Na
Ca^{2+}	+ $2e^-$	$\rightarrow$	Ca
K^+	+ e^-	$\rightarrow$	K
Li^+	+ e^-	$\rightarrow$	Li
Weakly oxidizing agent			*Strongly reducing agent*

The Electrochemical Series

THE ELECTROCHEMICAL SERIES REVEALS THE REDUCING STRENGTH OF SPECIES AND ALLOWS US TO PREDICT THE OUTCOME OF REDOX REACTIONS.

We have seen how to balance a range of redox reactions, but how can we predict which redox reactions will occur? The answer lies in the electrochemical series, a list of half-reaction reductions. **The lower the position of the half-reaction in the electrochemical series, the greater the reducing power of the species in the third column.**

What will be the result of placing a piece of zinc metal in a copper nitrate solution? The half-reaction involving zinc...

$$Zn^{2+}(aq) + 2e^- \rightarrow Zn(s)$$

...is lower in the electrochemical series thanthe half-reaction involving copper...

$$Cu^{2+}(aq) + 2e^- \rightarrow Cu(s)$$

Cu has a greater reducing power than Zn. Therefore, Zn has a greater oxidizing power than Cu. This means that a piece of zinc placed in a solution of Cu^{2+} (e.g., copper nitrate) will form Cu (s) and Zn^{2+} (zinc nitrate) ions in solution. The overall equation for this process is:

$$Cu^{2+}(aq) + Zn(s) \rightarrow Cu(s) + Zn^{2+}(aq)$$

KEY TERMS

Brønsted-Lowry acid: A species that is a proton donor.

Brønsted-Lowry base: A species that is a proton acceptor.

electrochemical series: A series of half-reactions listed in order of the reducing power of the species on the left-hand side of the half-reaction.

hydronium ion: The ion (H_3O^+) formed when water acts like a base and accepts a proton.

neutralization: The reaction between an acid and a base to produce a salt and water.

oxidation: The loss of electrons accompanied by an increase in oxidation number.

precipitate: A solid that forms from a solution.

redox reactions: Reactions in which one species loses electrons while another species gains electrons.

reduction: The gain of electrons accompanied by a decrease in oxidation number.

soluble: A solid that dissolves in water.

spectator ions: Ions not involved in chemical change, but present in a solution.

strong electrolyte: A solid that dissolves in water to produce 100% ions and conducts electricity.

THRILLS, CHILLS AND DRILLS

True or False

1. A strong electrolyte does not conduct electricity

2. All nitrates are insoluble.

3. The formation of sulfuric acid from SO_3 and H_2O involves a reduction, because the sulfur changes oxidation states from 0 to -2.

4. Silver halides are soluble.

5. A sample of tap water, exposed to electrodes, is found to strongly conduct electricity. This leads one to conclude that the water is de-ionized.

6. A strong electrolyte is one in which the positive and negative charges associate strongly and therefore form a precipitate.

7. A standard method of retrieving a halide from solution is by precipitating it out with silver nitrate.

8. A strong Brønsted-Lowry acid is one which stays protoned when dissolved in aqueous solution.

9. Na_2CO_3 is a strong acid.

10. HNO_3 is a strong acid.

11. Arrhenius defined an acid as a species that can donate it's protons to water.

12. The Arrhenius definition of acidity is more general (i.e. encompasses more species) than the Brønsted-Lowry definition.

13. Neutralization reactions between acids and bases produce a salt and water.

14. In NaCl, sodium has an oxidation number of +2.

15. In ClO_4^-, chlorine has an oxidation of +7, its maximum oxidation number.

16. In SO_2, sulfur has an oxidation number of +2.

17. $S_8(s) + 8O_2(g) \rightarrow 8SO_2(g)$ represents a redox reaction

18. The oxidation number of fluorine is always -1.

19. The oxidation number of oxygen is always -2.

20. The maximum oxidation number of an element is never greater than the group number of the element in the periodic table.

Multiple Choice

1. Silver nitrate is added to sodium chloride and a white precipitate immediately forms. Which of the following is the formula weight of the solid?
    a) 143 amu
    b) 169 amu
    c) 58 amu
    d) 85 amu

2. Strong electrolytes conduct electricity because they
    a) are made up of ions
    b) contain a solution of electrons
    c) form precipitates
    d) can plate an electrode
    e) contain soluble material

3. Your chemistry lab professor tells you that you can collect the product of your reaction by precipitation. In chemistry, precipitation is
    a) water from the heavens above
    b) the falling out of an insoluble compound
    c) falling off a cliff and hence precipitating through the sky
    d) the dissolution of a compound in a suitable solvent

4. In order to identify a precipitate after mixing two electrolytes, we need to
    a) have mystical insight
    b) identify the possible candidates and then consult the solubility rules
    c) use the VSEPR method

5. Acids can be defined as
    a) electron donors
    b) acceptors of electrons
    c) proton donors
    d) proton acceptors

6. Bases can be defined as
    a) electron donors
    b) acceptors of electrons
    c) proton donors
    d) proton acceptors

7. Ten molecules of HCl and 2 molecules of NaOH react. How many molecules of NaCl are produced?
    a) 1
    b) 2
    c) 1/2
    d) 4
    e) 1/4

8. Which of the following is a strong acid?
    a) H_2CO_3
    b) H_2SO_4
    c) NaOH
    d) H_2O
    e) NH_3

9. Arrhenius's bases are
    a) all Brønsted-Lowry bases
    b) sometimes Brønsted-Lowry bases
    c) proton donors
    d) electron acceptors
    e) Brønsted-Lowry acids

10. In which of the following two reactions does redox occur?
    $$2NO_2 \rightarrow N_2O_4$$
    $$2CrO_4{}^{2-} + 2H^+ \rightarrow Cr_2O_7{}^{2-} + H_2O$$
    a) The first is a redox reaction; the second is not.
    b) The first is not a redox reaction; the second is.
    c) Both are redox reactions.
    d) Neither are redox reactions.

11. In a certain reaction, the oxidation number of nitrogen changes from +3 to -2. Is the nitrogen oxidized, and how many electrons are gained?

    a) Yes, it is oxidized; 5 electrons are gained.

    b) No, it is reduced; 3 electrons are lost.

    c) Yes, it is oxidized; 3 electrons are lost.

    d) No, it is reduced; 5 electrons are gained.

12. A disproportionation reaction is one in which a portion of a molecule is oxidized while the rest of it is reduced. Which of the following are disproportionation reactions? Be careful: these reactions are not necessarily balanced, and there may be more than one.

    a) $Cl_2 \rightarrow Cl^- + ClO_3^-$

    b) $HCl \rightarrow H^+ + Cl^-$

    c) $MnO_4 \rightarrow MnO_2 + H_2O$

    d) $AlCl_3 \rightarrow Al_2Cl_6$

13. The oxidation number of chlorine in ClO^- is

    a) -1

    b) +2

    c) +3

    d) +1

    e) +4

14. What is the oxidation number of chlorine in ClO_3?

    a) -3

    b) +1

    c) -1

    d) +3

    e) +6

15. What is the oxidation number of oxygen in Cl_2O?

    a) +2

    b) -2

    c) -1

    d) +1

    e) +1/2

16. $KClO_3$ is a good

    a) acid

    b) base

    c) oxidizing agent

    d) reducing agent

17. Given that Zn^{2+} (aq) $+2e \rightarrow$ Zn(s) is lower in the electrochemical series than Cu_2^+(aq) $+2e \rightarrow Cu^{2+}$, what is the out come of mixing copper nitrate and zinc metal?

   a) No reaction.

   b) Zinc nitrate is formed.

   c) An acid base reaction occurs.

   d) A precipitation reaction occurs.

18. The reaction $2Mg + Cl_2 \rightarrow 2MgCl$ can be written as which of the following pairs of half-reactions?

   a) $Mg + e^- \rightarrow Mg^{2+}$; $Cl_2 + 2e^- \rightarrow 2Cl^-$

   b) $Mg \rightarrow Mg^{2+} + 2e^-$; $Cl_2 + 2e^- \rightarrow 2Cl^-$

   c) $Mg - 2e^- \rightarrow Mg_2^-$; $Cl_2 - 2e^- \rightarrow 2Cl^+$

Short Essays

1. Given your knowledge of solubility, how would you separate bromide, nitrate, and sulfate ions?

2. One liter of water collected from the Dead Sea (known to have an unusually high sodium chloride salt content) was treated with silver nitrate in order to analyze the ionic content.

   a. State and balance the full chemical equation of interest.

   b. Identify the spectator ions.

3. Your professor, investigating nitrous oxide, has approached you with a problem. He is trying to conduct the following equation, which seems balanced yet is not. Balance it and explain what is wrong.

$$NO_2 + H_2O \rightarrow NO_3^- + 2H^+$$

4. For each of the following, write a balanced ionic equation.

   a. $CuSO_4(aq) + BaCl_2(aq) \rightarrow CuCl_2(aq) + BaSO_4(s)$

   b. $Fe(NO_3)_3(aq) + LiOH(aq) \rightarrow LiNO_3(aq) + Fe(OH)_3(s)$

   c. $Na_3PO_4(aq) + CaCl_2(aq) \rightarrow Ca_3(PO_4)_2(s) + NaCl(aq)$

   d. $Na_2S(aq) + AgC_2H_3O_2(aq) \rightarrow NaC_2H_3O_2(aq) + Ag_2S(s)$

   Then list the spectator ions, and write a net ionic equation for each of the reactions in a) to d).

5. Using what you have learned from Questions 3 and 4, deduce the two conditions that must be fulfilled by a balanced ionic equation.

ANSWERS

True or False Answers

1. **False.** When a strong electrolyte is dissolved in water, the resulting solution can conduct electricity.

2. **False.** All nitrates are soluble.

3. **False.** The oxidation number of oxygen is -2. Therefore, the oxidation number of S in SO_3 must be +6. Since the sum of the oxidation numbers of the four oxygens in sulfuric acid is -8 and the sum of the oxidation numbers of the two hydrogens is +2, sulfer must also have an oxidation number of +6 in sulfuric acid. Sulfer does not change oxidation state.

4. **False.** Silver halides are insoluble.

5. **False.** Solutions that conduct electricity are electrolytes. The ions in the electrolyte are responsible for its ability to conduct electricity.

6. **False.** A strong electrolyte is a solution where positive and negative ions move about independently.

7. **True.** Silver nitrate will dissolve to form Ag^+ ions and NO_3^- ions. The Ag^+ ions will react with halide ions to form a silver halide. Silver halides are insoluble and will precipitate out of solution.

8. **False.** A strong Bronsted-Lowry acid will completely ionize in solution.

9. **False.** Sodium carbonate is a weak acid.

10. **True.**

11. **False.** The Arrhenius definition of acidity is a species which produces protons when dissolved in water.

12. **False.** The Bronsted-Lowry definition of acidity is more general than the Arrhenius definition.

13. **True.**

14. **False.** Sodium has an oxidation number of +1 in NaCl.

15. **True.** Oxygen has an oxidation number of -2. The ion has an oxidation number of -1. $4(-2) + ? = -1$ where ? is the oxidation number of Cl. Therefore, $? = +7$.

16. **False.** Oxygen has an oxidation number of -2. Because there are two oxygen atoms in SO_2, sulfur must have an oxidation number of +4 in this molecule.

17. **True.** A redox reaction is one where one species gains electrons (is reduced) and another species loses electrons (is oxidized.) The oxidation number of S in S_8 is zero. The oxidation number of O in O_2 is also zero. In SO_2, the oxidation number of O is -2, while the oxidation number of S is +4. Sulfur loses electrons in this reaction, while oxygen gains electrons.

18. **True.**

19. **False.** For example, the oxidation number of oxygen in O_2^- is -1.

20. **True.**

Multiple Choice Answers

1. (a) When silver nitrate is added to sodium chloride, silver chloride and sodium nitrate are formed. Silver chloride, which has a formula weight of 143 amu, is insoluble.

2. (a)

3. (b) A precipitate is a solid that forms on mixing two solutions.

4. (b)

5. (c) The Bronsted-Lowry definition of an acid is a species that can donate protons.

6. (d) The Bronsted-Lowry definition of a base is a species that can accept protons.

7. (b) $NaOH + HCl \rightarrow H_2O + NaCl$. If only two molecules of NaOH are reacted, only two molecules of NaCl can form.

8. (b) H_2SO_4 dissociates completely into $2H^+$ and SO_4^- in solution.

9. (a) The Bronsted-Lowry definition of a base is more general than the Arrhenius definition.

10. (d) The oxidation number of all elements in both reactions stays the same.

11. (d) Reduction is the gain of electrons with a resulting decrease in oxidation number.

12. (a) The oxidation number of Cl in Cl_2 is zero. The oxidation number of Cl in Cl^- is -1. The oxidation number of Cl in ClO_3^- is +5. Chlorine is both reduced and oxidized.

13. (d) The oxidation number of O is -2. The oxidation number of the ion is -1. Hence, the oxidation number of Cl must be +1.

14. (e) The sum of the oxidation numbers of oxygen in ClO_3 is 3(-2) = -6. Therefore, the oxidation number of Cl must be +6.

15. (d)

16. (c)

17. (b) Zn has a greater oxidizing power than Cu. A piece of zinc placed in a solution of Cu^{2+} (eg copper nitrate) will form Cu (s) and Zn^{2+} (zinc nitrate) ions in solution.

18. (b)

Short Essay Answers

1. Precipitate chloride ions with silver nitrate. Precipitate sulfate ions with barium nitrate.

2. a. $AgNO_3(aq) + NaCl(aq) \rightarrow AgCl(s) + NaNO_3(aq)$

    b. The spectator ions are Na^+ and NO_3^-.

3. $NO_2 + H_2O + e^- \rightarrow NO_3^- + 2H^+$

4. Balanced equations:

   a. $CuSO_4(aq) + BaCl_2(aq) \rightarrow CuCl_2(aq) + BaSO_4(s)$

   b. $Fe(NO_3)_3(aq) + 3LiOH(aq) \rightarrow 3LiNO_3(aq) + Fe(OH)_3(s)$

   c. $2Na_3PO_4(aq) + 3CaCl_2(aq) \rightarrow Ca_3(PO_4)_2(s) + 6NaCl(aq)$

   d. $Na_2S(aq) + 2AgC_2H_3O_2(aq) \rightarrow 2NaC_2H_3O_2(aq) + Ag_2S(s)$

   Spectator ions:

   a. Cu^{2+}, Cl^-

   b. Li^+, NO_3^-

   c. Na^+, Cl^-

   d. Na^+, $C_2H_3O_2^-$

   Net ionic equations:

   a. $SO_4^{2-}(aq) + Ba^{2+}(aq) \rightarrow BaSO_4(s)$

   b. $Fe^{3+}(aq) + 3OH^-(aq) \rightarrow Fe(OH)_3(s)$

   c. $2PO_4^{2-}(aq) + 3Ca^{2+}(aq) \rightarrow Ca_3(PO_4)_2(s)$

   d. $S^{2-}(aq) + 2Ag^+(aq) \rightarrow Ag_2S(s)$

5. The number of atoms of each element must be the same on both sides of a chemical equation. The number of electrons must also be the same.

CHAPTER

QUANTIFYING MATTER:

THE MOLE

OVERVIEW

How much fuel should the space shuttle take on its next mission? How much oxygen do we breathe in every day? How concentrated should liquid bleach be, and how can we set its concentration during the production process? Chemists can answer these questions, but to do so they need a way to quantify matter.

The central quantity that chemists use to quantify matter is the mole. This chapter introduces the mole and explains how to find the molar masses of elements and compounds. We will learn how to calculate the amounts of reactants and products in chemical reactions, and how to quantify the success of a reaction in terms of its percentage yield. Finally, we will examine how to make solutions of known concentration, and the stoichiometry of reactions in solution. In this chapter we will see how to combine the concept of the mole with the stoichiometry of equations (which we met in Chapter 3) to answer questions about how much of a reactant (or product) we need (or expect to gain) from a chemical reaction.

CONCEPTS

Moles and Molar Mass

Many of the calculations you will be asked to perform in chemistry involve moles of atoms or molecules. A mole of atoms contains 6.02×10^{23} atoms. This number is known as **Avagadro's number**. You might think of a mole as being like a boatful of rowers in a crew race. In each boat, there are, say, eight rowers. The rowers may be of different height, weight, and strength, but their number remains constant. Similarly, no matter what the size or type of objects involved, the number of objects in a mole is constant: 6×10^{23}.

If a boat's crew is made up of heavyweights with brawn and power it will weigh more than a crew made up of lighter people, but it will still contain eight people. In the same way, a mole of atoms with a large atomic weight will be heavier than a mole of atoms with a low atomic weight. A mole of iron will therefore weigh more than a mole of helium, **but both will contain the same number of atoms.**

Avagadro's number itself is defined as the number of atoms in exactly 12 grams of carbon-12.

THE MOLAR MASS OF AN ELEMENT IS THE NUMBER OF GRAMS OF THAT ELEMENT THAT CONSTITUTE ONE MOLE.

Let's continue our analogy to rowing and imagine a crew in which all eight people in the boat weigh the same. The mass of the crew would be eight times the mass of each individual. Similarly, the molar mass of an element is Avagadro's number times the mass of the one atom of the element. The molar mass of an element in grams per mole (g mol^{-1}) is the same number as the atomic weight of the element in amu. We can therefore write down the molar mass of an element by finding its atomic weight in the periodic table. For example, we can see that a mole of oxygen atoms weighs 16 grams, a mole of sodium atoms weighs 23 grams, and a mole of calcium atoms weighs 40 grams.

Since electrons have so much less mass than the nuclei they surround, a mole of ions weighs the same as a mole of atoms, for all practical purposes.

We can have a mole of anything as long as it contains Avagadro's number of that thing. In chemistry we are concerned with moles of compounds in addition to moles of atoms or ions, but we could also have moles of paper clips, moles of moon rocks, and moles of moles.

The molar mass of a compound is the number of grams of that compound that constitute one mole.

We calculate the molar mass of a compound by adding the atomic weights of the elements in the compound and converting the result to grams per mole (written g mol^{-1}).

How, for example, would we find the molar mass of H_2O?
> Strategy: Calculate the molecular weight. Convert to grams.
>> molecular formula: H_2O
>> molecular weight = (2 x 1.008 amu) + 16.000 amu = 18.016 amu
>> The molar mass of H_2O is 18.02 g mol^{-1}

What is the molar mass of NaCl?
> Strategy: Calculate the weight of a formula unit. Convert to grams.
>> formula unit: NaCl
>> formula weight = 22.99 amu + 35.45 amu = 58.44 amu
>> The molar mass of NaCl is 58.44 g mol^{-1}.

Many elements exist as molecules, and we can find the molar mass of molecules of an element in the same way that we find the molar mass for compounds. For instance, the molar mass of O_2 is 16 + 16 = 32 g mol^{-1}. For N_2, the molar mass is 14 + 14 = 28 g mol^{-1}.

TO FIND THE NUMBER OF MOLES IN A GIVEN MASS OF A SUBSTANCE, DIVIDE THE MASS OF A SAMPLE BY THE MOLAR MASS OF THE SUBSTANCE.

> number of moles (n) = mass of sample / molar mass of substance.

For example, how would we find the number of moles in 116.88 g of NaCl?
> Strategy: Use the equation: n = mass of sample / molar mass of NaCl

In our earlier example, we found that the molar mass of NaCl is 58.44.
>> n = 116.88 / 58.44
>> n = 2 moles

How many moles are in 31 grams of phosphorus atoms?
> Strategy: Use the equation: n = mass of sample / molar mass of P
>> n = 31 grams / 31 g mol^{-1}
>> n = 1 mole

How many moles are in 31 grams of P_4?
> Strategy: Use the equation: n = mass of sample / molar mass of P_4
>> n = 31 grams / 31 g mol^{-1} x 4
>> n = 1/4 mol = 0.25 moles

Moles and Stoichiometry

IN A CHEMICAL EQUATION, THE NUMBER OF MOLES OF A SPECIES IS EQUAL TO THE STOICHIOMETRIC COEFFICIENT OF THAT SPECIES.

In Chapter 3, we described stoichiometric coefficients as representing the relative numbers of atoms or units of a compound taking part in a reaction. Since it is the relative number of atoms or units that is important, we can multiply all the coefficients in an equation by any number. In particular, we can multiply all of the stoichiometric coefficients by Avagadro's number (N_A) and rewrite an equation in terms of the relative number of moles. For example:

> If we multiply...
> $N_2(g) + 3H_2(g) \rightarrow 2NH_3(g)$
> ... by N_A (Avagadro's number), we arrive at...
> 1 mole $N_2(g)$ + 3 moles $H_2(g) \rightarrow$ 2 moles $NH_3(g)$

When we look at a chemical equation, we can interpret the stoichiometric coefficients as the relative number of moles of each atom or compound taking part in a chemical reaction.

BALANCED EQUATIONS CAN BE USED TO FIND THE NUMBER OF MOLES OF REACTANTS AND PRODUCTS FOR A PARTICULAR REACTION.

If we take the equation:

$$N_2(g) + 3H_2(g) \rightarrow 2NH_3(g)$$

How many moles of N_2 and H_2 are needed to produce 2 moles of NH_3 ?

Looking at the equation, we can see that 1 mole of N_2 and 3 moles of H_2 combine to produce 2 moles of NH_3.

However, how many moles of N_2 and H_2 are required to produce 4 moles of NH_3? We realize that 4 moles of NH_3 is twice the number of moles of NH_3 represented in the equation. We would expect, therefore, that it would require twice the amount of the reactants to produce this amount of NH_3. 2 moles of N_2 and 6 moles of H_2 are required to produce 4 moles of NH_3. In the next example, we use a more general method for solving this type of problem.

Using the equation:

$$2H_2O \rightarrow 2H_2 + O_2$$

How many moles of a) H_2 and b) O_2 are produced from the decomposition of 3 moles of H_2O?

a) Hydrogen moles.

Two moles of H_2O yield one mole of H_2. We can represent this information in an equivalence statement.

$$2 \text{ mol } H_2O = 1 \text{ mol } H_2 \qquad 3/2$$

We can rewrite this statement into conversion factor between moles of H_2 and moles of H_2O:

$$1 \text{ mol } H_2 \text{ / } 2 \text{ mol } H_2O$$

We can then use this conversion factor to work out the number of moles of H_2 produced from 3 moles of H_2O:

$$3 \text{ mol } H_2O \times 1 \text{ mol } H_2 \text{ / } 2 \text{ mol } H_2O = {}^{3}/_{2} \text{ mol } H_2$$

b) Oxygen moles.

Two moles of H_2O yield one mole of O_2. We can represent this information in and equivalence statement:

$$2 \text{ mol } H_2O = 1 \text{ mol } O_2$$

As before, we can rewrite this as a conversion factor between moles of O_2 and moles of H_2O:

$$1 \text{ mol } O_2 \text{ / } 2 \text{ mol } H_2O$$
$$3 \text{ mol } H_2O \times 1 \text{ mol } O_2 \text{ / } 2 \text{ mol } H_2O = 3/2 \text{ mol } O_2$$

Decomposing 3 moles of H_2O gives 1.5 moles of H_2 and 1.5 moles of O_2. We can represent this information in the balanced equation:

$$3H_2O \rightarrow 1.5 \, H_2 + 1.5 \, O_2$$

The relationship between stoichiometric coefficients and the relative number of moles turns out to be quite useful in chemistry, as we will now examine.

WE CAN CONVERT THE MASS OF A SUBSTANCE TO THE NUMBER OF MOLES IT CONTAINS — AND VICE VERSA.

In the previous section, we saw how to use balanced equations to arrive at the number of moles of reactants and products for a particular reaction. In general, however, we do not measure the number of moles that react or are produced, but the mass of a reactant or product. We the need a way of converting between the masses we measure and the moles we represent in equations. Fortunately, we have such a conversion factor:

number of moles = mass / molar mass

WE CAN CALCULATE THE MASS OF A REACTANT REQUIRED TO REACT WITH A GIVEN MASS OF ANOTHER REACTANT.

In the space shuttle, lithium hydroxide is used to remove (absorb) unwanted carbon dioxide from the cabin. The reaction produces lithium carbonate and liquid water, following this balanced equation.

$$2LiOH + CO_2 \rightarrow Li_2CO_3 + H_2O$$

What mass of LiOH is required to remove 880g of CO_2 from the shuttle's cabin?

> Strategy: Convert the mass of CO_2 into moles of CO_2. Find the moles of LiOH necessary to absorb this mass of CO_2. Find the mass of LiOH corresponding to this number of moles.

To find the number of moles of CO_2:

> number of moles of CO_2 = mass CO_2 / molar mass of CO_2
> mass CO_2 = 880g (from question)
> molar mass of CO_2 = 12 g mol^{-1} + 2(16 g mol^{-1}) = 44 g mol^{-1}
> number of moles of CO_2 = 880g / 44 g mol^{-1} = 200 mol

From the balanced equation, we find the conversion factor: 2 mol LiOH / 1 mol CO_2. We can use this conversion factor to calculate the number of moles of LiOH required to react with the CO_2:

200 mol CO_2 × 2 mol LiOH / 1 mol CO_2 = 400 mol LiOH

Now we can calculate the mass of LiOH needed:

> The formula

n = mass / molar mass

> can be rearranged as

mass = n x molar mass.

Therefore:

mass LiOH = 400 mol × 24 g mol-1 = 400/24 g = 16.67 g

400/24 g of LiOH are required to absorb 880 g of CO_2 from the shuttle's cabin.

Limiting reagents control the maximum amount of product that can be formed in a chemical reaction.

The example above shows that when 16.67 g of LiOH reacts with exactly 880g of CO_2 both compounds are used up at the same time. There is exactly enough LiOH to react with all the CO_2, and vice versa. However, if 900g of CO_2 is mixed with the same amount of LiOH, then the LiOH is consumed before all the CO_2 used up. The CO_2 is in excess. In this case, the amount of product we can produce is controlled by the amount of LiOH. Once the LiOH is consumed, no more products can be made, even though some CO_2 still remains. In such a situation, where one reactant limits the amount of product that can be made, that reagent is known as a **limiting reagent**. In day-to-day practice, reactants are not mixed in stoichiometric amount, and it is essential to determine the limiting reagent in order to correctly calculate the amount of products that will be formed.

FOR A GIVEN CHEMICAL REACTION, WE CAN CALCULATE THE MASS OF A PRODUCT AS LONG AS WE KNOW THE MASSES OF THE REACTANTS.

Ammonia (NH^3) is a necessary raw material for fertilizers. It is produced in large quantities from nitrogen and hydrogen by a method known as the Haber process. The balanced equation for the Haber process is:

$$N_2(g) + 3H_2(g) \rightarrow 2NH_3(g)$$

Suppose that we react 10 grams of hydrogen and 14 grams of nitrogen. What is the maximum mass of ammonia that we can produce?

> **Strategy:** Use the mass and molar mass of reactants to calculate moles of reactants. Use the mole ratios to find the limiting reagent. Then use the mole ratios involving limiting reactant to calculate the moles of ammonia produced. Finally, use the molar mass of product to calculate the mass of products.

To calculate the moles of the reactants:

$$n\,H_2 = 10\,g\,/\,2\,g\,mol^{-1} = 5\,mol\,H_2$$

$$n\,N_2 = 14\,g\,/\,28\,g\,mol^{-1} = 0.5\,mol\,N_2$$

To find the limiting reactant we look at the mole ratio and the amount we have of each of the reactants. We can start with either, or in the case of a reaction with more than two reactants, any reactant. With this example, let's start by figuring out how much N_2 would be used in a reaction with 5 moles of H_2.

$$5\,mol\,H_2 \times 3\,mol\,N_2\,/\,1\,mol\,H_2 = 7.5\,mol\,N_2$$

Since 1.67 moles N_2 is greater than the 0.5 moles N_2 available, we conclude that N_2 is the limiting reagent.

Let's try it the other way, starting with the mass of N_2 (0.5 moles) available in order to see how much H_2 would be used in a reaction with 0.5 moles of N_2.

$$0.5 \text{ mol } N_2 \times 3 \text{ mol } H_2 / 1 \text{ mol } N_2 = 1.5 \text{ mol } H_2$$

Because 1.5 moles H_2 is less than the 5 moles H_2 available, we again conclude that N_2 is the limiting reagent.

Now that we have identified the limiting reagent (N_2), we are ready to find the amount of ammonia produced. We use the mole ratio 2 mol NH_3 / 1mol N_2.

Now, the amount of ammonia produced is dependent on the limiting reagent: N_2.

$$0.5 \text{ moles } N_2 \times 2 \text{ mol } NH_3 / 1 \text{ mol } N_2 = 1 \text{ mol } NH_3$$

The mass of NH_3 produced is calculated by rearranging

$$n = \text{mass} / \text{molar mass}$$
$$\text{as}$$
$$\text{mass} = n \times \text{molar mass}$$

NH_3 has a molar mass of 17 g mol^{-1}. The maximum mass of NH_3 we can produce is:

$$17\text{g mol}^{-1} \times 1 \text{ mol} = 17\text{g}.$$

Memorize the following steps to use when solving problems that involve limiting reagents:

- ◆ Write a balanced equation for the reaction.

- ◆ Use mass and molar mass of reactants to calculate moles of reactants.

- ◆ Use mole ratios to find the limiting reagent.

- ◆ Use mole ratios involving the limiting reagent to calculate moles of products.

- ◆ Use molar mass of product to calculate mass of products.

THE PERCENTAGE YIELD OF A REACTION IS A MEASURE OF ITS SUCCESS.

In the previous section, we saw how to calculate the amounts of products formed when specified amounts of reactants are combined.

The maximum mass of product that could be obtained from such calculations, based on the limiting reactant, is known as the **theoretical yield** of the reaction, since it is the calculated maximum amount of product obtainable from the given amount of reactants. The **actual**

yield of the reaction may be less than the theoretical yield for a number of reasons. Reactants may, for example, be used up in reactions other than those we are considering (side reactions). **A measure of the difference between actual and theoretical yield is the percentage yield:**

$$\text{percentage yield = mass produced / theoretical yield} \times 100\%$$

For example, when 14 g N_2 reacts with an excess of hydrogen gas, 15 g of NH_3 are produced. What is the percentage yield of the reaction?

From the previous calculations, we know that 14 g of N_2 as the limiting reagent leads to a theoretical yield of NH_3 of 17 g.

$$\text{percentage yield = 15g / 17g} \times 100\% = 88.23\%$$

Solution Reactions

Many reactions-including most of the reactions that keep our bodies functioning-occur in water. A substance that is dissolved in water (a solute) is said to be in **aqueous solution**. In this section, we describe how to find a solution's concentration (or molarity) and show how it is useful in dealing with reaction stoichiometry in solution.

THE MOLAR CONCENTRATION OF A SOLUTION OF AN ELEMENT OR COMPOUND, X, IS A MEASURE OF THE AMOUNT OF SOLUTE X THAT IS DISSOLVED IN A GIVEN VOLUME OF WATER.

The concentration of X is denoted [X] .
$\qquad$ [X] = moles of X / liters of solution
$\qquad$ [X] has units of mol liter^{-1}, abbreviated M

In other words, the molar concentration is the number of moles of X per liter of solution. For example, we could make a 1M NaCl solution by dissolving 1 mole of NaCl in a flask, and adding water to a total volume of 1 litre.

WE CAN MAKE SOLUTIONS OF KNOWN CONCENTRATION.

Rearranging the equation in terms of amount of solute...

$$\text{moles of X = volume of solution} \times \text{[X]}$$

...we see that the concentration of a solution is really just a conversion factor between the volume of a solution and the amount of solute it contains. Knowing this, we can prepare

solutions of defined concentration in a given volume, by calculating the appropriate number of moles.

For example, suppose that we want to prepare 250 mL (0.25 liters) of a 4M NaCl solution. The number of moles of solid NaCl required is:

$$0.25 \text{ liters} \times 4 \text{ mol l}^{-1} = 1 \text{ mole}$$

Since the molar mass of NaCl is 58 g mol^{-1}, we can go on to calculate the mass to which this number of moles corresponds:

$$\text{mass} = \text{molar mass} \times \text{n}$$
$$58 \text{ g mol}^{-1} \times 1 = 58\text{g}$$

Dissolving 58 g of NaCl in a small volume of water and filling the vessel to a total volume of 250 mL, will result in a 4M solution of NaCl. Such measurements are usually done in a flask specifically designed for this purpose-known as a volumetric flask.

WE CAN TRANSFER A KNOWN AMOUNT OF SOLUTE FROM ONE FLASK TO ANOTHER.

Given a stock solution of known concentration in one vessel, we can transfer a defined amount of solute to another vessel. Suppose that we want one mole of NaCl to use in a solution reaction. How do we calculate the appropriate volume of our 4M stock to transfer?

$$\text{volume of solution for transfer} =$$
$$\text{number of moles required} / \text{concentration of stock}$$
$$= 1 \text{ mol} / 4 \text{ mol L}^{-1} = 0.25 \text{ L}$$

STOCK SOLUTIONS CAN BE USED TO MAKE DILUTIONS.

To make a diluted (or less concentrated) solution, we take a portion of a stock solution and add more water to it. In this way, we can make specified dilutions of a stock solution.

For example, suppose we have a 4M stock solution of NaCl and want to make 500 mL of a 2M solution.

We first ask the question: How many moles of NaCl are in 500 mL of a 2M solution?

$$n = 2.0 \text{ mol L}^{-1} \times 0.5 \text{ L} = 1 \text{ mol.}$$

To what volume of 4M stock does this correspond? We found this answer, 250 mL, in the previous section.

To make 500 mL of 2M NaCl, we take 250 mL of 4M stock and add water to a final volume of 500 mL.

Stoichiometry of Solution Reactions

We can calculate the volume of solution required in a reaction.

We are now ready to calculate the volume of solution required for a reaction. Consider the neutralization reaction between hydrochloric acid (HCl) and sodium hydroxide (NaOH):

$$HCl \text{ (aq)} + NaOH \text{ (aq)} \rightarrow NaCl \text{ (aq)} + H_2O \text{ (l)}$$

How would we calculate the volume of 0.5M HCl required to react with 10mL of 0.25M NaOH?

Strategy: Calculate the number of moles of NaOH. Use the stoichiometry of reaction to find the number of moles of HCl required. Use the concentration of HCl to find the volume of HCl solution required.

First we calculate the number of moles in 10mL of 0.25M NaOH:

$$n = \text{concentration of stock} \times \text{volume}$$

$$n = 0.25 \text{ mol L}^{-1} \times .01 \text{ L}$$

$$= 0.0025 \text{ moles}$$

Since the equation tells us that 1 mole of NaOH reacts with 1 mole of HCl, it follows that 0.0025 moles of NaOH reacts with 0.0025 moles of HCl.

The volume of HCl we need is given by:

$$\text{Volume of HCl} = n \text{ HCl} / \text{Concentration of HCl} = 0.0025 \text{ mol} / 0.5 \text{ mol L}^{-1} = .005 \text{ L} = 5 \text{ mL}$$

KEY TERMS

Avagadro's number: Approximately 6×10^{23}. The number of things in a mole. This number is also the number of atoms in exactly 12g of carbon-12.

concentration: The ratio of solute to solvent in a solution.

dilution: The process of making less concentrated solutions.

limiting reagent: A reactant that controls the maximum amount of product that can be formed in a chemical reaction.

molar mass: The number of grams of an element or compound that constitute one mole.

mole: A unit containing Avagadro's number of objects. In chemistry, these objects are usually molecules.

percentage yield: A measure of the difference between the actual and theoretical yield of a reaction.

theoretical yield: A measure of the maximum possible yield of a reaction taking into account the amount of any limiting reagent.

THRILLS, CHILLS AND DRILLS

True or False

1. One mole of carbon atoms contains exactly the same number of atoms as one mole of oxygen atoms.

2. One mole of carbon atoms weighs exactly the same as one mole of oxygen atoms.

3. One mole of Ca^{2+} ions has a very different mass from one mole of Ca atoms.

4. The molar mass of an element is the number of kilograms of the element that constitute one mole.

5. The molar mass of N_2 is twice the molar mass of a nitrogen atom.

6. There are two moles of nitrogen atoms in 56 grams of N_2.

7. The mass of the chlorine atoms in 2 moles of sodium chloride (NaCl) is the same as that in 1 mole of methylene chloride (CH_2Cl_2).

8. In 2.57 moles of benzene (C_6H_6), the mass of carbon is approximately 12 times as great as the mass of hydrogen.

9. The balanced equation for the neutralization reaction between magnesium hydroxide and hydrochloric acid is:

$$Mg(OH)_2 + 2HCl \rightarrow MgCl_2 + 2H_2O(l)$$

This tells us that two moles of water are produced from one mole of $Mg(OH)_2$ and two moles of HCl.

10. The equation in Question 9 tells us that two mole of hydroxide ions are consumed for each mole of HCl.

11. The equation in Question 9 suggests that in order to make 10 moles of $MgCl_2$ we need at least 5 moles of HCl, assuming that $Mg(OH)_2$ is in excess.

12. The equation in Question 9 suggests that 2 moles of HCl will react with 58 g of $Mg(OH)_2$.

13. The balanced equation ...

$$3NO_2(g) + H_2O(l) \rightarrow 2HNO_3(aq) + NO(g)$$

...tells us that 30 g of NO_2 will react with 18 g of water.

14. When 30 g of NO_2 is reacted with 18 g of water, the limiting reagent is NO_2.

15. When 30 g of NO_2 is reacted with 18 g of water, $2/3$ moles of HNO_3 are produced.

16. When 30 g of NO_2 is reacted with 18 g of water, the theoretical yield of HNO_3 is $(2/3)$mol / 63 g mol^{-1}.

17. If the theoretical yield of a reaction is 25 g of NaCl and the actual yield is 15 g, then the percentage yield is 60%.

18. The molar concentration of a solution is defined as the number of grams of solute per liter of water.

19. If 200 mL of 5M NaCl is added to a volumetric flask, and the flask is then filled up to one liter, the concentration of Na^+ ions in solution is now 1M.

20. According to the balanced equation...

$$NaOH + HCl \rightarrow NaCl + H_2O$$

...200mls of 2M NaOH will exactly neutralize 250 mL of 5M HCl.

Multiple Choice

1. As he prepares to retire, Dr. Living B. Low is having trouble finishing off his last journal publication because he can't remember the formal definition of a mole! Help him get this last detail out of the way so he can take up golf instead. A mole is defined as
   a) exactly 6 of a given object
   b) a furry, brown creature living underground
   c) the number of atoms in 12 g of carbon-12
   d) the number of crooked politicians to have served Congress
   e) the number of atoms in 32 g of oxygen-16

2. The molar mass of an element equal to
   a) the mass of a mole of atoms the element
   b) the mass of a mole of molecules of the element
   c) the mass of 12 g of carbon-12

3. The molar mass of AlI_3 is
   a) 13 + 3(53)
   b) 13 + 3(53)
   c) 27 + 3(127)
   d) none of the above

4. The number of moles of water in 54 g of pure water is
   a) 1
   b) 2
   c) 3
   d) 4

5. The number of moles of hydrogen atoms in 54 g of pure water is
   a) 3
   b) 4
   c) 5
   d) 6

6. Ty Trayshun was studying a weak acid with a molar mass of 60 g mol^{-1}. Given that the ratio of carbon to hydrogen to oxygen atoms in the molecule is 1 : 2 : 1, what is the mass of oxygen found in 2.5 moles of the acid?
   a) 32 g
   b) 16 g
   c) 80 g
   d) 96 g

7. In 2.5 moles of ammonium nitrate, NH_4NO_3, there are
   a) 2 moles of nitrogen, 1 mole of nitrate
   b) 1 mole of nitrogen, 2.5 moles of nitrate
   c) 5 moles of nitrogen, 2.5 moles of nitrate
   d) 2.5 moles of nitrogen, 2.5 moles of nitrate

8. Given 125.32 g of $C_6H_{12}O_6$, which of the following expressions is equal to the mass (in grams) of carbon atoms present in the molecule?
   a) (125.32 x 72) / 180
   b) (125.32 x 180) / 72
   c) (72 x 180) / 125.32
   d) 72 x 180 x 125.32

9. Aluminum dissolves in sulfuric acid according to the following balanced equation:

$$2Al\ (s) + 3H_2SO_4(aq) \rightarrow Al_2(SO_4)_3\ (aq) + 6H^+\ (aq)$$

The minimum number of moles of sulfuric acid needed to dissolve 10 moles of aluminum is
   a) 10
   b) 7.5
   c) 15
   d) 20

10. According to the equation in Question 9, how many moles of aluminum are needed to give 15 moles of aluminum sulfate (assume molar excess of sulfuric acid)?

    a) 15 moles

    b) 7.5 moles

    c) 10 moles

    d) 30 moles

11. How much aluminum is needed to produce 684 g of aluminum sulfate, according to the equation in Question 9?

    a) 2 g

    b) 4 g

    c) 108 g

    d) 54 g

12. The limiting reagent in a reaction determines

    a) its percentage yield

    b) its theoretical yield

    c) the stoichiometry of the reaction

    d) the molar mass of reactants

13. The balanced equation for the reaction of sulfur dioxide with oxygen is:

$$2SO_2(g) + O_2(g) \rightarrow 2SO_3(g)$$

Therefore, if 5 moles of SO_2 react with 10 moles of O_2, the limiting reagent is

    a) SO_2

    b) O_2

    c) There is not a limiting reagent in this case.

14. If 32 g of SO_2 react with 100 g of O_2, what is the theoretical yield of SO_3?

    a) 20 g

    b) 80 g

    c) 40 g

    d) 100 g

15. If the actual yield of SO_3 under the conditions outlined in Question 15 is 40 g, then the percentage yield is

    a) 100%

    b) 80%

    c) 50%

    d) 10%

16. If x grams of $Mg(OH)_2$ is completely dissolved in 5 liters of water, and the resulting solution is measured to be 3M in magnesium ions, then x =
    a) 870 g
    b) 58 g
    c) 290 g
    d) 174 g

17. What volume of 4M NaCl solution constitutes 0.5 moles?
    a) 1 liter
    b) 0.5 liter
    c) 0.25 liter
    d) 0.125 liter

18. If 0.125 liters of a 4M solution of NaCl was evaporated, what mass of dry NaCl would be recovered?
    a) 58 g
    b) 29 g
    c) 116 g
    d) 464 g

19. Consider the following equation:

$$2Al \ (s) + 3H_2SO_4(aq) \rightarrow Al_2(SO_4)_3(aq) + 6H^+(aq)$$

What is the minimum volume of 2M H_2SO_4 required to react with 13.5 g of aluminum?
    a) 500mls
    b) 250mls
    c) 375mls
    d) 400mls

Short Essays

1. Palytoxin is produced by the marine colenterate **Palythoa mammillosa**, and it is one of the more potent marine toxins. Palytoxin has the molecular formula of $C_{145}H_{264}N_4O_{78}$. Calculate the number of grams in 3.0 moles of palytoxin.

2. Only four elements are recovered from the sea in commercially significant amounts: chlorine, sodium, magnesium, and bromine. Random samples have shown that the sodium concentration of seawater fluctuates between 0.6 and 0.8 moles per kilogram of seawater. What is the mass range of sodium (Na) we would expect to find in 3.0 kilograms of seawater?

3. Early refrigeration units used sulfur dioxide (SO_2) gas instead of the non-toxic freons that are currently used. The freons, such as freon-12 (CCl_2F_2), are likely to be replaced in the future because of the damage they cause to the ozone layer.

   a. How many moles of SO_2 gas were used in a refrigeration compressor charged with 156g of the gas?

   b. How many grams of freon-12 would correspond to the number of moles of SO_2 used?

4. Calcium chloride ($CaCl_2$) and sodium chloride (NaCl) are often used to melt ice and snow on roads and driveways. Chlorides-R-Us, a prominent salt company, is marketing a new mixture of the two. A chemist wishing to analyze the mixture dissolved a 100 g sample of it in water and precipitated the calcium using the oxalate ion ($C_2O_4^{2-}$). The calcium oxalate was then filtered out of solution, dissolved in sulfuric acid. $KMnO_4$ solution was added drop-by-drop to the solution until all the oxalate ions had reacted, according to the following equation:

$$6H^+ + 5H_2C_2O_4 + 2MnO_4^- \rightarrow 10CO2 + 2Mn^{2+} + 8H_2O.$$

100mls of 1M $KMnO_4$ was required.

   a. How many moles of oxalate ion were present?

   b. How many grams of $CaCl_2$ were in the original sample?

   c. What is the percentage by mass of $CaCl_2$ in the sample?

5. Your professor has conducted a reaction combining an unknown triprotic acid with sodium hydroxide. Assume the reaction goes to completion as described by the equation:

$$XH_3 + 3NaOH \rightarrow X^{3-} + 3H_2O$$

A sample of X weighing 0.200 g required 31.25 mL of 0.100 M NaOH for complete neutralization. What is the molecular mass of acid X based on this information?

6. One liter of water collected from the Dead Sea (known to have a high sodium chloride salt content) was treated with silver nitrate in order to analyze the ionic content.

   a. State and balance the full chemical equation.

   b. Given that 143.5 g of AgCl are collected after filtering away the aqueous layer, determine the initial salt concentration of the Dead Sea water.

7. Solder is an alloy containing the metals tin and lead. A sample of this alloy weighing 1.50 g was dissolved in acid. All the tin was converted to the +2 oxidation state. Next, it was found that 0.368 g of $Na_2Cr_2O_7$ was required to oxidize the all of the Sn^{2+} ion to the Sn^{4+} state in acidic solution. In the reaction, the chromium was reduced to $Cr^{3+}(Cr_2O_4^{2-})$.

a. Write a balanced net ionic equation for the reaction between the Sn^{2+} and the $Cr_2O_7^{2-}$ in acidic solution.

b. Identify which species is oxidized, and which is reduced.

c. Calculate the number of moles of tin involved in the reaction.

d. Calculate the number of grams of tin that were in the sample of solder.

e. What was the percentage by mass of the tin in the solder?

ANSWERS

True or False Answers

1. **True.** One mole of carbon or oxygen atoms contains 6.02×10^{23} atoms.

2. **False.** One mole of carbon atoms weighs $(1 \text{ mol})(12.01 \text{ g mol}^{-1}) = 12.01$ g. One mole of oxygen atoms weighs $(1 \text{ mol})(16.00 \text{ g mol}^{-1}) = 16.00$ g.

3. **False.** Electrons weigh much less than nuclei, so a mole of ions weighs the same as a mole of atoms.

4. **False.** The molar mass of an element is the number of grams of the element that constitute one mole.

5. **True.**

6. **True.** $56\text{g} / 2(14 \text{ g mol}^{-1}) = 2$ moles

7. **True.** There are 2 moles of chlorine atoms in both 2 moles of NaCl and 1 mole of CH_2Cl_2.

8. **True.** The mass of carbon is always 12 times the mass of hydrogen if carbon and mass are present in a 1:1 molar ratio.

9. **True.**

10. **False.** Two moles of hydroxide ions are consumed per two moles of HCl.

11. **True.**

12. **True.** The molar mass of $Mg(OH)_2$ is $24 \text{ g mol}^{-1} + 2(16 \text{ g mol}^{-1}) + 2(1.0 \text{ g mol}^{-1}) = 58.0 \text{ g mol}^{-1}$. So, 58 g of $Mg(OH)_2$ is 1 mol. From the balanced equation for the reaction, 1 mol of $Mg(OH)_2$ reacts with 2 moles of HCl.

13. **False.** The molar mass of NO_2 is $14 \text{ g mol}^{-1} + 2(16 \text{ g mol}^{-1}) = 46 \text{ g mol}^{-1}$. 30 g of NO_2 is $30 \text{ g} / 46 \text{ g mol}^{-1} = 0.65$ mol. The molar mass of water is $16 \text{ g mol}^{-1} + 2(1.0 \text{ g mol}^{-1}) = 18 \text{ g mol}^{-1}$. 18 g of H_2O is one mole. From the balanced equation, 3 mol NO_2 react with 1 mole of water. So 0.65 mol NO_2 will react with $(0.65 \text{ mol } NO_2)(1 \text{ mol } H_2O) / (3 \text{ mol } NO_2) = 0.22 \text{ mol } H_2O$.

14. **True.** 0.65 mol NO_2 will react with $(0.65 \text{ mol } NO_2)(1 \text{ mol } H_2O) / (3 \text{ mol } NO_2) = 0.22 \text{ mol } H_2O$. 0.22 mol is much less than the 1.0 mol of water which has been included in the reaction. NO_2 is the limiting reagent.

15. **False.** From the equation, you can determine the mole ratio 3 mol NO_2 / 2 mol HNO_3. The amount of HNO_3 produced is $(0.65 \text{ mol } NO_2)(2 \text{ mol } HNO_3) / (3 \text{ mol } NO_2) = 0.43 \text{ mol } HNO_3$.

16. **False.** The molar mass of $HNO_3 = 1.0 \text{ g mol}^{-1} + 14 \text{ g mol}^{-1} + 3(16 \text{ g mol}^{-1}) = 63 \text{ g mol}^{-1}$. The theoretical yield of HNO_3 is 0.43 mol HNO_3 (from the previous question) / 63 g mol^{-1}.

17. **True.** $(15\text{g} / 25\text{g}) \times 100\% = 60\%$

18. **False.** The molar concentration is the number of moles of solute per liter of solution.

19. **True.** 200 ml = 0.2 L. $(5 \text{ M NaCl})(0.2 \text{ L}) = 1 \text{ mol NaCl}$. 1 mol NaCl = 1 mol Na^+ because NaCl completely dissociates in water. When the volume is adjusted to 1 L, the molar concentration of Na^+ ions becomes 1 mol / 1 L = 1 M.

20. **False.** $(2\text{M NaOH})(0.2 \text{ L}) = 0.4 \text{ mol NaOH}$. $(5\text{M HCl})(0.25 \text{ L}) = 1.25 \text{ mol HCl}$. From the equation, one mole of NaOH will completely neutralize one mole of HCl. 0.4 mol NaOH is less than the 1.25 mol required to neutralize 250 mol of 5M HCl.

1. (c)

2. (a)

3. (c) The molar mass of Al is 13 g mol^{-1} and the molar mass of I is 127 g mol^{-1}. The mass of AlI_3 is therefore 13 g mol^{-1} + 3(127 g mol^{-1}).

4. (c) The molar mass of water is 2(1.0 g mol^{-1}) + 16 g mol^{-1} = 18 g mol^{-1}. 54g of water is 54g / 18 g mol^{-1} = 3 moles

5. (d) There are two moles of hydrogen atoms in one mole of water. From the previous question, 54g of water is 3 moles of water. 3 moles of water contains 6 moles of hydrogen.

6. (c) 60 g mol^{-1} = ? x (12 g mol^{-1} + 2(1.0 g mol^{-1}) + 16 g mol^{-1}). = ? x (30 g mol^{-1}). The formula of the acid must be $C_2H_4O_2$. Therefore, 2.5 moles of this acid contains 5 moles of oxygen. The mass of 5 moles of oxygen is 5(16 g mol^{-1}) = 80 g mol^{-1}.

7. (c) There are two moles of nitrogen and one mole of nitrate (NO_3^-) in one mole of ammonium nitrate. In 2.5 moles of ammonium nitrate, there are 5 moles of N and 2.5 moles of NO_3^-.

8. (a) The molar mass of $C_6H_{12}O_6$ is 180 g mol^{-1}. The number of moles of $C_6H_{12}O_6$ is 125.32 g / 180 g mol^{-1}. There are 6 moles of C, or 6 mol (12 g mol^{-1}) = 72g for each mole of $C_6H_{12}O_6$. So the mass of carbon atoms present in the molecule is (125.32g $C_6H_{12}O_6$ x 72g C)/ 180 g mol^{-1} $C_6H_{12}O_6$.

9. (c) The mole ratio 3 mol H_2SO_4 / 2 mol Al can be determined from the equation. The number of moles of sulfuric acid required to dissolve 10 mol Al is $(^3/_2)(10)$ = 15 mol H_2SO_4.

10. (d) The mole ratio 1 mol $Al_2(SO_4)_3$ / 2 mol Al tells us that 15 mol $Al_2(SO_4)_3$ (2 mol Al / 1 mol $Al_2(SO_4)_3$) = 30 mol Al are needed to give 15 moles of aluminum sulfate.

11. (c) 684 g of $Al_2(SO_4)_3$ is 684 g / (2 x 27 g mol^{-1}) + 3 x (32 g mol^{-1}) + 12 x (16 g mol^{-1}) = 2 moles. The amount of Al needed to produce 2 moles of aluminum sulfate is (27 g mol^{-1} Al) (2 mol $Al_2(SO_4)_3$) (2 mol Al / 1 mol $Al_2(SO_4)_3$) = 108g Al.

12. (b) Limiting reagents control the maximum amount of product that can be formed in a chemical reaction. The maximum mass of product that could be obtained from a reaction is the theoretical yield.

13. (a) The mole ratio 2 mol SO_2 / 1 mol O_2 can be determined from the equation. 5 moles of SO_2 will thus react with 2.5 moles of O_2. This is much less than the 10 moles of oxygen included in the reaction, so SO_2 is the limiting reagent.

14. (c) (32g SO_2) / (32 g mol^{-1} + 2 x (16 g mol^{-1})) = 0.5 mol SO_2. (100g O_2) / (2 x (16 g mol^{-1})) = 3 mol O_2. The limiting reagent is therefore SO_2. The molar ratio of SO_2 to SO_3 is 1. So 0.5 moles of SO_2 will react with oxygen to form 0.5 mol SO_3 = (0.5 mol SO_3) (32 g mol^{-1} + 3 x (16 g mol^{-1})) = 40g SO_3.

15. (a) 40g SO_3 / 40g SO_3 x 100% = 100%

16. (a) (3 M Mg^{2+})(5 L) = 15 mol. There is one mole of Mg^{2+} for one mole of $Mg(OH)_2$. The molar mass of $Mg(OH)_2$ is 24 g mol^{-1} + 2 x (16 g mol^{-1}) + 2 x (1 g mol^{-1}) = 58 g mol^{-1}. 15 moles of $Mg(OH)_2$ is 15 mol x 58 g mol^{-1} = 870g.

17. (d) 0.5 mol / 4 M = 8 L.

18. (b) 4 M x 0.125 L = 0.5 mol. 0.5 mol NaCl x (23 g mol^{-1} + 35 g mol^{-1}) = 29g NaCl.

19. (c) (13.5g Al) / (27g mol^{-1}) = 0.5 mol Al. 0.5 mol Al reacts with (0.5 mol Al)(3 mol H_2SO_4 / 2 mol Al) = 0.75 mol H_2SO_4. 0.75 mol / 2 M = 0.375 L H_2SO_4 = 375 mls.

Short Essay Answers

1. Palyotoxin has a molar mass of 3308 g mol^{-1}. Three moles of palyotoxin has a mass of 3 x 3308 = 9924g

2. The amount of sodium in 3kg of water varies between:

$$3(0.6 \text{ mol kg}^{-1}) = 1.8 \text{ mol}$$

and

$$3(0.8 \text{molkg}^{-1}) = 2.4 \text{mol}$$

molar mass of NaCl = 58 g mol^{-1}

mass = number of moles x molar mass

mass (lower limit) = 58 g mol^{-1} x 1.8 = 104.4g

mass (upper limit) = 58 g mol^{-1} x 2.4 = 139.2g

3. a. molar mass of SO_2 = 64 g mol^{-1}

   number of moles of SO_2 = mass of SO_2 / molar mass of SO_2 = 64/156 = 0.41mol

   b. molar mass of CCl_2F_2 = 121 g mol^{-1}

   mass corresponding to 0.41 moles = 0.41 x 121 = 49.6g of freon-12

4. a. 0.1 mole of MnO_4^- is required to react with all $C_2O_4^{2-}$ ions. From the stoichiometry of the equation, this number of moles corresponds to 5/2(0.1mol) = 0.25mol.

   b. We can deduce that calcium and oxalate ions react in a 1:1 ratio to give CaC_2O_4. Therefore, 0.25 moles of CaC_2O_4 were present, derived from 0.25 mole of $CaCl_2$. The molar mass of $CaCl_2$ is 111, and the mass present in the sample is equal to the number of moles of $CaCl_2$ multiplied by the molar mass:

   $$\text{mass} = 0.25 \times 111 = 27.75g$$

   c. 27.75/100 = 27.75%

5. Number of moles of NaOH used = 0.1 x 31.25/1000 = 0.003125 mol

   From the stoichiometry of the reaction we find the number of moles of tripotic acid, X, = 1/3 x 0.003125 = .00104mol.

   This corresponds to 0.2g of X.

   molar mass(X) = mass(X) / moles(X)

   molar mass(X) = .2g / 0.00104mol = 192 g mol^{-1}

6. a. $AgNO_3(aq) + NaCl(aq) \rightarrow AgCl(s) + NaNO_3(aq)$

   b. 143.5g of AgCl corresponds to one mole of AgCl. This resulted from 1 mole of NaCl, according the stoichiometry of the equation in a). 1 mole of NaCl was precipitated from one liter of water, so the concentration of NaCl in the seawater is 1M.

7. **a.** The half equations are:

$$6e + 6H+ + Cr_2O_7^{2-} \rightarrow Cr_2O_4^{2-} + 3H_2O$$

$$3Sn^{2+} + \rightarrow 3Sn^{4+} + 6e$$

Which combine to give:

$$6H^+ + Cr_2O_7^{2-} + 3Sn^{2+} \rightarrow Cr_2O_4^{2-} + 3 Sn^{4+} + 3H_2O$$

b. $Cr_2O_7^{2-}$ is reduced, Sn^{2+} is oxidized.

c. The molar mass of sodium dichromate is 262 g mol^{-1}.

Therefore, the number of moles of dichromate in the reaction is 0.368 g / 262 g mol^{-1} = 0.000468 mol. From the stoichiometry of the reaction, we can deduce that the number of moles of Sn is 3 x 0.000468 = $.001404$ mol.

d. This corresponds to $.001404$ x 119 = 0.17 g

e. 0.17 / 0.368 x 100 = 45%

CHAPTER

THE PROPERTIES
OF GASES

OVERVIEW

In Chapter 1 we defined a gas as a substance that can fill any container, and is easily compressible into a smaller volume. We saw that these properties can be explained by thinking about the molecules that make up the gas. The molecules in a gas are widely separated and move around independently and randomly, colliding with each other and with the walls of their container. When a gas is compressed into a smaller volume, the molecules simply move closer together.

In this chapter we consider experiments that lead to our understanding of how gases repond to changes in conditions. We will look at macroscopic properties of gases, such as pressure, temperature and volume, and find that a remarkable, underlying natural law relates these properties. We will attempt to understand these macroscopic properties, and the relations between them, in terms of the molecular properties of a model or 'ideal' gas. Finally, we will consider how mixtures of gases can be understood.

CONCEPTS

PRESSURE IS DEFINED AS FORCE PER UNIT AREA.

We use the word "pressure" frequently in everyday conversation: we add pressure to the air in our car tires; weather forecasters refer to "high" and "low" pressure; end-of semester exams (especially in chemistry) put a lot of pressure on students. Scientist define the pressure of a gas as the force it exerts on a given area of a surface.

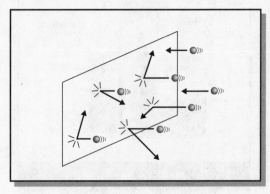

$$\text{Pressure (P)} = \frac{\text{Force (F)}}{\text{Area (A)}}$$

PRESSURE CAN BE EXPLAINED IN TERMS OF MOLECULES.

We can understand differences in pressure by thinking about the molecules that make up a gas. A high gas pressure results from the molecules in a gas bombarding the surface of their container with frequency and vehemence. Low pressure results from less energetic or less frequent collisions with a surface.

THE PRESSURE OF THE ATMOSPHERE IS MEASURED USING A BAROMETER.

The air that we breathe exerts a pressure on our bodies and on everything in the atmosphere. This pressure is called atmospheric pressure. In 1643, Evangelista Torricelli developed the barometer, a device to measure the atmospheric pressure. The barometer consists of an inverted glass tube placed in a dish. Both the tube and the dish are filled with mercury. The mercury in the tube does not drain out into the dish, but instead settles in the tube at the level at which the atmospheric pressure bearing down on the mercury in the dish can support the weight of the mercury in the tube. The height of the mercury in the tube is proportional to the pressure of the atmosphere, and for this reason pressure is sometimes measured in millimeters (mm) of mercury. One mm Hg is also known as 1 torr, in honor of Torricelli, who was a student of the famed astronomer Galileo. The height of mercury in the tube at standard atmospheric pressure is 760 mmHg or 760 torr. (The pressure of the atmosphere is not, however, constant. It is lower at high altitude.)

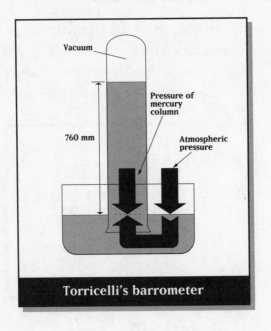

Torricelli's barrometer

 Pressure is measured according to a variety of units. Aside from torr, two other units of pressure are commonly used: the standard-atmosphere and the pascal. However, it is easy to convert between these units given the appropriate conversion factors.

One standard atmosphere (atm) is equivalent to 760 mmHg or 760 torr:

1 atm = 760 mmHg = 760 torr

One standard atmosphere is equal to 101,325 pascals (Pa):

1atm = 101,325Pa   or   101.325 KPa (kilopascals)

Since all of these units are in common use, we need to be able to convert between them. We can use the equations above to derive conversion factors.

For example: How many standard atmospheres are equivalent to 10 torr?

We know that the conversion factor from torr to atm is

[1 atm / 760 torr]

Multiplying this conversion factor by 10 torr, we arrive at the number of atmospheres.

$$10 \text{ torr} \times 1 \text{ atm} / 760 \text{ torr} = 1 / 76 \text{ atm}$$

Notice that we have arrived at the units we are looking for — atm.

You can always check your conversions between pressure scales by showing they result in the right units for your answer.

"Three Law Men" and an Ideal Law: Boyle, Charles and Avagadro

Now we will consider the three empirically-derived gas laws: Boyle's Law, Charles' Law, and Avagadro's Law. These laws can be combined to formulate the ideal gas law.

BOYLE'S LAW RELATES THE PRESSURE AND VOLUME OF A GAS.

The first person to experimentally determine the relationship between the pressure of a gas and its volume was Robert Boyle. Boyle found that the pressure of a gas (P) is inversely proportional to the volume of the gas (V) at a constant temperature (T) and with a constant amount of gas (n = number of moles). In other words:

$P \propto 1 / V$ (P is proportional to 1 / V) or $PV = a$ a = constant when T and n are fixed

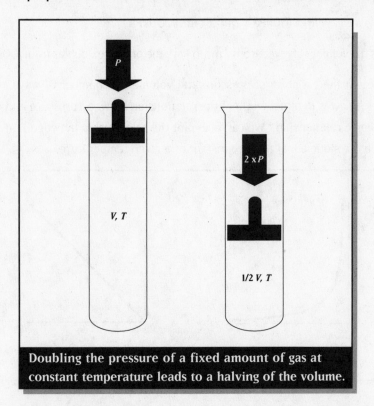

Doubling the pressure of a fixed amount of gas at constant temperature leads to a halving of the volume.

Boyle's Law tells us that if we know the pressure of a gas at a given volume, we can find its pressure at a different volume – and vice-versa. For example, if we represent the initial pressure and volume by P_i and V_i, and the final pressure and volume by P_f and V_f, then we can write:

$$P_i V_i = a$$
$$\text{and}$$
$$P_f V_f = a$$

We can therefore write:

$$P_i V_i = P_f V_f$$
$$\text{and}$$
$$P_f = P_i V_i / V_f$$

Consider this problem: A gas in a large syringe has an initial volume of $2\,m^3$. The pressure of the gas is 100 kPa. The piston in the syringe is pushed down compressing the gas to a volume of $1 m^3$. The temperature is unchanged. What is the pressure of the gas at this new volume?

Initial conditions	Final Conditions
$P_i = 100kPa$	$P_f = ?$
$V_i = 2\,m^3$	$V_f = 1\,m^3$

$$P_f = P_i V_i / V_f$$

Solving for P_f, we have $P_f = 100kPa \times 2\,m^3 / 1\,m^3 = 200kPa$

Notice that as the volume is halved from $2\,m^3$ to $1\,m^3$, the pressure doubles from 100Pa to 200Pa.

We can represent the variation of pressure and volume in a number of ways. One way to visualize Boyle's Law is to plot a graph of the relationship between pressure and volume that shows the inverse relationship. We can also plot the relationship between P and $1/V$, which is linear and has a slope equal to the constant at a given temperature.

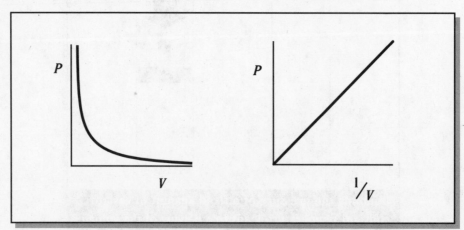

We can explain Boyle's Law based on our understanding of the way molecules, colliding with a surface, create pressure upon a surface.

Imagine a large box filled with gas. The gas will exert a pressure on the walls of the box due to collision of gas molecules with them. Now imagine shrinking the box — decreasing the volume in which the gas is contained. In the smaller box, the molecules that make up the gas are more likely to hit the walls of the box. The gas exerts a greater pressure.

We expect the pressure that a gas exerts to increase as its volume decreases. We expect the pressure that a gas exerts to **decrease** as the volume increases. This is exactly the sort of behavior that Boyle's Law predicts.

CHARLES' LAW RELATES THE VOLUME AND TEMPERATURE OF A GAS.

Charles' Law was formulated in 1787 by Jaques Charles, a French physicist who also made the first solo hot air balloon flight. The law states that for a fixed amount of gas, the volume of the gas is proportional to its temperature at constant pressure.

$$V \; \alpha \; T \qquad or \qquad V \, / \, T = b \qquad b = \text{constant when P and n are fixed}$$

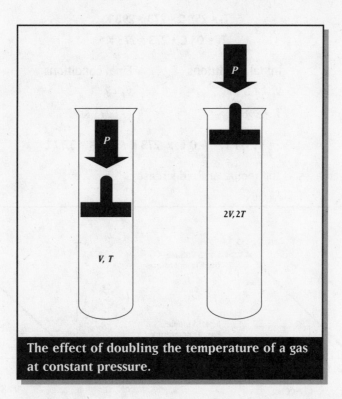

The effect of doubling the temperature of a gas at constant pressure.

Chemists often measure temperature in Kelvin (K). The conversion from Celsius to Kelvin is a simple one: **K = °C + 273**

Charles' Law tells us that if we know the volume of a gas at a given temperature, we can calculate its volume at another temperature – and vice versa – providing the pressure and amount of gas is unchanged. For example, if we label the initial volume and temperature V_i and T_i and the final volume and temperature V_f and T_f, then we can write:

$$V_i / T_i = b$$
$$\text{and}$$
$$V_f / T_f = b$$

Therefore:

$$V_i / T_i = V_f / T_f$$
$$V_f = V_i T_f / T_i$$
$$T_f = T_i V_f / V_i$$

Let's look at an example. In an experiment, 4.0 L of air is collected in a balloon at 25 C°. The balloon is then cooled to 0 C°. The pressure is held constant at 1 atm. What is the volume of the gas at this new temperature?

First, we need to convert the temperatures to the Kelvin scale:

$$T_i = 25° \text{ C} + 273 = 298 \text{ K}$$
$$T_f = 0° \text{ C} + 273 = 273 \text{ K}$$

Initial conditions	Final conditions
V_i = 4.0 L	V_f = ?
T_i = 298 K	T_f = 273 K

$$V_f = V_i T_f / T_i = 4.0 \text{ L} \times 273 \text{ K} / 293 \text{ K} = 3.77 \text{ L}$$

The volume decreases as the temperature decreases.

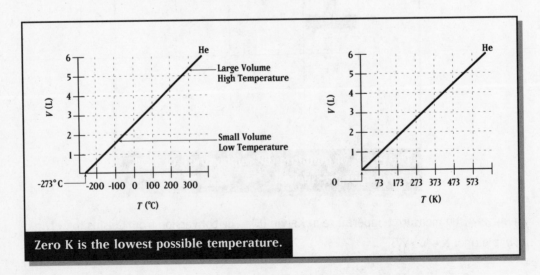

Zero K is the lowest possible temperature.

From a graph plotting the relationship between T/K and V, we expect the temperature of a gas to approach zero Kelvin as the volume shrinks. Since a volume cannot be negative, we deduce that zero Kelvin, known as **absolute zero**, is the coldest possible temperature.

Charles' Law can be explained in terms of the molecules that make up a gas.

Think of the temperature of a gas as the speed of the molecules of which it is composed; high temperatures correspond to high-speed molecules. Increasing the temp-erature of a gas leads to increased molecular speed. Increased speed in the same volume leads to an increase in the frequency with which molecules hit the walls — an increased pressure. Therefore, we expect pressure to increase with a rise in temperature at a given volume. However, we might also expect that the same pressure could be maintained by arranging the faster moving molecules in a larger volume.

AVAGADRO'S LAW RELATES THE AMOUNT OF GAS TO ITS VOLUME.

The final rule we want to consider is Avagadro's Law, named after a 19th century Italian chemist, which asserts that the volume of a gas is proportional to the number of atoms or molecules it contains at a given temperature and pressure. In other words:

$$V \alpha\ n \text{ (V is proportional to n)} \quad \text{or} \quad V / n = \text{constant at fixed T and P}$$

THE IDEAL GAS LAW COMBINES THE LAWS OF BOYLE, CHARLES, AND AVAGADRO.

Avagadro's Law is the final piece of information we need to formulate a general law relating the pressure, volume, temperature, and number of moles of a gas. In fact, we can think of Boyle's, Charles', and Avagadro's laws as merely special cases of this more general ideal gas law. We derive the form of the ideal gas law by combining the simpler laws.

Boyle's	$V = a / P$	(at constant T and n)
Charles'	$V = bT$	(at constant P and n)
Avagadro's	$V = cn$	(at constant T and P)
Ideal	$V = R(Tn / P)$ or $PV = nRT$, $R = 8.3145 \text{ J K}^{-1} \text{mol}^{-1}$	

R is a new constant called the **universal gas constant.** It is universal in the sense that it has the same value for all gases. The ideal gas law relates four properties: pressure, temperature, volume, and number of moles. If we know any three of these, we can find the fourth using this equation. You should commit the ideal gas law to memory.

In this next section we consider how to use the ideal gas law in a number of calculations.

Calculating volume changes with changing pressure:

As a stage prop for the latest Rolling Stones tour, the aging rockers have requested a large neon sign in the shape of a pair of lips. The neon used to fill the lips comes in a 50 liter cylinder at a pressure of 2 atm. Assume the whole cylinder of gas is used to fill the glass lips, the temperature of the gas does not change, and the final pressure of the gas in the lips is 1 atm.

What is the volume of the lips?

Begin by writing down all the values that we know:

Initial conditions	Final Conditions	Unchanging
$V_i = 50L$	$V_f = ?$	$T_i = T_f;\ n_i = n_f$
$P_i = 2$ atm	$P_f = 1$ atm	

The ideal gas law is:

$$PV = nRT$$

For the gas in the cylinder we can write:

$$P_i V_i = n_i RT_i$$

When the gas is transferred to the lips:

$$P_f V_f = n_f RT_f$$

Since all the gas is transferred, n is the same in the lips and in the cylinder. Furthermore, we have been told the temperature does not change ($n_i RT_i = n_f RT_f$). Therefore, we can write:

$$P_i V_i = P_f V_f$$

Dividing both sides by P_f, we arrive at:

$$V_f = P_i V_i / P_f$$

$V_f = 2$ atm $\times$ 50L / 1 atm = 100 L (pretty big lips)

Calculating pressure from volume:

A millionaire who craves publicity is attempting to break the world altitude record for balloon flight. You are a member of the ground crew about to pump the helium gas from a 1000 L cylinder at 5 atm into a balloon capable of holding 5000 L of gas. What is the pressure of the gas when the contents of the cylinder are transferred to the balloon?

Initial conditions	Final conditions	Unchanging
$P_i = 5$ atm	$P_f = ?$	$T_i = T_f; n_i = n_f$
$V_i = 1000$ L	$V_f = 5000$ L	

Using the ideal gas law:

$$PV = nRT$$

As in the example above, we can write:

$$P_iV_i = P_fV_f$$

Dividing each side by V_f, we arrive at:

$$P_f = P_i \, V_i \, / \, V_f$$
$$P_f = 5 \text{ atm} \times 1000 \text{ L} / 5000 \text{ L} = 1 \text{ atm}$$

Calculating volume from temperature:

A sample of gas at 20°C and 1 atm has a volume of 2 L. What volume will the gas occupy after being heated at constant pressure to 40°C?

First, we need to remember to convert the temperature to the Kelvin scale using:

$$\text{Temperature in Kelvin} = °C + 273$$
$$T_i = 20 + 273 = 293 \text{ K}$$
$$T_f = 40 + 273 = 313 \text{ K}$$

Now write down what we know:

Initial conditions	Final conditions	Unchanging
$T_i = 293$ K	$T_f = 313$ K	$P_i = P_f; n_i = n_f$
$V_i = 2$ L	$V_f = ?$	

The ideal gas law:

$$PV = nRT \text{ or } V / T = nRP$$

Or:

$$V_i / T_i = n_i RP_i \text{ and } V_f / T_f = n_f RP_f$$

Since neither the number of moles nor the pressure of the gas change $(n_i RP_i = n_f RP_f)$, we can write:

$$V_i / T_i = V_f / T_f$$

Multiplying each side by T_f gives:

$$V_f = V_i T_f / T_i$$
$$V_f = 2 \text{ L} \times 313 \text{ K} / 293 \text{ K} = 2.14 \text{ L}$$

Calculating changes in volume after changes in both pressure and temperature at constant composition:

A gas in a 0.25 L cylinder is at a 25°C and under a pressure of 5 atm. What volume does the gas occupy when it is transferred to a balloon that is sealed and heated to 50°C at l atm?

Initial conditions	Final conditions	Unchanging
$V_i = 0.25$ L	$V_f = ?$	$n_i = n_f$
$T_i = 25 + 273 = 298$ K	$T_f = 50 + 273 = 323$ K	
$P_i = 5$ atm	$P_f = l$ atm	

The ideal gas law:

$$PV = nRT$$

or:

$$PV / T = nR$$

or:

$$P_i V_i / T_i = n_i R \text{ and } P_f V_f / T_f = n_f R$$

At constant composition $(n_i = n_f)$, then:

$$P_i V_i / T_i = P_f V_f / T_f$$

or:

$$V_f = T_f P_i V_i / P_f T_i$$
$$V_f = (323 \text{ K} \times 5 \text{ atm} \times 0.25 \text{ L}) / (1 \text{ atm} \times 298 \text{ K}) = 1.35 \text{ L}$$

CHAPTER 10: THE PROPERTIES OF GASES

Reacting Gases and Stoichiometry

THE MOLAR VOLUME OF A GAS UNDER STANDARD CONDITIONS IS 22.4 L MOL^{-1}.

The molar volume of a substance (V_m) is the volume occupied per mole of the substance:

$$V_m = V / n$$

But the ideal gas law can be written:

$$V/n = RT / P$$

Therefore:

$$V_m = RT / P$$

For stoichiometric calculations, it is useful to define a standard set of conditions. The set of conditions that have been chosen are called the **standard temperature and pressure (STP)**. STP is defined as 273.15 K and 1 atm. Under these conditions, the molar volume of any gas is given by the ideal gas law:

$$V_m = RT / P = 0.08206 \text{ L atm K}^{-1} \text{ mol}^{-1} \times 273K / 1 \text{ atm} = 22.4 \text{ L}$$

The molar volume of any gas is approximately 22.4 L at STP, so 22.4 L of gas contains approximately 1 mole of an ideal gas. The molar volume is useful for making stoichiometric calculations with gases.

Consider the reaction in which ozone O_3 is produced from oxygen gas O_2. A balanced equation representing this process is:

$$3O_2 (g) \rightarrow 2O_3(g)$$

What volume of ozone can be produced from 1.5 moles of O_2 gas at STP?

Strategy: We need to find out the number of moles of ozone produced and use this to find the corresponding volume.

$$3 \text{ mol } O_2 = 2 \text{ mol } O_3$$
$$1.5 \text{ mol } O_2 \times 2 \text{ mol } O_3 / 3 \text{ mol } O_2 = 1 \text{ mol } O_3$$

the volume (V) of gas produced $= V_m \times n$

$$= 22.4 \text{ L mol}^{-1} \times 1 \text{ mol} = 22.4 \text{ L}$$

Example:

Calcium carbonate decomposes into calcium oxide (quicklime). The process is described by the balanced equation:

$$CaCO_3(s) \rightarrow CaO(s) + CO_2(g)$$

What is the volume of CO_2 produced from the decomposition of 400 g of carbonate at STP?

Strategy: First we need to determine the number of moles of $CaCO_3$, then we need to find the number of moles of carbon dioxide produced; and then we can determine the corresponding volume at STP.

The number of moles of $CaCO_3$ can be found using the equation:

n = mass / molar mass

The mass is 400g , and the molar mass is 100g. There are, therefore, 4 moles of calcium carbonate decomposed – which means that 4 moles of CO_2 are produced. The volume of CO_2 produced at STP is equal to the molar volume times the number of moles of CO_2 produced.

$$V = V_m \times n = 22.4 \text{ L mol}^{-1} \times 4 = 89.6 \text{ L}$$

Mixtures of Gases

Dalton's Law of Partial Pressures describes the behavior of mixtures of ideal gases.

The air that surrounds us is a mixture of gases: oxygen, nitrogen, carbon dioxide, water vapor, and argon. Dalton's law of partial pressures tells us how to treat mixtures of gases mathematically. Before we examine Dalton's law, it is worth considering what we expect the properties of gas mixtures to be. We have seen that the pressure, volume, and temperature of a gas do not depend on its identity. We can conclude that the types of molecules that make up a gas mixture does not determine its properties. It is therefore unimportant if some of the molecules in a gas are different. We expect the mixture to behave as if it was a single, pure gas. We expect the pressure of each individual gas in a mixture of gases to behave as if that gas were alone in the container. Dalton introduced the term **partial pressure** to describe the pressure a gas in a mixture would exert if it were alone in a container. **Dalton's Law of Partial Pressures** states that:

The total pressure of a mixture of gases is the sum of the **partial pressures** (P_a, P_b, P_c) of its components.

We express this mathematically as:

$$P = P_a + P_b + P_c$$

We denote that n moles of gas a (n_a) would have a pressure P_a, if alone in a container. The partial pressure P_a can therefore be calculated, using the ideal gas law in the form:

$$P_a = n_a RT / V$$

Let's look at an example of how to deal with calculations involving mixtures of gases, consider the following problem:

The gas in a scuba diver's tank is a mix of helium and oxygen. A typical tank has a five-liter capacity. If such a tank contains 1.0 mol of O_2 and 0.5 mol helium, what is the partial pressure of each gas, and what is the total pressure of the gas in the cylinder at 20°C?

First, we convert the temperature to Kelvin:

Temperature in Kelvin = °C + 273 = 20 + 273 = 293

The partial pressure of each gas can be found using the ideal gas law. The total pressure is found by adding the two partial pressures. Recall that the partial pressure can be calculated with a form of the ideal gas law:

$$P_a = n_a RT/V$$

For oxygen (O_2), the quantities are:

$$pO_2 = ? \qquad nO_2 = 1.0mol \qquad T = 293K \qquad V = 5L$$
$$R = 0.08206 \text{ L atm K}^{-1} \text{mol}^{-1}$$

$$pO2 = nO_2RT/V$$
$$pO_2 = 1.0 \text{ mol} \times 0.08206 \text{ L atm K}^{-1} \text{mol}^{-1} \times 273 \text{ K} / 5 \text{ L}$$
$$pO_2 = 4.4805 \text{ atm}$$

For helium (He), the quantities are:

$$pHe = ? \qquad nHe = 0.5 \qquad T = 293 \qquad V = 5L$$
$$R = 0.08206 \text{ L atm K}^{-1} \text{mol}^{-1}$$

$$pHe = 0.5 \text{ mol} \times 0.08206 \text{ L atm K}^{-1} \text{mol}^{-1} \times 293 \text{ K} / 5 \text{ L}$$
$$pHe = 2.4043 \text{ atm}$$

We calculate the total pressure by adding the partial pressures.

$$P \text{ (total)} = pO_2 + pHe = 6.8848 \text{ atm}$$

KEY TERMS

Avagadro's Law: The volume of gas is proportional to the amount of gas.

Boyle's Law: The pressure of a gas at a constant temperature and composition is inversely proportional to its volume.

Charles' Law: The volume of a gas is proportional to its temperature, given a constant pressure and composition.

Dalton's law of partial pressures: The pressure of a mixture of ideal gases is the sum of the partial pressures of the individual gases in the mixture.

gas constant: The gas constant is represented by R in the ideal gas law. R has the same value for all gases.

ideal gas law: $PV = nRT$

molar volume: The volume occupied by one mole of a substance. The molar volume of an ideal gas is 22.4 L mol^{-1}.

partial pressure: The pressure exerted by one gas in a mixture of ideal gases. The partial pressure is the pressure that the gas would exert were it alone in the container.

pascal (Pa): A unit of pressure. 1 atm = 101,325 Pa = 760 mm Hg = 760 torr

pressure: The average force per unit area exerted upon a surface.

torr: A unit of pressure. 760 torr = 760 mm Hg = 1 atm = 101,325Pa

THRILLS, CHILLS AND DRILLS

True or False

1. The pressure of a gas is defined as the average force per unit area exerted by the gas.

2. According to Boyle's Law a graph plotting P versus T would be linear.

3. Boyle's Law states that P / T is constant for a given amount of gas in a sealed container.

4. A consequence the ideal gas law is that 1 mole of gas molecules will always fill the same volume under standard conditions.

5. Charles' Law states that the volume of a fixed mass of gas is directly proportional to the pressure — provided that temperature is kept constant.

6. A graph plotting V versus T is linear, in accordance with Charles' Law.

7. Charles' Law suggests that at zero Kelvin, the volume of a gas would go to infinity.

8. Temperature in Kelvin = °C + 273

9. Assuming that gas molecules are, on average, equally distributed in space, the average distance between H_2 molecules in a lab (at 1 atm) is greater than in outer space (at 10^{-21} atm).

10. The volume of a mole of H_2 and F_2 gas under identical conditions is the same.

11. Air is a mixture of gases, therefore 22.4 L of air at STP will contain 1 mole of oxygen gas.

12. The behavior of an ideal gas can be completely described by knowledge of its volume, pressure, and temperature.

13. A decrease in the temperature of a sample of gas can always be expected to lead to decrease in both the pressure and the volume of the sample.

14. The partial pressure of an ideal gas in a mixture is different from the pressure the gas would exert if alone in the container.

15. The oxidation of carbon to carbon dioxide and carbon monoxide yields a lower mass than the starting materials carbon and oxygen.

16. The ideal gas law predicts that an increase in the pressure of a system will results in a proportional increase in the average velocity of the gas molecules.

17. The temperature of a gas is a measure of the average speed of the molecules present in the gas.

18. Slower moving gas molecules exert a greater pressure than fast moving ones.

19. R, the gas constant, is different for different gases.

20. At STP, the volume of CO_2 produced when one mole of $CaCO_3$ decomposes completely is unknowable.

Multiple Choice

1. According to Boyle's Law, a graph plotting P against V
   a) is linear
   b) shows inverse proportion
   c) is parabolic
   d) is quadratic
   e) is symmetrical

2. Charles' Law relates
   a) P and T
   b) P and V
   c) n and T
   d) V and T

3. Ordinary high-performance auto engines have "compression ratios" of about 8. This means that the pressure on the gasoline-air mixture in the top of the cylinder is approximately 8 atm. If, through combustion, the temperature of the mixture rises from 20°C to 700°C, what will the final pressure be?
   a) 10 atm
   b) 15 atm
   c) 19 atm
   d) 27 atm
   e) 30 atm

4. Venus, known as the cloudy planet, has an atmosphere of carbon dioxide. Given that the surface temperature is 470°C and the pressure is 1 atm, what is the molar volume of CO_2 in the lower Venusian atmosphere, measured in m^3?

   a) R x 470 / 1

   b) R x (470+273) / 1

   c) R x (1) / 470

   d) R x (470+273) / 101325

5. A syringe on the planet Mercury is filled with H_2 gas. During the day, the temperature on the planet is 350°C, and the volume of the gas is 2 m^3. At night, the temperature on the planet drops to -170°C. Assuming H_2 is still a gas at this low temperature, and that the pressure on Mercury does not vary, what is the volume of the gas at night?

   a) 2 x 170 / 350

   b) 2 x 350 / 170

   c) 2 x (-170 + 273) / (350 + 273)

   d) (-170 + 273) / (350 + 273)

   e) (350+ 273) / (170 + 273)

6. Ozone (O_3) decomposes at 100°C to yield pure oxygen. Pure ozone is sealed in a bottle at 760 mmHg and 0°C and then heated to 100°C. What is the final pressure of the container ?

   a) (373 x 3 x 760) / (273 x 2)

   b) (273 x 3 x 760) / (273 x 2)

   c) 0

   d) (273 x 3) / (760 x 273 x 2)

   e) (373 x 3) / (760 x 373 x 2)

7. What is the volume occupied by 3 moles of gas at STP?

   a) 22.4 L

   b) 7.47 L

   c) 44.8 L

   d) 67.2 L

8. O_2 at a pressure of 1 atm in a 1 L cylinder is added to a 1 L cylinder container of He at a pressure of 2 atm. What is the pressure of the mixture of gases?

   a) 4 atm

   b) 1 atm

   c) ½ atm

   d) 3 atm

   e) 2 atm

9. When a gas is collected over water, the pressure exerted due to water vapor is an important consideration. A 350 mL sample of gas is collected over water at 40 degrees Celsius and a barometric pressure of 756.7 torr. What is the pressure due to the dry gas at that temperature given that the vapor pressure of pure water vapor at 40 degrees Celsius is 55.3 torr?

   a) 602 torr

   b) 701 torr

   c) 802 torr

   d) 901 torr

10. 1 atm corresponds to 101325 P_a and 760 torr. How many Pascals are equal to 1520 torr?

   a) ½ (101325)

   b) 2 (101325)

   c) 101325

   d) 1

   e) 2 (760)

11. A certain gas is being released from the tailpipe of your automobile. A sample takes up 3.187 liters at 478 Kelvin and a pressure of 758.2 mm Hg. The sample also has a mass of 2.24 g. Identify the gas.

   a) CO, carbon monoxide

   b) CO_2, carbon dioxide

   c) NH_3, ammonia

   d) O_2, oxygen

12. One way of forming carbon dioxide is through the decomposition of ammonium carbonate [$(NH_4)_2CO_3(s)$] to $CO_2(g)$ + $2NH_3(g)$ + $H_2O(l)$. If collected at STP, what volume of carbon dioxide can be formed from 1.7 g of ammonium carbonate?

   a) 0.20 L

   b) 0.40 L

   c) 1.20 L

   d) 1.60 L

13. The ideal gas law is an approximation. It relies on the fact that gas molecules generally do not interact. In order to interact, molecules must come close together. In light of this we expect the ideal gas law to be a better approximation at

   a) high P, small V

   b) low P, large V

   c) low T, small V

   d) all the above

   e) none of the above

14. How can you explain the pressure of a gas in terms of the activity of its molecules?

   a) Molecules in a gas line up and all fire themselves at a surface simultaneously.

   b) Molecules in a gas move around randomly, occasionally colliding with the surface and exerting a pressure on it.

   c) The pressure cannot be explained.

   d) The cosmic ether that pervades all things is responsible.

   e) None of the above.

15. At high temperatures molecules move

   a) more slowly

   b) more quickly

   c) at the same speed as at lower temperatures

   d) not at all

   e) none of the above

16. Avagadro's Law states which of the following?

   a) V is proportional to n.

   b) V is proportional to T.

   c) V is proportional to P.

   d) I think therefore I am.

Short Essays

1. Given that a 4.5 g sample of gas at 0°C and 1 atm occupies 5.6 L, guess the identity of the gas. Furthermore, what mass of gas would be required to fill a 7.0 L balloon at 3 atm and 15°C?

2. The human lung has an average temperature of 37°C. If one inhales Alaskan air at 1 atm and -20°C, to what pressure will the air in the lungs rise? If the human lung bursts at 2 atm, will the lungs be safe on an Alaskan expedition?

3. A 6 gsample of impure graphite (a form of carbon) is taken from pencil lead. Upon combustion, 7.05 L of CO_2 is measured at 740 mm Hg and 20°C. How pure is the sample (as a percent yield of purity)?

4. Use your knowledge of the ideal gas law to explain why, on the absolute temperature scale, the zero value was set at -273°C, rather than at a more convenient value (such as -300°C).

ANSWERS

1. **True.**

2. **False.** According to Boyle's Law, a graph of P vs. 1/V is linear.

3. **False.** Boyle's Law says that the product PV is constant for a given amount of gas in a sealed container.

4. **True.** At STP, a mole of gas will always fill a volume of 22.4 liters.

5. **False.** Charles' Law states that the volume of a fixed mass of gas is directly proportional to the temperature provided that volume is kept constant.

6. **True.**

7. **False.** According to Charles' Law, a graph of V vs. T is linear, which suggests that at zero Kelvin the volume of a gas would go to zero.

8. **True.**

9. **False.** The pressure in outer space is much lower than the pressure in the lab. Boyle's Law states that the volume of a gas is inversely proportional to the pressure of a gas. Thus, according to Boyle's Law, the volume of a fixed amount of gas is larger at a low pressure (i.e., in space) than at a higher pressure (i.e., in lab). So the distance between molecules will be greater in space than in the lab.

10. **True.** The volume of a mole of H_2 or F_2 gas, under identical conditions, is 22.4 liters.

11. **False.** 22.4 L of air at STP will contain 1 mol of all gases combined. Since air is a mixture of gases, 22.4 L of air will contain less than 1 mol of oxygen gas.

12. **True.** The ideal gas law is $PV = nRT$. Thus, if you know its volume, pressure and temperature, you can determine the amount of gas present, and fully describe the gas.

13. **False.** $PV = nRT$. If the temperature of a gas is decreased, the product PV must decrease. This can occur in three ways: the pressure can decrease and the volume can remain constant, the pressure can remain constant and the volume can decrease, or both the pressure and volume can decrease.

14. **False.** The partial pressure of an ideal gas in a mixture is equal to the pressure the gas would exert if alone in the container.

15. **False.** According to conservation of mass, the mass of the starting materials will be the same as the mass of the products.

16. **True.** $PV = nRT$. An increase in the pressure of an ideal gas, at a constant volume, will result in an increase in the temperature of the gas. At a higher temperature, the average speed of the molecules in the gas will be higher.

17. **True.**

18. **False.** At a constant volume, fast moving gas molecules exert a greater pressure than slower moving ones because they collide with the walls more frequently.

19. **False.** The gas constant R is the same for different gases.

20. **False.** You can write down the balanced chemical equation:

$$CaCO_3 \rightarrow CaO + CO_2$$

From this equation, it is possible to determine that one mole of CO_2 results from the decomposition of one mole of $CaCO_3$. One mole of gas at STP occupies a volume of 22.4 L.

Multiple Choice Answers

1. (b) The volume of an ideal gas is inversely proportional to the pressure of the gas, according to Boyle's Law.

2. (d) Charles' Law states that the volume of an ideal gas is proportional to its temperature.

3. (d) Temperature in Kelvin = °C +273. So, T_i = 20°C + 273 = 293 K and T_f = 700°C + 273 = 973 K. $P_i / T_i = P_f / T_f$. Therefore, P_f = (8 atm)(973 K) / (293 K) = 27 atm.

4. (d) T = 470 + 273. PV = nRT. V/n = RT/P = R x (470 + 273) / 1 atm x 101325 Pa/atm.

5. (c) $V_i / T_i = V_f / T_f$. T_i = 350/°C + 273 and T_f = -170/°C + 273. V_f = 2 m^3 x (-170 + 273) / (350 + 273).

6. (a) The balanced equation for this reaction is 2 O_3 → 3 O_2. $P_i / n_i T_i = P_f / n_f T_f$. 0 degrees C = 273 K, and 100 degrees C = 373 K. P_f = (760 mm Hg)(3 mol)(373 K) / (2 mol)(273 K).

7. (d) 1 mol of an ideal gas takes up 22.4 L at STP. 3 moles therefore occupies 3(22.4 L) = 67.2 L.

8. (d) The pressure of a mixture of gases is the sum of the partial pressures of each gas. pO_2 = 1 atm and pHe = 2 atm. The pressure of the mixture of the gases is therefore 3 atm.

9. (b) P = pH_2O + p(dry gas). p(dry gas) = 756.7 torr - 55.3 torr = 701 torr.

10. (b) ? Pa = (1520 torr)(1 atm/760 torr)(101325 Pa / 1 atm) = 2(101325).

11. (a) PV = nRT. n = PV/RT. n = (758.2 mm Hg)(1 atm/760 mm Hg)(3.187 L) / (0.08206 L atm mol^{-1} K^{-1})(478 K) = 0.081 mol. Molar mass of the gas = (2.24 g) / (0.081 mol) = 28 g mol^{-1}. The molar mass of CO is 12 g mol^{-1} + 16 g mol^{-1} = 28 g mol^{-1}.

12. (b) PV = nRT. 1.7 g of ammonium carbonate is 1.7 g / 96 g mol^{-1} = 0.018 mol. One mole of carbon dioxide is produced from one mole of ammonium carbonate. Therefore, V = nRT/P = (0.018 mol)(0.08206 L atm mol^{-1} K^{-1})(273 K) / (1 atm) = 0.40 L ammonium carbonate.

13. (b) Molecules would not interact at a low P and large V because they would be very far apart.

14. (b) Pressure results from the molecules in a gas moving around randomly and occasionally bombarding the surface of their container.

15. (b)

16. (a) Avagadro's Law states that the volume of a gas is proportional to the number of atoms or molecules it contains at a given temperature and pressure

17. (a) He is a noble gas so it will not form molecules. He atoms are constantly moving around randomly.

Short Essay Answers

1. Temperature in Kelvin = °C + 273 = 0 + 273 = 273

   (1 atm)(5.6 L) = (4.5 g / x g mol^{-1})(0.08206 L atm mol^{-1} K^{-1})(273 K)

   where x is the molecular weight of the unknown gas.

   So, x = (4.5 g)(0.08206 L atm mol^{-1} K^{-1})(273 K) / (1 atm)(5.6 L)

   = 18.0 g mol^{-1}.

   The gas is likely to be water vapor.

   Temperature in Kelvin = °C + 273 = 15 + 273 = 288

   (1 atm)(5.6 L) / (4.5 g)(273 K) = (3 atm)(7.0 L) / (x g)(288 K)

   where x is the mass of gas.

   x = (3 atm)(7.0 L)(4.5 g)(273 K) / (1 atm)(5.6 L)(288 K)

   = 16 g.

2. T_1 (in Kelvin) = °C + 273 = -20 + 273 = 253.

   T_2 (in Kelvin) = °C + 273 = 37 + 273 = 310.

   $P_2 = P_1 T_2 / T_1$ = (1 atm)(310 K) / (253 K) = 1.23 atm

   Yes, the lungs will be safe on an Alaskan expedition.

3. $C + O_2 \rightarrow CO_2$

   740 mm Hg = (740 mm Hg)(1 atm / 760 mm Hg) = 0.97 atm

   Temperature in Kelvin = °C + 273 = 20 + 273 = 293

   (0.97 atm)(7.05 L) = (x mol CO_2)(0.08206 L atm mol^{-1} K^{-1})(293 K)

   where x is the moles of CO_2.

   x = (0.97 atm)(7.05 L) / (0.08206 L atm mol^{-1} K^{-1})(293 K)

   = 0.29 mol CO_2

   There is one mole of C for every one mole of CO_2, according to the balanced equation above.

   0.29 mol C = x g / 12.0 g mol^{-1}

   where x is the mass of C converted to CO_2 upon combustion.

   x = 3.48 g C

   % purity = (3.48 g C / 6.0 g C) x 100% = 58%

4. The ideal gas Law states that PV = nRT. At constant pressure and amount of gas (n), V = c T , where c is a constant (Charles' Law). Therefore, a graph plotting V against T is linear, and it shows that when V = 0, T = 273°C. Since the molecules in a gas occupy a definite volume, a sample of gas cannot have a negative volume. The temperature of 273°C is the smallest possible temperature, because it corresponds to the smallest sensible value for the volume of matter.

CHAPTER

CONDENSED STATES OF MATTER: SOLIDS AND LIQUIDS

11

OVERVIEW

Why do pipes burst in winter? Why does water boil at 100°C? Why is salt a solid? The answers to these, and many other questions can be found in this chapter.

This chapter looks at solids and liquids — which are collectively known as the condensed states of matter. For condensed phases, the forces between molecules are important (in contrast to the forces between molecules in a gas). We will describe the forces that bind atoms and molecules together in condensed states and the signs of interaction. It is important to understand these forces because they are invoked in the explanation of many of the properties of condensed matter.

We will examine the ionic and intermolecular forces that hold condensed phases together. For liquids, we will learn the signs that indicate the strength of intermolecular forces: the boiling point of a liquid and its vapor pressure. For solids, we will learn to describe the ionic, covalent and network solids that can be formed.

CONCEPTS

THE ATOMS, IONS, OR MOLECULES IN A SOLID OR A LIQUID ARE CLOSE TO THEIR NEIGHBORS.

Gases fill their container, and are easily compressible. The particles that form a gas are relatively far apart and fly about the container with few forces holding them together.

A solid, in contrast to a gas, is not compressible and maintains its shape regardless of the container it occupies. In general a solid consists of closely-packed, well-ordered particles.

Liquids are in between solids and gases, but resemble solids more than gases. A liquid consists of particles that are more disordered and not quite as tightly-packed as the particles in a solid. However, the particles in a liquid are much closer together than those in a gas. Solids and liquids are referred to collectively as the **condensed** phases.

Intermolecular and Interionic Forces

INTERMOLECULAR FORCES AND INTERACTIONS AMONG IONS HOLD CONDENSED PHASES TOGETHER.

For particles to pack closely against one another in a condensed phase, the particles must be bound by forces of attraction. Ionic solids are held together by ionic bonds between oppositely-charged ions. Condensed phases composed of molecules are held together by forces between the molecules, known as intermolecular forces.

ION-ION INTERACTIONS HOLD IONIC SOLIDS TOGETHER. THE INTERACTIONS ARE STRONG AND ACT OVER A LARGE DISTANCE.

Ionic solids are held together by the attraction of oppositely-charged ions to one another. These attractive forces have a long range of influence, so ions not only attract their nearest neighbor, but also oppositely-charged ions further away. The strong attraction between ions in an ionic solid is responsible for the high melting points of such solids (to melt a solid we must break down the attractive forces between the particles of which it is composed. The stronger the forces the higher the melting temperature). This attraction is strongest for small, highly charged ions. MgO and Al_2O_3, which are made up of small highly charged ions, melt at 2015°C and 2800°C, respectively.

ION-DIPOLE INTERACTIONS RESULT FROM IONS INTERACTING WITH ONE END OF THE ELECTRIC DIPOLE OF A NEUTRAL MOLECULE.

Though ionic solids are held together by strong forces, many readily dissolve in water to produce their constitutive ions. Sodium chloride, for example, dissolves in water to form Na^+ ions and Cl^- ions. One reason salts are soluble is that water molecules have an electric dipole: one end of a water molecule is negative while the other is positive. The oxygen atom in water has a partial negative charge, while the hydrogen atoms have partial positive charges. The partial negative charge on the oxygen atom of water is attracted to the positive charge of the cation (Na^+), and an ion-dipole interaction is established, helping the salt to dissolve.

In general, an ion-dipole interaction may result from (1) the attraction between either a cation and the negative end of an electric dipole, or (2) an anion and the positive end of an electric dipole.

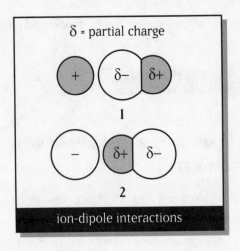

ion-dipole interactions

HYDRATES OF SALTS CAN BE EXPLAINED BY THE STRENGTH OF ION-DIPOLE INTERACTIONS.

When some salts crystallize from aqueous solution, they take a few water molecules with them. Salts that have associated water molecules are known as **hydrates.** Copper sulfate, for example, crystallizes with five molecules of water for every one of copper sulfate. The hydrate is denoted as: $CuSO_4 \cdot 5H_2O$.

The hydration of salts can be explained by the persistence of ion-dipole interactions between cations and water molecules in the solid. The strength of ion-dipole interactions increases with decreasing cation size. For example, lithium (the smallest member of Group

I in the periodic table) forms a number of hydrated salts. On the other hand, the heavier metals of Group I rarely form hydrated salts.

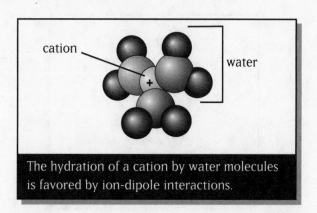

cation

water

The hydration of a cation by water molecules is favored by ion-dipole interactions.

 MOST CLOSED-SHELL NEUTRAL MOLECULES OR ATOMS ARE HELD TOGETHER BY A COLLECTION OF NON-IONIC FORCES THAT ARE COLLECTIVELY KNOWN AS INTERMOLECULAR FORCES.

There are a number of intermolecular forces: dipole-dipole interactions, London dispersion forces, and hydrogen bonds. We will consider the origin of each type of force below.

 POLAR MOLECULES HAVE ASSOCIATED ELECTRIC DIPOLES.

Recall from Chapter 5 that the bonds between atoms with intermediate differences in electronegativity are described as polar. One element (the less electronegative one) in a polar bond has a slight, or "partial" positive charge. The other (more electronegative) element has a "partial" negative charge.

For example, in the polar molecule HCl, the H atom has a partial positive charge, while the Cl atom has a partial negative (represented -ve) charge. Using δ +/- to denote "partial" positive or negative charges we can write:

$$\delta^+ H \text{——} Cl \, \delta^-$$

A dipole exists in any object that has one positive and one negative end. Polar bonds such as the bond in HCl have an associated electrid dipole moment, or dipole.

Dipoles are often represented by an arrow. The tail of the arrow indicates the center of positive charge; the head of the arrow indicates the center of the negative (-ve) charge. For HCl, we write:

$$\delta^+ H \xrightarrow{} Cl \, \delta^-$$

Whole molecules can have associated dipoles. For example, water molecules have a dipole, as shown in the figure below.

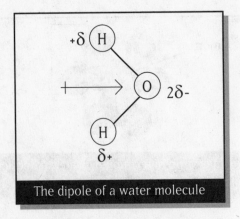

The dipole of a water molecule

DIPOLE-DIPOLE INTERACTIONS DESCRIBE THE INTERACTIONS BETWEEN THE ELECTRIC DIPOLES OF POLAR MOLECULES.

Recall that bonds between atoms can have an associated electric dipole. Whole molecules can also have associated electric dipoles. This phenomena is most obvious when the molecule consists of two atoms with a polar bond between them. Examples of such molecules include HCl, HF, and HI.

In the condensed phases of substances made up of polar compounds, such as HCl, the dipoles on the molecules may line up so that there is an attraction between the positive end of a dipole on one molecule and the negative end of the dipole on a neighboring molecule. Two such arrangements are illustrated in the figure below. Dipole-dipole interactions are weaker than ion-ion interactions since they result from the attraction of the **partial** charges of dipoles, as opposed to the **full** charges of ions.

Two arrangements showing how the electric dipoles of molecules can form attractive interactions between their positive and negative ends. Arrows represent electric dipoles.

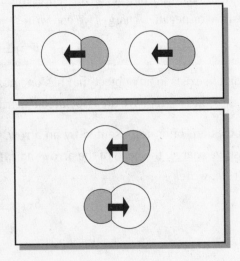

LONDON DISPERSION FORCES HOLD NON-POLAR MOLECULES TOGETHER IN CONDENSED PHASES.

Noble gas atoms are known to form liquids and solids at low temperatures. Dipole-dipole interactions cannot account for the attraction between the monatomic noble gas atoms because isolated atoms cannot have permanent dipoles. So some other attractive force must be holding noble gas atoms together in the condensed phase. The force responsible is known as the London dispersion force.

THE FIRST STEP IN UNDERSTANDING LONDON DISPERSION FORCES IS REALIZING THAT NON-POLAR MOLECULES MAY HAVE INSTANTANEOUS DIPOLES.

In non-polar molecules, the electrons associated with the atom or molecule are, on average, evenly distributed. However, at any instant, there may be more electrons on one side of an atom or molecule than on the other side.

WE CAN UNDERSTAND LONDON DISPERSION FORCES IN TERMS OF THE INTERACTION BETWEEN INSTANTANEOUS DIPOLES.

Consider two neighboring molecules, molecule 1 and molecule 2. At any instant there may be a dipole on molecule 1. Molecule 2 will tend to respond to the complementary dipole so that when an instantaneous partial positive charge occurs on molecule 1, the part of molecule 2 nearest to molecule 1 will gain a partial negative charge. The interaction of these two instantaneous dipoles leads to an attractive force between molecules 1 and 2. These interactions are called London dipersion forces.

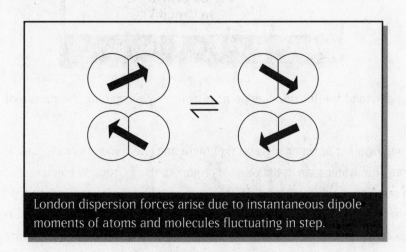

London dispersion forces arise due to instantaneous dipole moments of atoms and molecules fluctuating in step.

While London dispersion forces occur for all molecules, they are the dominant intermolecular force for non-polar molecules. London dispersion forces are stronger for larger atoms or molecules, because larger molecules have more electrons and can therefore achieve larger instantaneous dipoles, which lead to stronger London dispersion forces. Since London dispersion forces fall off rapidly with distance, molecules need to be close to one another to feel their effect.

Hydrogen bonding accounts for the high boiling point of water.

When we look at the boiling points of the hydrogen compounds in Group VI, it is apparent that water has an unusually high boiling point. While H_2S boils at -60°C, water (H_2O) boils at a steamy +100°C. (Similarly, we find high boiling points for NH_3 in the Group V H_3 compounds and for HF in the Group VII H compounds.)

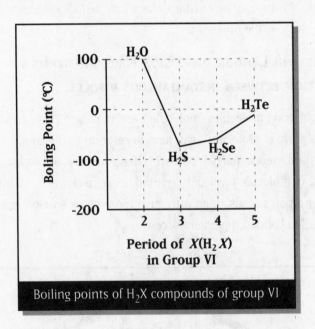

Boiling points of H_2X compounds of group VI

We can understand the high boiling point of water by examining the nature of hydrogen bonds.

The high boiling point of water suggests that there must be some intermolecular force that is much stronger in water than in the other H_2 compounds of Group VI elements. This force is hydrogen bonding. Hydrogen bonding occurs when a hydrogen atom is bonded to a highly electronegative atom. The hydrogen atom has a large partial positive charge and can form a strong dipole-dipole interaction with the electronegative atom on a neighboring molecule. Hydrogen bonds are represented by a dotted line.

The Liquid State

A commuter on a busy New York subway can move past other passengers, but cannot escape their proximity. In the same way, molecules in a liquid can move past each other, but cannot escape completely from their neighbors. The stronger the forces between molecules in a liquid, the higher the boiling point of the liquid and the lower its vapor pressure.

EVAPORATION OF A LIQUID RESULTS FROM MOLECULES ESCAPING THE LIQUID SURFACE TO FORM THE GAS PHASE. EVAPORATION DECREASES THE VOLUME OF A LIQUID.

When we place a liquid sample in a closed container, the amount of liquid initially decreases. This decrease in liquid volume occurs because some of the molecules on the surface can escape the intermolecular forces in the liquid and form the gas or vapor phase. This process is known as **evaporation** of the liquid.

CONDENSATION OCCURS WHEN MOLECULES FORM A LIQUID FROM THE GASEOUS STATE. CONDENSATION INCREASES THE VOLUME OF A LIQUID.

As the number of molecules in the vapor phase increases it becomes more likely that some of them will return to the liquid phase. This process is known as **condensation** of the vapor phase.

A DYNAMIC EQUILIBRIUM BETWEEN EVAPORATION AND CONDENSATION IS ESTABLISHED FOR A LIQUID IN A CLOSED CONTAINER.

At some point, the volume of the liquid stops decreasing. At this point, the same number of molecules are leaving the liquid surface as are rejoining the liquid; the rate of evaporation and the rate of condensation are equal. Chemists say the system has now reached equilibrium. Equilibrium is not static; both evaporation and condensation are still occurring. The equilibrium is described as a **dynamic equilibrium**.

THE VAPOR PRESSURE IS THE PRESSURE EXERTED BY A VAPOR ABOVE A LIQUID AT EQUILIBRIUM.

The pressure exerted by the gas above a liquid at equilibrium is known as the **vapor pressure** of the liquid. The vapor pressure of a liquid is defined as the pressure of a liquid due to its vapor, when the two phases are in dynamic equilibrium.

The vapor pressure of a liquid correlates to the strength of intermolecular forces in the liquid.

The lower the vapor pressure, the stronger the intermolecular forces in the liquid. For example, water, which has strong intramolecular hydrogen bonds, has a low vapor pressure. In contrast, liquid chloroform, which is held together by London dispersion forces (weaker than hydrogen bonds) has a high vapor pressure.

Solids

Solids are generally categorized into three types: ionic solids, molecular solids, and molecular networks. As we will see the properties of solids are determined in large part by the type of bonding used. Solids held together by strong intermolecular forces have high melting points; melting points can be used to gauge the strengths of bonding forces.

Ionic solids are held together by strong ionic bonds.

Ionic solids are held together by strong ion-ion attraction forces. They have high melting points and are very stable. The structure of an ionic solid is best described by thinking of the ions as spheres packed together in a way that minimizes the space between them. This arrangement also maximizes the number of cations surrounding an anion, or the number of anions surrounding a cation. For example, in NaCl the chlorine ions pack closely together and the smaller sodium ions fit into the holes between the chlorine atoms.

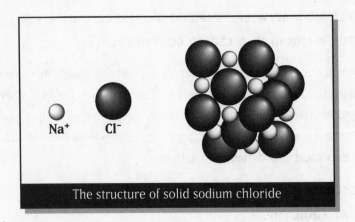

The structure of solid sodium chloride

Molecular solids are composed of molecules (as opposed to ions). They are held together by intermolecular forces.

There are several types of molecular solids, and this variety reflects the diversity of intermolecular forces. Molecular solids, in contrast to ionic solids, melt at low temperatures, since intermolecular forces are generally weaker than ionic forces. Common examples of molecular solids include white phosphorus (P_4) and ice (H_2O).

In white phosphorous, the non-polar P_4 units are held together by London dispersion forces. Recall that only London dispersion forces can hold together non-polar molecules. A section of the P_4 structure is represented below. Notice that the distance between phosphorus atoms in the same molecule is much shorter than the distance between P_4 molecules. This is because phosphorus atoms within a molecule are held together by covalent bonds, whereas P_4 molecules are held together by much weaker London dispersion forces.

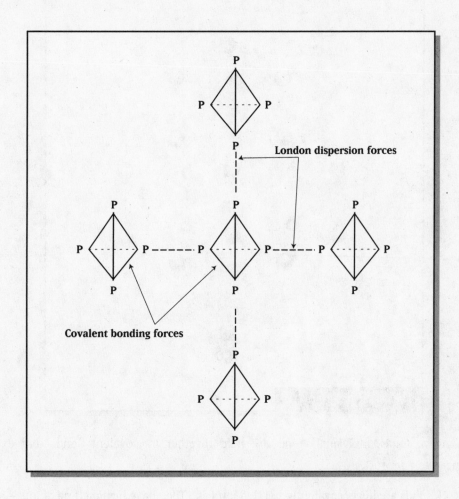

In ice, the H_2O molecules are held together by hydrogen bonds. Each water molecule forms four hydrogen bonds. Two hydrogen bonds are formed between a molecule's hydrogen atoms and the oxygen atoms of a neighboring molecule. Another two hydrogen bonds are formed between a molecule's oxygen atom and the hydrogen atoms of a neighboring water molecule. Water forms an open network of hydrogen bonds in the solid state. In liquid water, a number of hydrogen bonds collapse. Water molecules in the liquid are less ordered than in the solid, but more tightly packed. In fact, water is unique in that the solid (ice) is less dense than the liquid. For other substances, the reverse is true. For example, solid carbon dioxide, "dry ice," has a higher density than liquid carbon dioxide.

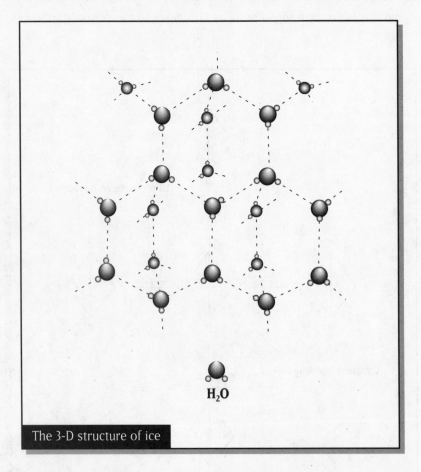

H_2O

The 3-D structure of ice

In network solids, individual atoms are held together by covalent bonds that extend throughout a network.

Network solids are huge, covalently-bonded lattices. They have high melting points – since to melt a network solid we must break all the covalent bonds in the network. In general, network solids are rigid and hard.

Diamond, a form of carbon, is an example of a network solid. In a sample of diamond, each carbon atom is connected to four other carbon atoms, forming a tetrahedron. Diamonds melt only at very high temperatures and are very hard.

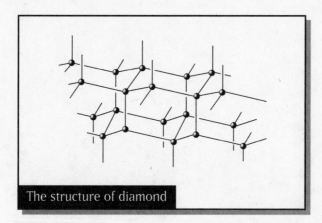

The structure of diamond

Forms of the same element, which differ in the way their atoms are linked, are known as allotropes. Diamond is one allotrope of carbon; another allotrope of carbon is known as graphite.

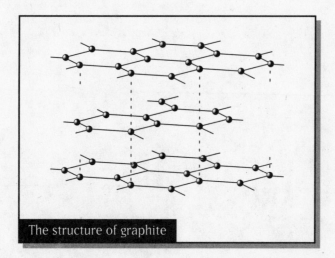

The structure of graphite

Graphite, like diamond, is a network solid. Unlike diamond, graphite is composed of sheets of carbon atoms. The atoms in a sheet are covalently bonded in a hexagonal network resembling chicken wire. In this arrangement, sheets lie on top of one another, and the covalent bonds between the sheets are weak. Therefore, the sheets can move over each other relatively freely.

KEY TERMS

allotropes: Forms of an element that differ in the way their of atoms are linked.

condensation: The process by which gas becomes liquid.

dipole-dipole interactions: An intermolecular force that binds molecules with permanent electric dipoles.

dipole moment: A property of a bond or molecule that can be represented by a line connecting a center of positive charge and a center of negative charge.

dynamic equilibrium: When two opposing processes occur at exactly the same rate, the processes are said to be in dynamic equilibrium.

evaporation: The process by which liquid becomes gas.

hydrogen bonding: A type of intermolecular force between a hydrogen atom and a strongly electronegative atom, such as nitrogen, fluorine, or oxygen.

intermolecular forces: The forces that hold molecules together. Intermolecular forces are most prevalent in solids and liquids. Intermolecular forces include dipole-dipole interactions, London dispersion forces, and hydrogen bonding.

ion-dipole interaction: An interaction between the charge of an ion and the partial charge of one end of an electric dipole. The classic example is the attraction between metal ions and dipolar water molecules.

ion-ion interaction: A relatively long range force between two ions. When the ions are oppositely-charged, the forces are attractive.

ionic solid: A solid held together by the attraction of oppositely-charged ions.

London dispersion forces: The forces between molecules that result from the attraction of their instantaneous dipoles.

molecular solids: Solids composed of molecules and held together by intermolecular forces, such as London dispersion forces.

network solids: Solids composed of individual atoms held together by covalent bonds that extend throughout a network. A type of molecular solid.

polar: For an object to be polar it must have a permanent dipole moment.

vapor pressure: The pressure exerted by a vapor above a liquid in a closed container.

THRILLS, CHILLS AND DRILLS

True or False

1. Ionic solids melt at low temperatures.

2. The high melting points of ionic solids reflect their weak ionic bonds.

3. Ionic solids composed of large ions with low charges have higher melting points than those composed of small, highly-charged ions.

4. Ion-ion interactions account for the ability of salts to dissolve in water.

5. Polar molecules have an associated electric dipole.

6. HCl, HF, and HI are examples of polar ions.

7. Polar molecules may have dipole-dipole interactions.

8. Dipole-dipole interactions are stronger than ion-ion interactions.

9. London dispersion forces result from the interaction of permanent electric dipoles.

10. All molecules experience London dispersion forces.

11. London dispersion forces act over a long range.

12. London dispersion forces are strongest for large molecules.

13. Hydrogen bonding is responsible for the high boiling point of water.

14. Hydrogen bonding is an intermolecular force.

15. Evaporation tends to increase the volume of a liquid.

16. Condensation tends to increase the volume of a liquid.

17. The larger the vapor pressure of a liquid, the stronger the intermolecular forces in the liquid.

18. P_4 molecules are held together by London dispersion forces.

19. The existence of liquid xenon is attributable to London dispersion forces.

20. Network solids have low melting points.

21. Network solids are generally hard and brittle.

Multiple Choice

1. Solid MgO is held together by
   a) covalent bonds
   b) ionic bonds
   c) hydrogen bonds
   d) Van der Waals forces

2. Hydrates of salts are favored by
   a) ion-dipole interactions
   b) hydrogen bonding
   c) covalent metal-water bonds
   d) alpha hydroxy compounds

3. Dipole-dipole interactions result from the interaction of
   a) full charges
   b) anions and cations
   c) partial charges on polar molecules
   d) non-polar molecules

4. Ion-ion interactions are
   a) short range
   b) long range
   c) weak
   d) rare

5. Which of the following is a polar molecule?
   a) H_2
   b) F_2
   c) HI
   d) K_2

6. London dispersion forces are
   a) long range
   b) only found in liquids
   c) only found in solids
   d) caused by the interaction of instantaneous dipoles

7. Hydrogen bonding occurs in

   a) CO_2

   b) H_2

   c) BF_3

   d) H_2O

8. The vapor pressure of a liquid

   a) is the pressure exerted by a vapor above its liquid at dynamic equilibrium

   b) is unrelated to the strength of intermolecular forces

   c) depends solely on the rate of evaporation of the liquid in a closed container

   d) is the pressure exerted by a liquid beneath a vapor

9. At the dynamic equilibrium between a liquid and its vapor

   a) the amount of liquid changes

   b) the amount of vapor is constant

   c) the rates of evaporation and condensation are different

   d) evaporation and condensation cease

10. In winter pipes often freeze, which causes them to burst. The fact most relevant in explaining this phenomenon is that

    a) Liquid water occupies a greater volume than solid water.

    b) Water is not ionically bonded

    c) Water is covalently bonded

    d) Water has the formula H_2O

11. Network solids, such as diamond, are held together by

    a) ionic bonds

    b) covalent bonds

    c) intermolecular forces

    d) dipole-dipole interactions

12. The boiling points of diatomic halogens increase with increased intermolecular forces. It follows that

    a) the boiling point of $F_2 > Cl_2 > Br_2 > I_2$

    b) the halogens are held together by London dispersion forces

    c) the boiling point of $I_2 > Br_2 > Cl_2 > F_2$

    d) the molecules are held together by hydrogen bonding

13. The vapor pressure of CH$_3$-O-CH$_3$ (ether) is greater than the vapor pressure of CH$_3$-CH$_2$-OH (ethanol). This is because

   a) there are stronger intermolecular forces in ether

   b) ether molecules can form hydrogen bonds with their neighbors

   c) ether is an anesthetic

   d) ethanol can form hydrogen bonds in the liquid

14. One form of solid sulfur is composed of S$_8$ rings. We expect the length of the S-S bonds between adjacent sulfur atoms in the ring to be

   a) shorter than the length of the S-S bonds between sulfur atoms in different rings

   b) greater than the length of the S-S bonds between sulfur atoms in different rings

   c) equal to the length of the S-S bonds between sulfur atoms in different rings

15. Chloroform molecules do not have a permanent electric dipole. It follows that

   a) chloroform molecules are polar

   b) chloroform molecules are non-polar

   c) chloroform is a liquid

   d) chloroform is a good anesthetic

Short Essays

1. Liquids have low boiling points if there are weak forces between the particles that make up the liquid. Arrange the following lists compounds in terms of decreasing boiling points and explain your reasoning.

   a. NaCl, NO, N$_2$

   b. C (diamond), H$_2$O, Ne

2. Solids can be classed as ionic, molecular, or network.

   a. Give an example of each type of solid.

   b. Name the types of forces or bonding that hold together the particles in each type of solid.

3. If crystals of moth repellent (the unfortunately named paradichlorobenzene) are placed in an open container, they will gradually disappear by evaporation. If placed in a sealed bottle, some crystals will remain indefinitely. Explain this phenomenon.

ANSWERS

True or False Answers

1. **False.** Ionic solids melt at high temperatures. This is due to the strong attraction between ions in an ionic solid.

2. **False.** The high melting points of ionic solids reflect the strong ionic bonds.

3. **False.** Small highly charged ions will be held together by stronger ionic interactions than large ions with low charges. Thus, an ionic solid made up of small highly charged ions will have a higher melting point.

4. **False.** The ability of salts to dissolve in water is due to the strength of ion-dipole interactions formed in solution.

5. **True.**

6. **False.** The molecules in the polar bear may have associated electric dipoles, but an entire polar bear does not have an overall electric dipole!

7. **True.** Dipole-dipole interactions describe the interactions between the electric dipoles of polar molecules.

8. **False.** Ion-ion interactions are stronger than dipole-dipole interactions. Dipole-dipole interactions are weaker than ion-ion interactions since they result from the attraction of the partial charges of dipoles, as opposed to the full charges of ions.

9. **False.** London dispersion forces result from the interaction of instantaneous electric dipoles.

10. **True.**

11. **False.** London dispersion forces act only over very short distances.

12. **True.**

13. **True.**

14. **True.** Hydrogen bonding occurs when a hydrogen atom is bonded to a highly electronegative atom. The hydrogen atom has a large partial positive charge and can form a strong dipole-dipole interaction with the electronegative atom on a neighboring molecule.

15. **False.** Evaporation of a liquid results from molecules escaping the liquid surface to form the gas phase. Evaporation tends to decrease the volume of a liquid.

16. **True.** Condensation occurs when molecules form a liquid from the gaseous state.

17. **False.** The larger the vapor pressure of a liquid, the weaker the intermolecular forces in the liquid.

18. **True.** P_4 is a nonpolar molecule.

19. **True.** Xe is a noble gas, and does not form ions or molecules easily.

20. **False.** Network solids have high melting points because to melt these solids, all the covalent bonds in the lattice must be broken.

21. **True.**

Multiple Choice Answers

1. (b) MgO is an ionic solid.

2. a) The hydration of salts can be explained by the persistence of ion-dipole interactions between cations and water molecules.

3. (c)

4. (c) Ions do not attract just their nearest neighbor, but also oppositely charged ions further away.

5. (c) HI is polar due to the large difference in electronegativity between H and I.

6. (d)

7. (d) A hydrogen atom in water has a large partial positive charge and can form a strong dipole-dipole interaction with the oxygen atom on a neighboring water molecule.

8. (a)

9. (b) The rates of condensation and evaporation are equal at equilibrium, and so the amounts of vapor and liquid are constant.

10. (a) Liquid water is more dense than ice, and hence occupies a smaller volume.

11. (b) In network solids, individual atoms are held together by covalent bonds that extend throughout a network.

12. (c) I_2 is larger than Br_2, which is larger than Cl_2, which is larger than F_2. The larger the molecules, the stronger London dispersion forces that hold the molecules together.

13. (d) The higher the vapor pressure, the weaker the intermolecular forces in the liquid. Ethanol can form hydrogen bonds, which are much stronger than the forces which hold ether molecules together.

14. (a) Sulfur atoms within a molecule are held together by covalent bonds, while the adjacent sulfur rings are held together by much weaker London dispersion forces.

15. (b)

Short Essay Answers

1. **a.** $NaCl > NO > N_2$.

   NaCl is held together by strong ionic bonds. N_2 is non-polar and held together by London dispersion forces. NO is about the same size as N_2, and so the London dispersion forces that hold NO together are of comparable strength to those in N_2. However, NO has an electric dipole, so it is also held together by dipole-dipole interactions.

   b. $C > H_2O > Ne$

   The carbon atoms in diamond are held together by strong covalent bonds in an extended network. Water molecules are held together by London dispersion forces and also by hydrogen bonding. Neon is of comparable size to water and has comparable London dispersion forces, but neon is not hydrogen bonded.

2. **a.** Ionic: sodium chloride

   Molecular: white potassium (P_4)

   Network: diamond (C)

   b. Ionic solids are held together by ionic bonds.

   Molecular solids are held together by intermolecular forces.

   Network solids are held together by covalent bonds.

3. In a closed container, a dynamic equilibrium between solid paradichlorobenzene and its vapor can be achieved. In an open container, evaporation still occurs, but the vapor does not accumulate and condense back into the solid. The solid is therefore depleted until it disappears entirely.

CHAPTER

NATURE'S BALANCING ACTS: CHEMICAL EQUILIBRIA

12

OVERVIEW

Hemoglobin, the molecule that transports oxygen through our bodies absorbs different amounts of oxygen in different environments. For example, those living at high altitude — where there is less oxygen in the air — have more efficient hemoglobin than those living at sea level. This is why athletes often train at high altitudes — doing so improves the ability of their hemoglobin to capture oxygen.

The ability of hemoglobin to capture oxygen depends on (is balanced with) the amount of oxygen available. Indeed, many of the chemical processes that sustain life are finely balanced with the conditions in which they take place.

In this chapter, we will see how to describe the balance between reactants and products in chemical reactions. Often, this balance is exquisitely sensitive to changes in conditions. In fact, we will see that we can predict the effects of changing the pressure, volume, temperature or amounts of reactants or products on the balance in chemical reactions. Finally, we will see that we can apply the ideas developed in this chapter to quantify the solubility of salts, or the strengths of acids.

CONCEPTS

EQUILIBRIUM IS A STATE OF BALANCE.

Imagine walking down an "up" escalator. If you walk down faster than the stairs move up, you make progress toward the bottom of the stairs. If you move too slowly, you are carried up the stairs in spite of your efforts. However, if you walk at just the right speed you can maintain your position on the stairs. At this speed, the rate at which you walk down the stairs is exactly balanced by the rate at which the stairs come up to meet you. A chemist would say that you and the upward-moving are in equilibrium. In general, equilibrium occurs when the rates of two processes are exactly balanced.

REACTIONS REACH EQUILIBRIUM AND DO NOT ALWAYS CONTINUE TO COMPLETION.

Thus far we have thought about reactions as continuing until the limiting reagent runs out. For many reactions, this actually occurs. Yet other reactions stop far short of completion. For example, when nitrogen and hydrogen gas are mixed to form ammonia...

$$N_2 + 3H_2 \rightarrow 2NH_3$$

...the concentrations of nitrogen and hydrogen initially drop, as the concentration of ammonia increases from zero. If the reaction continued to completion, we would expect the concentration of ammonia to continue increasing until there was no more nitrogen or hydrogen to use up. However, this does not occur. Rather, after a period of time, the concentrations of ammonia, nitrogen and hydrogen, all become constant.

Why does this reaction — like many others — stop short of completion?

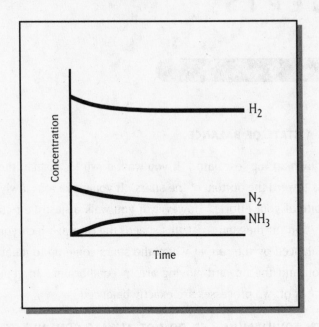

To answer this question, we need first to consider the forward reaction:

$$N_2 + 3H_2 \rightarrow 2NH_3$$

Initially, when we mix nitrogen and hydrogen, they are at high concentrations. The rate at which nitrogen and hydrogen react to form ammonia decreases as their concentrations decrease. As the forward reaction proceeds, the concentration of ammonia increases.

But this is not the whole story. As soon as the first drop of ammonia is formed, we must consider a reverse reaction. The reverse reaction, in this case, is the decomposition of NH_3 into N_2 and H_2:

$$2NH_3 \rightarrow N_2 + 3H_2$$

The greater the concentration of ammonia, the faster this reaction occurs.

As the forward reaction proceeds, the concentration of ammonia increases, so the rate at which ammonia turns into nitrogen and hydrogen gas (the reverse reaction) also increases.

Finally, the rate at which ammonia decomposes and the rate at which ammonia is formed become equal. At this point, there is no net change in the concentration of ammonia or in the concentrations of nitrogen and hydrogen. The reaction appears to have stopped. Chemists describe the reaction as having reached equilibrium. **It is important to realize that the reaction has not actually stopped.** If we could look at the reaction in microscopic detail, we would see that for each molecule of ammonia formed, one molecule is broken down into nitrogen and hydrogen. The apparent stasis of equilibrium is, in fact, maintained by constant change in opposite directions.

Chemical equilibria are dynamic. Equilibria result when forward and reverse reactions have equal rates.

The dynamic equilibrium between compounds is denoted using a double headed arrow. For the equilibrium between nitrogen, hydrogen and ammonia, we write:

$$3H_2 + N_2 \rightleftharpoons 2NH_3$$

The equilibrium constant quantifies equilibria.

Cato Maximilian Guldberg and Peter Waage, two Norwegian chemists, proposed that equilibria follow a simple mathematical relation. For a reaction that is represented by the balanced equation:

$$aA + bB \rightleftharpoons cC + dD,$$

where a, b, c, and d are the stoichiometric coefficients for the chemical species A, B, C and D, respectively, we can define an equilibrium constant K, at a constant temperature, in terms of the following equilibrium expression:

$$K = \frac{[C]^c[D]^d}{[A]^a[B]^b} \qquad \text{(constant temperature)}$$

where [X] represents the concentration of species X at equilibrium.

The equilibrium expression tells us that for a given reaction, the ratio of products and reactants defined by the equilibrium constant will always be the same (at a given temperature).

It is a simple matter to write down an equilibrium constant from a balanced equation. For example, for the reaction:

$$N_2(g) + 3H_2(g) \rightleftharpoons 2NH_3(g)$$

The equilibrium constant is defined as:

$$K = \frac{[NH_3]^2}{[N_2][H_2]^3}$$

THERE MAY BE MANY EQUILIBRIUM POSITIONS, BUT ONLY ONE EQUILIBRIUM CONSTANT FOR A REACTION.

There is only one equilibrium constant for a reaction (at a given temperature). However, there are many sets of concentrations of products and reactants that satisfy the equilibrium expression. The equilibrium expression speaks to the ratios the concentrations of species — not to the concentration of any one of the species.

Consider the reaction of NO_2^- with itself to give $N_2O_4^{2-}$:

$$2NO_2^- \rightleftharpoons N_2O_4^{2-}$$

Imagine that a number of different NO_2^- and $N_2O_4^{2-}$ solutions with different concentrations (measured in molarity) are allowed to reach equilibrium at 100°C. The equilibrium concentrations of NO_2^- and $N_2O_4^{2-}$ are then measured. The results are given below.

INITIAL (M)		EQUILIBRIUM (M)		$K = \dfrac{[N_2O_4^{2-}]}{[NO_2^-]^2}$
$[NO_2^-]$	$[N_2O_4^{2-}]$	$[NO_2^-]$	$[N_2O_4^{2-}]$	
2.00	0	0.54	0.73	$0.73/\,0.54^2 = 2.5$
2.36	0.32	0.68	1.16	$1.16/\,0.68^2 = 2.5$
0.72	0.64	0.54	0.73	$0.73/\,0.54^2 = 2.5$

Notice in the above table that a range of equilibrium concentrations of each species are observed. Each set of concentrations corresponds to one equilibrium position. However, at the given temperature (100°C) only one equilibrium constant is observed (2.5). A range of equilibrium positions satisfy the equilibrium constant.

The concentration of pure solids or pure liquids are not included in the equilibrium expression.

So far we have only considered equilibria involving one state of matter. These equilibria are described as **homogeneous**. When more than one state of matter is involved in an equilibria, it is described as **heterogeneous**. A subtle but important point concerns the equilibrium constants for heterogeneous equilibria involving pure liquids or solids. Consider the equilibria between $CaCO_3$ and the products of its decomposition into CO_2 and CaO.

$$CaCO_3(s) \rightleftharpoons CaO(s) + CO_2(g)$$

The expected equilibrium expression K' is as follows.

$$K' = \frac{[CaO]\,[CO_2]}{[CaCO_3]}$$

However, the equilibrium position cannot depend on the concentration of a solid, since the concentration of a solid is a constant. Both CaO and $CaCO_3$ are solids.

If the concentration of CaO is a constant, **a**, and the concentration of $CaCO_3$ is **b**, we can write the equilibrium expression as:

$$K' = a\,[CO_2]\,/\,b$$
$$\text{or } bK'\,/\,a = [CO_2]$$

Given that we can simply redefine our equilibrium constant – now represented by (K') – to take into acount a and b, we let K = aK'/b

$$K = [CO_2]$$

Similarly, the equilibrium position does not depend on the pure liquids involved in the reaction. For example, for the reaction:

$$2H_2O(l) \rightleftharpoons 2H_2(g) + O_2(g)$$

the equilibrium expression is...

$$K = [H_2]^2\,[O_2]$$

...because the concentration of H_2O is constant.

We have seen how to describe chemical equilibria in terms of equilibrium constants and positions. But, how does the equilibrium constant or the equilibrium position respond to changes in the reaction conditions?

Le Chatelier's principle states that when a change is imposed on a system at equilibrium such as a change in temperature, pressure, or amount of reactants, the position of the equilibrium shifts to reduce the effect of that change.

Le Chatelier's principle is a general statement about the qualitative effects of changes imposed on a system that has already established equilibrium. This idea enables us to consider the way changes in concentration, volume, and temperature affect the equilibrium position.

IF MORE REACTANTS ARE ADDED TO AN EQUILIBRIUM MIXTURE OF REACTANTS AND PRODUCTS, THE SYSTEM REACTS BY MAKING MORE PRODUCT. THE EQUILIBRIUM CONSTANT FOR THE REACTION IS UNCHANGED.

Consider the reaction between N_2 and H_2 to produce NH_3

$$N_2(g) + 3H_2(g) \rightleftharpoons 2NH_3(g)$$

At equilibrium, the concentration of each substance is constant. If more N_2 and H_2 are added to the equilibrium reaction mixture, the concentration of N_2 and H_2 increase. The reaction is, therefore, no longer at equilibrium. Equilibrium is re-established after some period of time. Le Chatelier's principle tells us that at the new equilibrium position, the concentration of NH_3 is greater than at the initial equilibrium position. Since the equilibrium constant is a constant at a given temperature, it is unchanged at the new equilibrium position.

IN THE SAME WAY, IF THE PRODUCT OF A CHEMICAL REACTION IS REMOVED, THE SYSTEM REACTS BY MAKING MORE PRODUCT.

Now imagine removing ammonia from the equilibrium mixture of nitrogen, hydrogen, and ammonia. Le Chatelier's principle suggests that a new equilibrium position will be established by an increased concentration of ammonia. Again, because the equilibrium constant is a constant at a given temperature, it is unchanged at the new equilibrium position.

A DECREASE IN VOLUME FAVORS THE SIDE OF A REACTION WITH THE LEAST NUMBER OF GAS MOLECULES. CHANGING THE VOLUME CHANGES THE EQUILIBRIUM POSITION, BUT NOT THE EQUILIBRIUM CONSTANT.

When we decrease the volume of a reaction vessel, we increase the pressure of any gases in the vessel. Le Chatelier's principle tells us that the system will shift in a direction that reduces its pressure.

As an example of using Le Chatelier's principle to predict the effect of a change in volume, consider (once again) the reaction between nitrogen and hydrogen gas to give ammonia.

$$N_2(g) + 3H_2(g) \rightleftharpoons 2NH_3(g)$$

Imagine conducting the reaction in a syringe. We let the reaction reach equilibrium in a given volume, V. Then we push the plunger into the barrel of the syringe, which decreases the volume of the reaction vessel (the syringe barrel) and increases the pressure. The system is no longer at equilibrium. According to Le Chatelier's principle, the system will return to equilibrium by decreasing its pressure. The pressure results from gas molecules bombarding the syringe walls. The fewer the number of gas molecules, the lower the pressure of the gas. Le Chatelier's principle suggests that the system will find a new equilibrium position with a decreased number of gas molecules.

We can predict the direction of the change in equilibrium position by finding the number of molecules on each side of the equation. Increased pressure will favor the side of the reaction with the fewest number of gas molecules.

On the left hand side, there are four gas molecules ($N_2 + 3H_2$). On the right hand side of the equation, there are two gas molecules ($2NH_3$). Increasing the pressure, therefore, favors the right hand side of the equation, the production of ammonia.

The reverse is also true; decreasing the pressure favors more gas molecules and would therefore favor the production of nitrogen and hydrogen gas from ammonia.

The value of the equilibrium constant K changes with temperature. The direction of the change can be predicted by Le Chatelier's principle.

Some reactions give off heat; these are classed as **exothermic.** Other reactions consume heat; these are classed as **endothermic.**

You can think of heat as a product of an exothermic reaction and as a reactant in an endothermic reaction.

$$X + Y \rightarrow Z + heat \quad \text{(exothermic)}$$

$$X + Y + heat \rightarrow Z \quad \text{(endothermic)}$$

Le Chatelier's principle tells us that when we increase the temperature of an exothermic reaction, the system reacts by favoring the reactants. (Think of increasing the temperature of an exothermic reaction as being like increasing the amount of a product in a chemical reaction.)

Decreasing the temperature favors products in an exothermic reaction. Similarly, the products in an endothermic reactions are favored by increased temperature.

Applications of the equilibrium constant

SALT DISSOLVING IN WATER CAN BE CONSIDERED AN EQUILIBRIUM REACTION.

When an ionic solid dissolves in water, it dissociates into separate anions and cations. For example, when AgI dissolves in water we can write:

$$AgI(s) \rightleftharpoons Ag^+(aq) + I^-(aq)$$

The **solubility** of a salt (such as AgI) is a measure of the maximum amount (number of moles) of salt that can dissolve in a liter of water. It is reported in units of $mol\ L^{-1}$.

SOLUBILITY EQUILIBRIA ARE TREATED QUANTITATIVELY USING THE SOLUBILITY CONSTANT, ALSO CALLED THE SOLUBILITY PRODUCT, K_{SP}.

The solubility constant for the equilibrium between AgI and Ag^+ and I^- ions is expressed below.

$$K_{sp} = [Ag^+][I^-]$$

Remember: Because AgI is a pure solid, it is not included in the equilibrium expression.

As examples of how to write solubility products, we will derive the solubility products for the following compounds dissolving in water:

$$\text{a) } BaSO_4 \quad \text{b) } CaCl_2 \quad \text{c) } Ca(NO_3)_2$$

Strategy: Write a balanced equation for the solubility equilibrium. Use the balanced equation to determine the solubility product K_{sp}.

a) $BaSO_4(s) \rightleftharpoons Ba^{2+}(aq) + SO_4^{2-}(aq)$

$$K_{sp} = [Ba^{2+}][SO_4^{2-}]$$

b) $CaCl_2(s) \rightleftharpoons Ca^{2+}(aq) + 2Cl^-(aq)$

$$K_{sp} = [Ca^{2+}][Cl^-]^2$$

c) $Ca(NO_3)_2 \rightleftharpoons Ca^{2+}(aq) + 2NO_3^-(aq)$

$$K_{sp} = [Ca^{2+}][NO_3^-]^2$$

Solubility products for a compound can be calculated given a knowledge of solubility of the compound.

The solubility of AgI(s) is 1.2×10^{-8} $molL^{-1}$.

The equation describing AgI dissolving in water is:

$$AgI(aq) \rightleftharpoons Ag^+(aq) + I^-(aq)$$

Therefore, for every mole of AgI in solution, we have one mole of Ag^+ ions and one mole of I^- ions.

It follows that :

$$[Ag] = 1.2 \times 10^{-8} \text{ mol } L^{-1}$$

$$[I^-] = 1.2 \times 10^{-8} \text{ mol } L^{-1}$$

The solubility product $K_{sp} = [Ag^+][I^-] = (1.2 \times 10^{-8})(1.2 \times 10^{-8}) = 1.5 \times 10^{-16}$

By convention, the solubility constant is not measured with any unit. It's just a lonely number.

The solubility of a salt can be derived from its solubility product.

As an example, let's find the solubility of $CaSO_4$ in the following reaction. The K_{sp} for $CaSO_4$ is 2×10^{-5}.

$$CaSO_4(s) \rightleftharpoons Ca^{2+}(aq) + SO_4^{2-}(aq)$$

$$K_{sp} = [Ca^{2+}][SO_4^{2-}] = 2 \times 10^{-5}$$

The number of moles of Ca^{2+} in solution is equal to the number of moles of SO_4^{2-}. Setting these concentrations equal to x, we have:

$$K_{sp} = (x)(x) = x^2$$

$$x = \sqrt{K_{sp}} = \sqrt{2 \times 10^{-5}}$$

Since the concentration of each ion is equal to the concentration of the dissolved salt, x is equal to the solubility.

The solubility of $CaSO_4$ is $\sqrt{2 \times 10^{-5}}\, mol\ L^-$.

Acid-base Reactions Reach Equilibrium

Acid-base reactions are often discussed in terms of chemical equilibria.

When an acid, HA, (where A represents an element or ion) is added to water, the following equilibrium is established:

$$HA(aq) + H_2O(l) \rightleftharpoons H_3O^+(aq) + A^-(aq)$$

| acid 1 | base 2 | | conjugate acid 2 | conjugate base 1 |

For example, when HCl reacts with water, we can write:

$$HCl(aq) + H_2O(l) \rightleftharpoons H_3O^+(aq) + Cl^-(aq)$$

This reaction can occur in both directions. In the forward reaction, HCl (the acid HA) protonates water (donates a proton) to give H_3O^+ and its conjugate base Cl^-. In the reverse reaction, H_3O^+ acts as an acid-protonating Cl^- to give HCl, the conjugate acid of Cl^-.

For a strong acid, the equilibrium will favor the ions on the right-hand side of the equation. Remember that the strong acids are HCl, HI, HBr, HNO_3, H_2SO_4, and $HClO_4$.

When a base, HB, is added to water, the following equilibrium is established:

$$B(aq) \quad + \quad H_2O(l) \quad \rightleftharpoons \quad HB^+(aq) \quad + \quad OH^-(aq)$$

base 1   acid 2   conjugate acid 1   conjugate base 2

An example is the reaction of ammonia and water:

$$NH_3(aq) \quad + \quad H_2O(l) \quad \rightleftharpoons \quad NH_4^+(aq) \quad + \quad OH^-(aq)$$

base 1   acid 2   conjugate acid 1   conjugate base 2

In the forward reaction, ammonia (base B) is protonated by H_2O, now acting as an acid, to give the conjugate acid of ammonia, NH_4^+ (HB^+), and OH^-. In the reverse reaction, NH_4^+ (HB^+) protonates OH^- to give water and ammonia (base B).

THE IONIC PRODUCT OF WATER IS A CONSTANT AT 25°C

Notice that in the first equilibrium, water acts first as a base (with HCl), while in the second equilibrium, water acts as an acid (with NH_3). In general, substances that can function as both acids and bases are called **amphoteric.** Another example of the amphoteric behavior of water is in its auto ionization, which is defined by the process:

$$H_2O(l) + H_2O(l) \rightleftharpoons H_3O^+(aq) + OH^-(aq)$$

In this reaction, one molecule of water protonates another molecule of water, giving a hydroxide ion (OH^-) and a hydronium (H_3O^+)ion.

The equilibrium constant for this process is denoted K_w. The equilibrium expression is:

$$K_w = [H_3O^+][OH^-]$$

In pure water, K_w has a value of 1×10^{-14} at 25°C.

Because pure water produces one molecule of H_3O^+ for every molecule of OH^-, it follows that

$$[OH^-] = [H^+]$$

Setting both concentrations equal to x, we can write:

$$K_w = x^2$$
$$x = \sqrt{K_w} = 1 \times 10^{-7}$$
$$[OH^-] = [H^+] = 1 \times 10^{-7}$$

THE RELATIVE CONCENTRATIONS OF H^+ AND OH^- DETERMINE WHETHER AN AQUEOUS SOLUTION IS ACIDIC OR BASIC.

The ionic product of water is equal to 1×10^{-14} in any aqueous solution at 25°C. However, the concentrations of H^+ and OH^- may vary with the addition of an acid or a base. In a neutral solution: $[H_3O^+] = [OH^-]$.

In an acidic solution: $[H_3O^+] > [OH^-]$.

In basic solution: $[H_3O^+] < [OH^-]$.

The pH of a solution is a measure of its acidity.

pH is defined as $-\log[H_3O^+]$

Common substances have pH values between 0 (acidic) and 14 (basic). A pH of 7 is neutral.

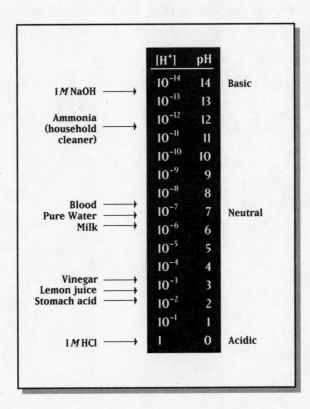

As examples of how to use the pH calculation, let's find the pH of the following solutions:

a) A solution in which $[H^+] = 1.0 \times 10^{-4}$

   $pH = -\log 1.0 \times 10^{-4} = 4$

b) A solution in which $[OH^-] = 5.0 \times 10^{-5}$

   We know that $K_w = [H^+][OH^-] = 1 \times 10^{-14}$

Rearranging this expression, we get:

$[H^+] = K_w / [OH^-]$

$[H^+] = 1 \times 10^{-14} / 5.0 \times 10^{-5}$

$[H^+] = 1.0 \times 10^{-9}$

$pH = -\log [H^+] = -\log (1 \times 10^{-9}) = 9.$

The solution is basic.

c) What is the pH of a 1.0M HCl solution?

To answer this question, we must recall that HCl is a strong acid. It is therefore completely ionized in solution. A 1.0M HCl solution contains few HCl molecules; instead, it contains 1.0M of H^+ ions and 1.0M of Cl^- ions.

The pH = $-\log [H^+] = -\log 1 = 0$

KEY TERMS

conjugate acid: The protonated form of a base.

conjugate base: The deprotonated form of an acid.

equilibrium constant (K): The product of the equilibrium concentrations of the products of a chemical reaction raised to the power of their stoichiometric coefficients divided by the product of the equilibrium concentration of reactants raised to the power of their stoichiometric coefficients. In a reaction where $aA + bB \rightleftharpoons cC + dD$, $K = [C]^c[D]^d/[A]^a[B]^b$.

equilibrium position: The concentrations of reactants and products at equilibrium.

heterogeneous equilibria: Equilibria involving more than one state of matter.

homogeneous equilibria: Equilibria involving only one state of matter.

ionic product of water, (K_w): $K_w = [H_3O^+][OH^-]$

Le Chatelier's principle: When a change is imposed on a system at equilibrium, the position of equilibrium shifts to reduce the effect of the change.

pH: A measurement of the acidity of a solution. $pH = -\log[H_3O^+]$. Below pH7 is acidic; above pH 7 is basic; and pH7 is neutral.

the solubility product, K_{sp}: Used to calculate the solubility of a compound.
For a reading of the form $X_nY_m(s) \rightarrow nX(aq) + mY(aq)$, $K_{sp} = [X]^n [Y]^m$
where [X] and [Y] are equilibrium concentrations.

THRILLS, CHILLS AND DRILLS

True or False

1. All reactions continue to completion.

2. Chemical reactions reach equilibrium when the forward and reverse reactions stop.

3. A reaction has a single equilibrium position.

4. For the reaction:

$$2HI(g) \rightarrow H_2(g) + I_2(g)$$

The equilibrium constant $K = [H_2][I_2] / [HI]$

5. The equilibrium constant for the reaction:

$$CaCO_3(s) \rightarrow CaO(s) + CO_2(g)$$

The equilibrium constant $K = [CaO][CO_2] / [CaCO_3]$

6. A reaction has a single equilibrium constant at a given temperature.

7. If ammonia is removed from an equilibrium mix of ammonia, nitrogen, and hydrogen, more ammonia will be synthesized.

8. Exothermic reactions are favored by an increase in temperature.

9. Endothermic reactions are favored by an increase in temperature.

10. Decreasing the volume of a reaction favors the side of the reaction with the most number of gas molecules.

11. Decreasing the concentration of a reactant in a reaction that has previously reached equilibrium changes the value of K for a reaction.

12. For the reaction

$$Ba(NO_3)_2 \rightarrow Ba^{2+} + 2NO_3^-$$

The solubility product $K_{sp} = [Ba_2^+][NO_3^-]^2$

13. If the solubility of $Ba(NO_3)_2$ is X, then the solubility product $= 4X^3$.

14. If the solubility product in Question 12 is Y, then the concentration of barium ions $= \sqrt[3]{Y}$.

15. The conjugate base of an acid is the deprotonated form of the acid.

16. The ionic product of water is dependent on the pH of a solution.

17. Acidic solutions have a low concentration of H+ ions.

18. pH = -log[H+]

19. If a solution has a pH of 14, it is basic.

20. A solution with a pH of 7 is neutral.

Multiple Choice

1. Find K for the following reaction.

$$N_2O_4(g) \rightleftharpoons 2NO_2 (g)$$

 a) $[N_2O_4] / [NO_2]$
 b) $[NO_2] /[N_2O_4]$
 c) $[NO_2]_2$
 d) $[NO_2]_2 / [N_2O_4]$

2. Find K for the following reaction.

$$H_2(g) + I_2(g) \rightleftharpoons 2HI (g)$$

 a) $[H_2] [I_2] / [_2HI]$
 b) $[H_2] [I_2] / [HI]_2$
 c) $[H_2] [I_2] / [HI]_2$
 d) $[HI]_2 / [H_2] [I_2]$

3. Find K for the following reaction.

$$N_2(g) + 2H_2(g) \rightleftharpoons N_2H_4(g)$$

 a) $[N_2H_4]$
 b) $[N_2H_4] / [H_2][N_2]$
 c) $[N_2H_4] / [H_2]^2[N_2]$
 d) $[H_2]_2[N_2] / [N_2H_4]$

4. Find K for the following reaction.

$$NH_4Cl(s) \rightleftharpoons NH_3(g) + HCl(g)$$

 a) $[NH_3] [HCl] / [NH_4Cl]$
 b) $[NH_3] [HCl]$
 c) $[NH_4Cl] / [HCl] [NH_3]$
 d) $[NH_4Cl]$

5. An example of a homogeneous equilibria is
    a) $P(s,red) \rightleftharpoons P(s,white)$
    b) $H_2O(s) \rightleftharpoons H_2O(l)$
    c) $CaCO_3(s) \rightleftharpoons CaO(g) + CO_2(g)$
    d) $N_2O_4(l) \rightleftharpoons 2NO_2(g)$

6. An example of a heterogeneous equilibria is
    a) $2N_2(g) + O_2(g) \rightleftharpoons 2N_2O(g)$
    b) $N_2(g) + O_2(g) \rightleftharpoons 2NO(g)$
    c) $N_2O_4(l) \rightleftharpoons 2NO_2(g)$
    d) $P_4(g) + Cl_2(g) \rightleftharpoons 4PCl_3(g)$

7. A and B react to form C according to the equation:

$$A + B \rightleftharpoons 2C$$

In one vessel, we react 5 moles of A and 3 moles of B. In another vessel, we have only 7 moles of C. If equilibrium positions are obtained in both pots, it follows that

    a) K and the equilibrium position are necessarily the same in both pots
    b) K and the equilibrium position are different in each pots
    c) K is different in each pot, but the equilibrium position necessarily is the same
    d) K is the same in both pots, but the equilibrium position may be different

8. Methanol can be made through the reaction of CO and H_2 according to the following equation:

$$CO(g) + 2H_2(g) \rightleftharpoons CH_3OH(g)$$

Based on this information, the production of methanol might be improved by

    a) removing methanol from the reaction as it is formed
    b) adding methanol to the reaction
    c) performing the reaction under reduced pressure
    d) performing the reaction at higher temperature

9. Water can be made from H_2 and O_2 according to the following equation.

$$H_2(g) + O_2(g) \rightleftharpoons H_2O(g)$$

If this reaction has already reached equilibrium, and a scrubber that removes oxygen is added, then

    a) the equilibrium position will shift to the left
    b) the equilibrium position will shift to the right
    c) the equilibrium position will not change
    d) the equilibrium constant will change

10. Smelling salts decompose to give ammonia, carbon dioxide, and water according to the equation

$$(NH_4)_2CO_3(s) \rightleftharpoons 2NH_3(g) + CO_2(g) + H_2O(g)$$

The decomposition will be favored by

  a) an increase in temperature

  b) a decrease in pressure

  c) the addition of ammonia

  d) the addition of water

11. The equation in Question 10 represents an endothermic reaction. The production of ammonia will be favored by

  a) an increase in temperature

  b) a decrease in temperature

  c) a catalyst

  d) none of the above

12. The following is an unbalanced equation.

$$NOCl(g) \rightleftharpoons Cl_2(g) + NO(g)$$

The equilibrium constant corresponding to a balanced equation is

  a) $[Cl_2] [NO] / [NOCl]$

  b) $[Cl_2] [NOCl]$

  c) $[NO]^2[Cl_2] / [NOCl]^2$

  d) $[2NO] [Cl_2] / [NOCl]$

13. The decomposition of NOCl in Question 12 would be favored by

  a) a decrease in pressure

  b) an increase in pressure

  c) the removal of NOCl

  d) none of the above

14. The following reaction is studied:

$$NO(g) + H_2(g) \rightleftharpoons N_2(g) + H_2O(g)$$

At a particular temperature, the equilibrium concentration of each species is measured with the following results.

$$[NO] = 0.07M \quad [H_2] = 0.01M \quad [N_2] = 0.02M \quad [H_2O] = 0.15M$$

The equilibrium constant is

a) 0.07M x 0.01M / 0.02M x 0.15M

b) 0.02M x 0.15M / 0.07M x 0.01M

c) 0.01 x (0.15)^2 / 0.07 x 0.01

d) 0.01 x (0.15)^2 / (0.07)^2 x (0.01)^2

15. What is the solubility constant for the equation

$$PbI_2(s) \rightleftharpoons Pb^{2+}(aq) + 2I^-(aq)$$

a) $[PbI_2] / [Pb^{+2}] [2I^-]$

b) $[Pb^{+2}] [2I^-]$

c) $[Pb^{+2}] [I^-]^2$

d) none of the above

16. The solubility product of the reaction in Q.15 is 6.5 x 10^{-9} at 25°C. It follows that the solubility of PbI$_2$ is

a) $((6.5 \times 10^{-9}/4)^{1/3})$

b) $(6.5 \times 10^{-9})^{-1/3}$

c) 6.5×10^{-9}

d) $(6.5 \times 10^{-9})^{1/2}$

17. Silver phosphate dissolves in water according to the following equation.

$$Ag_3PO_4(s) \rightleftharpoons 3Ag^+ + PO_4^{3-}$$

The concentration of silver ions at equilibrium [Ag$^+$] has been observed to be 4.8 x 10^{-5}M

It follows that the concentration of phosphate ions is

a) $3 \times (4.8 \times 10^{-5}M)$

b) $4.8 \times 10^{-5}M$

c) $(4.8 \times 10^{-5}M) / 3$

d) unknown

18. Given the data in Question 17, the solubility constant for silver phosphate is

a) $(4.8 \times 10^{-5}M) / 3$

b) $(4.8 \times 10^{-5}M)^3 \times (4.8 \times 10^{-5}M) / 3$

c) $4.8 \times 10^{-5}M$

d) unknown, due to insufficient data

NATURE'S BALANCING ACTS: CHEMICAL EQUILIBRIA

19. In an acidic solution
   a) $[H_3O^+] < [OH^-]$
   b) $[H_3O^+] > [OH^-]$
   c) $[H_3O^+] = [OH^-]$
   d) none of the above

20. The pH of 1M HNO_3 is
   a) 0
   b) 1
   c) 10
   d) 5

21. Strong acids
   a) have strong conjugate bases
   b) have high pH's
   c) are never ionized
   d) are completely ionized in water

Short Essays

1. At a certain temperature, it is found that K= 5×10^{-3} for the reaction represented by the following equation.

$$PCl_5(g) \rightleftharpoons PCl_3(g) + Cl_2(g)$$

At equilibrium, the concentration of PCl_5 is twice that of PCl_3.

   a. Write an expression for the equilibrium constant in terms of the concentration of PCl_3.

   b. What is the concentration of PCl_5 under these conditions?

2. Bromine molecules decompose into bromine atoms at high temperatures according to the equation below.

$$Br_2(g) \rightleftharpoons 2Br(g)$$

The reaction is endothermic.

a. State Le Chatelier's principle.

b. What is the effect on the position of equilibrium of a decrease in volume of the reaction vessel?

c. What is the effect on the equilibrium position of removing bromine molecules?

d. What is the effect of decreasing the temperature of this reaction?

e. Is there an effect on the equilibrium constant of the actions described above?

3. H_2 and F_2 react to form HF, according to the equation below.

$$H_2(g) + F_2(g) \rightleftharpoons 2HF(g)$$

The equilibrium constant for the reaction is 5×10^3 at a given temperature. One equilibrium position has $[F_2] = [H_2] = 0.5M$

Write a numerical expression for the concentration of HF at this equilibrium position.

4. Calcium phosphate $Ca_3(PO_4)_2$, the substance of which our teeth is made, is very insoluble. (Good thing or our teeth would dissolve every time we drink.) For calcium phosphate, K_{sp} = 1.3×10^{-32} at 25°C.

a. Write an equation for calcium phosphate dissolving in water.

b. Write an expression for K_{sp}.

c. Calculate the concentration of calcium ions in a saturated solution of calcium phosphate.

d. Calculate the solubility of calcium phosphate.

5. a. Name four strong acids.

b. Explain the distinction between a strong acid and a concentrated acid.

c. Calculate the pH of a IM solution of HNO_3.

ANSWERS

True or False Answers

1. **False.** Reactions reach equilibrium and do not always go to completion.

2. **False.** Chemical reactions reach equilibrium when the forward and reverse reactions rates are equal.

3. **False.** A reaction can have multiple equilibrium positions.

4. **False.** $K = [H_2] [I_2]/[HI]_2$

5. **False.** $K = [CO_2]$. The concentrations of pure solids are not included in the equilibrium constant.

6. **True.**

7. **True.** $2NH_3 \rightarrow N_2 + 3H_2$. By Le Chatelier's principle, if you remove ammonia, more ammonia will be synthesized.

8. **False.** Le Chatelier's principle tells us that when we increase the temperature of an exothermic reaction, the system reacts by favoring the reactants.

9. **True.** Le Chatelier's principle tells us that when we increase the temperature of an endothermic reaction, the system reacts by favoring the products.

10. **False.** A decrease in volume favors the side of a reaction with the least number of gas molecules.

11. **False.** If the concentration of a reactant is decreased, the system will react by making more of that reactant. The equilibrium constant for the reaction is unchanged.

12. **True.**

13. **True.** One mole of $Ba(NO_3)_2$ yields one mole of Ba^{2+} and two moles of NO_3^-. Thus $[Ba^{2+}] = x$, $[NO_3^-] = 2x$ and $K_{sp} = x(2x)2 = 4 x 3$.

14. **False.** If $K_{sp} = Y$, then $[Ba^{2+}] = (Y/4)^{1/3}$ since $K_{sp} = [Ba^{2+}][NO_3^-]_2$ and $2[Ba^{2+}] = [NO_3^-]$.

15. **True.**

16. **False.** The ionic product of water is a constant at $25°C$.

17. **False.** Acidic solutions have a high concentration of H^+ ions.

18. **True.**

19. **True.** A solution with pH between 7 and 14 is basic. A solution with pH between 0 and 7 is acidic.

20. **True.** At pH 7, $[H_3O^+] = [OH^-]$.

Mulitple Choice Answers

1. (d)

2. (d)

3. (c)

4. (c)

5. (a) Homogeneous equilibria are equilibria involving only one state of matter.

6. (c) Heterogeneous equilibria are equilibria involving more than one state of matter.

7. (d) K would be the same for both reactions, but since the first pot contains 8 moles total and the second pot contains 7 moles, the equlibrium positions in the two pots are likely to be different.

8. (a) If the concentration of a product is decreased, the system will react by making more of that product. Thus, removing methanol as it is formed will improve the production of methanol.

9. (a) If the concentration of a reactant is decreased, the system will react by making more of that reactant. Thus, the equilibrium will shift to the left.

10. (b) A decrease in pressure favors the side of a reaction with the greatest number of gas molecules. In this reaction, a decrease in pressure would favor decomposition.

11. (a) Le Chatelier's principle tells us that when we increase the temperature of an endothermic reaction, the system reacts by favoring the products.

12. (c) The balanced equation is $2NOCl(g) \rightarrow Cl_2(g) + 2NO(g)$.

13. (a) A decrease in pressure favors the side of a reaction with the greatest number of gas molecules. In this reaction, a decrease in pressure would favor decomposition.

14. (d) The balanced equation for this reaction is $2NO(g) + 2H_2(g) \rightarrow N_2(g) + 2H_2O(g)$. $K = [N_2][H_2O]^2 / [NO]^2[H_2]^2$.

15. (c)

16. (a) $K_{sp} = [Pb^{+2}][I^-]^2$. $2[Pb_2^+] = [I^-]$. If $x = [Pb_2^+]$, then $K_{sp} = 4x^3$. $[Pb_2^+] = ((6.5 \times 10^{-9}/4)^{1/3})$. Since one mole of PbI_2 yields one mole of Pb, the solubility of PbI_2 is $((6.5 \times 10^{-9}/4)^{1/3})$.

17. (c) By stoichiometry, $[PO_4^{3-}] = 1/3 [Al^+]$.

18. (b) $K_{sp} = [Al^+]^3[PO_4^{3-}]$.

19. (b)

20. (a) HNO_3 completely dissociates into H^+ and NO_3^-. $[H^+] = [HNO_3] = 1M$. $pH = -\log [H^+] = 0$.

21. (d)

Short Essay Answers

1. a. $K = [PCl_3][Cl_2] / [PCl_5]$

   We are told that $[PCl_5] = 2[PCl_3]$

   $K = [PCl_3][Cl_2] / 2[PCl_3]$

   From the stoichiometry of the equation $[PCl_3] = [Cl_2]$

   Therefore, substituting for $[Cl_2]$:

   $K = [PCl_3][PCl_3] / 2[PCl_3] = [PCl_3]/2$

b. Since $[PCl_5] = 2[PCl_3]$:

$[PCl_3] = [PCl_5] / 2 (1)$

Since from a) $[PCl_3] / 2 = K$

$[PCl_3] = 2K$ (2)

Equating (1) and (2) we have:

$[PCl_5] / 2 = 2K$

$[PCl_5] = 4K$

Substituting the given value of K,

$[PCl_5] = 4(5x10^{-3})$

2. a. When a change is imposed on a system at equilibrium, the position of equilibrium shifts to reduce the effect of that change.

b. Equilibrium position shifts to the left (less gas molecules).

c. Equilibrium position shifts to the left.

d. The reaction is endothermic, so the equilibrium position shifts to the left.

e. b) no effect; c) no effect d) there is an effect.

3. $K = [HF]^2 / [H_2] [F_2]$

$[HF] = \sqrt{(K [H_2] [F_2])}$

$[HF] = \sqrt{\{(5x10^3)(0.5x0.5)\}}$

4. a. $Ca_3(PO_4)_2 \rightleftharpoons 3Ca^{2+} + 2PO_4^{3-}$

b. $K_{sp} = [Ca^{2+}]^3[PO_4^{3-}]^2 / Ca_3(PO_4)_2$

c. $\sqrt[3]{\{[Ca_3(PO_4)_2]K_{sp} / [PO_4^{3-}]^2\}} = [Ca^{2+}]$.

d. There are three moles of calcium ions per mole of calcium phosphate. The solubility is one third the concentration of calcium ions.
Because...

$[Ca^{2+}] = \sqrt[3]{\{[Ca_3(PO_4)_2]K_{sp} / [PO_4^{3-}]^2\}} = [Ca^{2+}]$

...the solubility of calcium phosphate $= 1/3(\sqrt[3]{\{\{[Ca_3(PO_4)_2]K_{sp} / [PO_4^{3-}]^2\}\}})$

5. a. HNO_3, HCl, H_2SO_4, HBr

b. A concentrated acid has a large number of acid molecules per unit volume of solution. The concentration of an acid tells us nothing about the position of the equilibrium between an acid molecule and its ions.

The strength of an acid tells us about the position of the equilibrium between an acid and its ions. Strong acids are completely dissociated into ions, whereas weak acids are barely dissociated. An acid may be concentrated and weak, concentrated and strong, dilute and weak, or dilute and strong.

c. HNO_3 is a strong acid. The solution is 1.0M, so the H+ concentration is 1.0M. pH= -log[H$^+$] = -log(1) = 0.

GLOSSARY

GLOSSARY

allotropes: Forms of an element that differ in the way atoms are linked.

anion: A negatively-charged ion.

atom: The smallest particle with the chemical properties of an element. Atoms are made up of protons, neutrons, and electrons.

atomic mass: The mass of an atom, measured in amu.

atomic number (Z): The number of protons in the nucleus of an atom. Elements are defined by their atomic numbers.

atomic radii: Half the distance between the nearest atoms in a solid sample of an element.

atomic symbol: The one or two letters chemists use to denote an element.

atomic weight: The average atomic mass of an element calculated by taking into account the relative abundance of each of its isotopes.

Avagadro's number: Approximately 6×10^{23}. The number of things in a mole. This number is also the number of atoms in exactly 12g of carbon-12.

azimuthal quantum number (l): This number takes values from zero to n - 1. The value of l defines which subshell an electron occupies.

balanced equation: An equation in which the number of atoms of a given type is equal in the products and reactants. Equations are balanced by the choice of stoichiometric coefficients.

bond angle: The angle between any two bonds that includes a common atom.

bond length: The distance between two chemically-bonded atoms along a straight line between their nuclei.

bonding electrons: Valence electrons of an atom that are involved in a covalent bond.

Bronsted-Lowry acid: A chemical species that is a proton donor.

Bronsted-Lowry base: A chemical species that is a proton acceptor.

building-up principle: A method of finding the electron configuration of an atom or monatomic ion.

cation: A positively-charged ion.

chemical equation: A representation of the rearrangement of atoms that occurs during a chemical reaction.

chemical property: A description of the way that matter behaves in chemical change.

chemical reaction: The transformation of one substance into another.

compound: A substance of two or more elements combined in a specific and uniform ratio.

concentration: The ratio of solute to solvent in a solution.

condensation: The process by which a gas becomes a liquid.

conjugate acid: The protonated form of a base.

conjugate base: The deprotonated form of an acid.

covalent bonds: Chemical bonds in which elements share electrons.

degenerate orbitals: Electron orbitals of equal energy.

dilution: The process of making less concentrated solutions.

dipole: The property of covalently bonded molecules with slight, or "partial" positive ends and "partial" negative ends. The electric imbalance is caused by an unequal sharing of electrons.

dipole-dipole interactions: An intermolecular force that binds molecules with permanent electric dipoles.

dipole moment: A property of a bond or molecule that can be represented by a line connecting a center of positive charge and a center of negative charge.

dynamic equilibrium: When two opposing processes occur at exactly the same rate, the processes are said to be in dynamic equilibrium.

electrochemical series: A series of half-reactions listed in order of the reducing power (power to gain electrons) of the species on the left-hand side of the half-reaction.

electron affinity: A measure of the energy necessary to add an electron to a gaseous atom to form an anion.

electron configuration: A description of the way in which electrons are organized in an atom or monatomic ion.

electron dot structure: A representation of the valence electrons in an atom or molecule.

electronegativity: A measure of the ability of elements to attract and hold on to electrons in a chemical bond.

electrons: Light, negatively-charged particles that orbit the nucleus of an atom.

element: A pure substance that cannot be decomposed by a chemical change. A sample of an element is composed of many identical atoms.

equilibrium constant (K): The product of the equilibrium concentrations of the products of a chemical reaction raised to the power of their stoichiometric coefficients divided by the product of the equilibrium concentration of reactants raised to the power of their stoichiometric coefficients. In a reaction where $aA + bB \iff cC + dD$, $K = [C]^c[D]^d/[A]^a[B]^b$.

equilibrium position: The concentrations of reactants and products at equilibrium.

evaporation: The process by which a liquid forms a gas.

extensive properties: The physical properties of matter that are dependent on the amount of matter.

formula unit: A description of the ratio of elements in an ionic compound.

gas: Fluid matter that fills its container and is compressible.

group: A vertical column in the periodic table.

heterogeneous equilibria: Equilibria involving more than one state of matter.

heterogeneous mixture: A mixture in which the composition varies within the sample.

homogeneous equilibria: Equilibria involving only one state of matter.

homogeneous mixture: A mixture in which the composition does not vary within the sample.

Hund's first rule: If more than one orbital of a subshell is available, add electrons with parallel spins to different orbitals in that subshell.

hydrogen bonding: A type of intermolecular force between a hydrogen atom and a strongly electronegative atom, such as nitrogen, fluorine, or oxygen.

hydronium ion: The ion (H_3O^+) formed when water acts like a base and accepts a proton.

intensive properties: The physical properties of matter that are independent of the amount of matter.

intermolecular forces: The forces that hold molecules together. Intermolecular forces are most prevalent in solids and liquids. Intermolecular forces include dipole-dipole interactions, London dispersion forces, and hydrogen bonding.

ion: Charged particles formed by the loss or gain of electrons from atoms.

ion-dipole interaction: An interaction between the charge of an ion and the partial charge of one end of an electric dipole. The classic example is the attraction between metal ions and dipolar water molecules.

ionic bonds: Chemical bonds in which elements are held together by the electrostatic attraction between their oppositely-charged ions.

ion-ion interaction: A relatively long range force between two ions. When the ions are oppositely-charged, the forces are attractive.

ionic product of water, (Kw): $Kw = [H_3O^+][OH^-]$

ionic solid: A solid held together by the attraction of oppositely-charged ions.

ionization: The process of removing an electron from an atom or ion.

ionization energy: The energy associated with ionization (either gaining or losing an electron).

isotopes: Elements with the same atomic numbers, but different atomic masses.

Le Chatelier's principle: When a change is imposed on a system at equilibrium, the position of equilibrium shifts to reduce the effect of the change.

Lewis structures: Diagrams in which each covalent bond between two atoms is represented by a line between their atomic symbols.

limiting reagent: A reactant that controls the maximum amount of product that can be formed in a chemical reaction.

liquid: Fluid matter that takes the shape of the part of its container it fills and is not easily compressed.

London dispersion forces: The forces between molecules that result from the attraction of their instantaneous dipoles.

lone pair electrons: Pairs of electrons in the valence shell that are uninvolved in chemical bonding.

magnetic spin quantum number (ms): The magnetic spin number may take the value $+\frac{1}{2}$ or $-\frac{1}{2}$.

magnetic quantum number (ml): The magnetic quantum number has $2l + 1$ values from $+l$ to $-l$. The magnetic quantum number defines the orbital an electron occupies.

mixture: A combination of pure substances.

molar mass: The number of grams of an element or compound that constitute one mole.

mole: A unit containing Avagadro's number.

molecular formula: A description of the number of atoms of each element in a molecule.

molecular solids: Solids composed of molecules and held together by intermolecular forces.

molecular structure: A description of the three-dimensional shape of a molecule in terms of its bond lengths and bond angles.

molecule: A definite, discrete group of bonded atoms.

network solids: Solids composed of individual atoms held together by covalent bonds that extend throughout a network.

nucleus: The center of an atom, comprised of protons and neutrons.

neutralization: The reaction between an acid and a base to produce a salt and water.

neutrons: Heavy, uncharged particles in the nuclei of atoms.

octahedral: The arrangement of six electron pairs predicted by VSEPR. Here, the angle between electron pairs is 90°.

octet: An atom with eight electrons in its valence shell is said to have completed its octet.

octet rule: Atoms proceed as far as possible to complete their octets.

orbital: A region around the nucleus in which electrons are free to move. Each orbital can hold up to two electrons in accordance with the Pauli exclusion principle.

oxidation: The loss of electrons accompanied by an increase in oxidation number.

oxoacid: An acid containing an oxoanion.

oxoanion: An anion that contains oxygen.

Pauli exclusion principle: No two electrons may occupy the same orbital unless they have opposite spins.

percentage yield: A measure of the difference between the actual and theoretical yield of a reaction.

period: A horizontal row in the periodic table.

periodic table: A chart that arranges all the known elements into a useful form for chemists.

pH: A measurement of the acidity of a solution. $pH = -\log[H_3O^+]$. Below pH7 is acidic; above pH 7 is basic. pH7 is neutral.

physical properties: The properties of matter that are observable without changing its chemical properties.

polar: For an object to be polar it must have a permanent dipole moment.

polyatomic ion: A molecule that has a charge (either positive or negative).

precipitate: A solid that forms from a solution.

principal quantum number (n): The principal quantum number can take values from 1 to infinity. It defines the shell of an atom in which an electron is found.

products: Chemical species on the right-hand side of a chemical equation.

protons: Heavy, positively-charged particles in the nuclei of atoms.

quantized: A description of the discrete values the energy of an electron in an atom may take.

quantum number: The quantum number defines the state of a particle. The four quantum numbers of an electron define its state.

reactants: Chemical species on the left-hand side of a chemical equation.

redox reactions: Reactions in which one species loses electrons while another species gains electrons.

reduction: The gain of electrons accompanied by a decrease in oxidation number.

resonance structures: Lewis structures having the same arrangement of atoms, but different arrangements of valence electrons.

shell: The orbitals in an atom or monatomic ion with the same value of n.

solid: Matter with shape independent of its container that is not compressible.

the solubility product, Ksp: Used to calculate the solubility of a compound. For a reading of the form XnYm(s) $\rightarrow$ nX(aq) + mY(aq), Ksp = $[X]^n$ $[Y]^m$ where [X] and [Y] are equilibrium concentrations.

soluble: A solid that dissolves in water.

spectator ions: Ions not involved in chemical change, but present in a solution.

stoichiometric coefficients: Numbers that precede chemical formulae in chemical equations. Equations are balanced by the choice of correct stoichiometric coefficients.

strong electrolyte: A solid that dissolves completely in water to produce 100 percent ions and conducts electricity.

subshell: Degenerate orbitals with the same value of n and l.

tetrahedral: The arrangement of four electron pairs predicted by VSEPR. The angle between electron pairs in a tetrahedron is approximately 109°.

theoretical yield: A measure of the maximum possible yield of a reaction taking into account the amount of any limiting reagent.

trigonal bipyramid: The arrangement of five electron pairs predicted by VSEPR. The angles between electron pairs in this arrangement are either 90° or 120°.

trigonal planar: The arrangement of three electron pairs predicted by VSEPR. The angle between electron pairs in a trigonal plane is 120°.

trigonal pyramidal: The arrangement of three atoms and one lone pair predicted by VSEPR.

VSEPR: Valence Shell Electron Pair Repulsion Theory. A theory used to predict the bond angles in molecules based on the minimization of repulsion between electron pairs.

valence electrons: Electrons that occupy the valence shell.

valence shell: The outermost shell of electrons in an atom or monatomic ion.

vapor pressure: The pressure exerted by a vapor above a liquid in a closed container.

Jason Chin was born in London and educated at Oxford University. He is currently a Fulbright Scholar at Yale University. He has written for *New Scientist* magazine on matters of general medical and scientific interest. Jason received a masters in chemistry at Oxford and has taught chemistry for several semesters at Yale while pursuing his PhD. Jason enjoys mountain biking and tennis in the summer and snowboarding in the winter.

LOOKING TO PUT YOUR KNOWLEDGE OF CHEMISTRY TO GOOD USE? VISIT VAULT REPORTS ON THE WEB

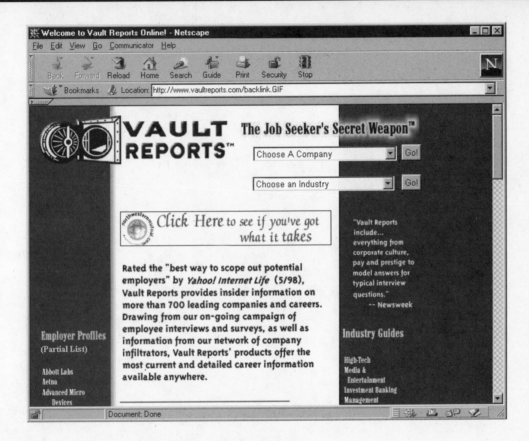

- ◆ **EMPLOYER PROFILES**
- ◆ **INDUSTRY GUIDES**
- ◆ **FREE CAREER NEWSLETTER**
- ◆ **EXPERT CAREER ADVICE**
- ◆ **CELEBRITY INTERVIEWS AND PROFILES**

www.vaultreports.com

VAULT REPORTS™

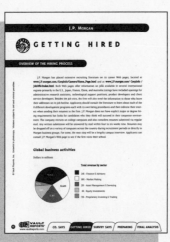